Horizons on
Catholic Feminist Theology

Horizons on
Catholic Feminist Theology

EDITED BY

Joann Wolski Conn and Walter E. Conn

GEORGETOWN UNIVERSITY PRESS / WASHINGTON, D.C.

Georgetown University Press, Washington, D.C.   20057
© 1992 by Georgetown University Press. All rights reserved.
Printed in the United States of America
10 9 8 7 6 5 4 3 2 1   1992
THIS VOLUME IS PRINTED ON ACID-FREE OFFSET BOOK PAPER.

Library of Congress Cataloging-in-Publication Data

Horizons on Catholic feminist theology / edited by Joann Wolski Conn
    and Walter E. Conn.
            p.   cm.
        Includes bibliographical references.
            1. Feminist theology.   2. Women in the Catholic Church.
        3. Catholic Church--Doctrines.   I. Conn, Joann Wolski.   II. Conn,
        Walter E.
        BT83.55.H67   1992   230' .2'082--dc20   92-30435
        ISBN 0-87840-534-8 (pbk.)

for
all our Catholic feminist theological colleagues,
especially Denise and John Carmody

Contents

Preface

Our goal in this book is to illustrate feminist theological awareness within the Catholic tradition. Since feminism is experienced and understood in different ways, we begin the preface by noting some basic definitions and identifying our perspective. Then we link the tasks of feminist studies with theoogy and, finally, identify which essays illustrate specific tasks.

In broadest outline, as Sandra Schneiders explains, feminism is "a comprehensive ideology which is rooted in women' experience of sexual oppression, engages in a critique of patriarchy as an essentially dysfunctional system, embraces an alternative vision for humanity and the earth, and actively seeks to bring this vision to realization."[1] It is not an ideology in the sense of an uncritical absorption of cultural values, nor a false consciousness. Rather, it is both a coordinated set of ideas and a practical plan of action rooted in critical awareness of the way a culture controlled by men for their own perceived advantage oppresses women and dehumanizes men. Although comprehensive, this ideology is expressed in a variety of forms (e.g., socialist, ecological, romantic) that reveal two basic types.[2]

These primary types of feminism, according to Karen Offen, are "relational" and "individualist."[3] Ideas and projects in the *relational feminist* tradition feature a nonhierarchical couple as the basic unit of society and promote an egalitarian vision of social organization. Relational feminism emphasizes women's rights *as women*, defined principally by their childbearing or nurturing qualities, or by their assumed affinity with nature. It insists on women's distinctive contributions to society. Whether these qualities are rooted in nature or socialization is an open question. Carol Gilligan's position resembles this line of argument.[4] *Individualist* views and aims, on the other hand, posit the individual as the basic unit of society regardless of sex (biology) or gender (social construction of the meaning of sex as "masculine" or "feminine"). This tradition emphasizes more abstract concepts of individual human rights, celebrates autonomy, downplays all socially defined roles, and minimizes discussion of sex-linked qualities. Enactment of the Equal Rights Amendment is a political priority of these feminists. Different political aims are dear to relational feminists: governmental programs that bolster women's performance of procreative functions (e.g., parental leave from the work place), even as other avenues for life-work are made available.

In summary, the case for feminism is made from two perspectives. Individualists argue for the moral equality of women and men who share the same human nature and, therefore, deserve equal rights. Relational feminists affirm equality, yet stress "the difference difference makes." That is, they respect the unique socialization our culture gives women and men and insist that society value women's special contribution with the same status and rewards it confers on men for their contribution.

Drawing attention to these two types of feminism does not imply a need to choose between them; rather, it promotes awareness of the strengths and weaknesses of whatever kind of feminism informs any theological position. Relational values, for example, sometimes romanticize women's qualities, and individual values can exaggerate autonomy. We believe that authentic feminism promotes autonomy for the sake of genuine relationship.

When feminists wish to identify themselves as Christian and Catholic (the focus of this book) they face the issues described above in a religious context that has related to them in contradictory and conflicting ways. While affirming women as baptized into Christ as fully as men, and elevating "woman" to heavenly heights in the person of Mary, church teaching and practice has also demeaned, ignored, and even oppressed women. It is this experience and these interpretations that diverse feminist theologians address in a comprehensive project.

Mary Jo Weaver has schematized the general feminist project in six logical steps or tasks that are exemplified in the field of theology by the essays in this collection.[5] The first task of feminist theology is to notice and demonstrate the fact that women have been ignored in the field (J. W. Conn, Keightley). Second, one shows that what we do know about women in Christian tradition is characterized by much hostility, diminishment, frivolity, or romantic mystification (Gudorf, Johnson, Ross). Third, scholars search out and write about women lost in the field or overlooked in scholarship regarding a theological topic, such as discernment or prophetic mysticism (Schneiders, F. E. Weaver). The fourth task is to revise the reading of old texts by asking new questions which cause the texts to lose their power to exclude or restrict women (Johnson, O'Connor). Fifth is the challenge to the discipline methodologically in order to force it to redefine borders, goals, and consequences (Carr, J. W. Conn, Keightley). Last is the work toward an integrated field which is not reduced by its prejudices against women, lower classes, variant sexual preferences, ethnic groups or anything else, but which represents humanity in all its messy diversity (M. J. Weaver).

Regarding this last task, readers will notice that these essays are written by feminist theologians who are white, middle-class academics, speaking within a certain experience of the Catholic tradition, writing, for the most part, as "loyal opposition" within the church. Different perspectives, for example Afro-American Christian, would modify or expand the positions taken here. This collection of essays—which were published originally in *Horizons*, the journal of the College Theology Society—is our contribution to the long struggle and invigorating challenge of the Catholic feminist theological project.

JOANN WOLSKI CONN
WALTER E. CONN

NOTES

1. Sandra Schneiders, *Beyond Patching* (New York: Paulist, 1991), 15.
2. Ibid., 15-31.
3. Karen Offen, "Defining Feminism: A Comparative Historical Approach," *Signs* 14/1 (Autumn 1988), 119-154.
4. Carol Gilligan, *In A Different Voice* (Cambridge, MA: Harvard University Press, 1982).
5. Mary Jo Weaver, *New Catholic Women* (San Francisco: Harper & Row, 1985). In "Widening the Sphere of Discourse," contained in our present collection of essays, Weaver explains and elaborates on these six tasks.

I

Theological Visions

1

A Discipleship of Equals:
Past, Present, Future

Joann Wolski Conn*

ABSTRACT

This chapter clarifies the foundation for a discipleship of equals by bringing feminist scholarship to bear upon conflicting religious assumptions regarding women. To this end, it surveys significant scholars as well as issues: past, present, and future. It evaluates the outcome of the three phases of study in women's history (I); it urges present action in four areas which are essential for equality in the Church (II); and it speaks words of hope for difficult times to come (III).

> For . . . those who have put on Christ,
> There is neither Jew nor Greek;
> There is neither slave nor free;
> There is no male or female;
> For you are all one.
> (Gal 3:27-28)

This text is best understood as a communal Christian self-definition, an affirmation that within the Christian community no structures of domination can be tolerated.[1] Of all the structures of domination, it

---

*Joann Wolski Conn (Ph.D., Columbia University) is Professor of Religious Studies at Neumann College (Aston, PA 19014), where she also teaches in the Graduate Program in Pastoral Counseling. She is the editor of *Women's Spirituality: Resources for Christian Development* (New York: Paulist, 1986) and the author of *Spirituality and Personal Maturity* (New York: Paulist, 1989) as well as many articles in such journals as *Cross Currents, Horizons, Spirituality Today, Spiritual Life*, and *Theology Today*. This paper was presented at the 1987 Villanova University Theology Institute, which holds its copyright. It was published in *A Discipleship of Equals: Towards a Christian Feminist Spirituality*, Volume XX of the Proceedings of the Theology Institute, and appears here with the kind permission of Francis A. Eigo, O.S.A., Director of the Institute and Editor of its Proceedings.

3

has been argued that the patriarchal oppression of women is the deepest and most pervasive.[2] Therefore, to expose its roots and abrogate its
claim to legitimacy is not only to liberate women and evangelize men,
but also to loosen the bonds of racism, classism, and every other structural obstacle to a Christian discipleship of equals.

How can we promote this discipleship of equals, this new Christianity beyond patriarchy? We can build its foundation: the dialogue
of religiously committed women and men, the energy of reciprocal
consciousness. Together, we must unpack, examine, and evaluate the
baggage of our conflicting religious assumptions. Because religion is
the single most important shaper and enforcer of women's role as either equal or subordinate in society, such religious dialogue becomes
an instrument not only of religious transformation but also of wider
social reform.[3]

Until very recently, Christianity had been interpreted and communicated from an almost exclusively male-centered point of view so
that we had a monologue rather than dialogue. Now the emerging
discipline of women's studies is recovering the forgotten or neglected
history of women in every field, including the Christian religion. Consequently, a genuine Christian dialogue becomes possible, one that
frees men and women, like Lazarus, from being "bound head and
foot" by patriarchy's distortions. "Untie yourselves," Jesus is telling
us, "and let yourselves go free" (Jn 11:45).

This essay will survey the issues that feminist scholars judge important for discussion in the Christian tradition. Its method is collaborative, in the sense that it selects some of the best feminist scholars as
spokespersons for each issue. Therefore, it surveys significant scholars
as well as central issues. It will interpret and evaluate the past (Part I)
and the present (Part II) in order to imagine the future (Part III) in a
way that inspires both action and patience, according to the Spirit's
leading. My advisor about how to approach the future is Teresa of
Avila, who notices the pattern of God's interaction with humanity:
"Oh, what a good friend You make, my Lord! How you proceed by favoring and enduring. You wait for the other to adapt to Your nature,
and in the meanwhile you put up with his!"[4]

I believe that God is now favoring us with the gift of Christian
feminist spirituality and enduring our struggles to walk in its light.
The term spirituality, here, refers to our deepest self lived in relation
to God, the sustainer of all, and so, literally, it touches everything. As
feminist, spirituality is that way of relating to God, and to everyone
and everything, lived by those who are aware of the history of
women's restriction and oppression and now work to ensure women's
equality in every sphere. Sensitivity to women's oppression alerts

feminists to the wider dimensions of human oppression, especially to the relationship of sexism, racism, classism, and elitism in our society. As Christian, feminist spirituality is that mode of relating to God, in Christ Jesus, through the Spirit, which is, like the gospel, inclusive of women and men, universal in its vision, and prophetic in its call to be converted from the sins of domination and self-righteousness.[5] Christian feminist spirituality relies on *contemplation* in *action for justice* as its only hope for the future.

I. INTERPRETING THE PAST

Christian women's and men's spiritual growth requires knowledge of women's history. It is necessary, first of all, in order to satisfy the basic human need for meaning and identity. Because meaning requires imagination, we all need an accurate picture of women's own past and role models to support an inclusive vision for the future. Second, knowledge of this history promotes action. When women perceive their condition as deprivation, history demonstrates that they act to change this condition.[6]

Although the field of women's history is young, it has already developed through three phases of approaches. As in human growth, tasks of earlier stages remain significant even when later tasks emerge.[7]

Compensatory history was naturally the first phase. Because so many notable women are missing from traditional history, especially from religious history, this continues to be a long-term undertaking. Here, two questions are basic. To what extent did Judaism and Christianity directly promote misogynism? To what extent were they combating earlier denigration of women and helping women's gradual rise to respect?

Phase two moves from documenting oppression and exploitive interpretations of women's role to investigating how women operated in a male-defined world on their own terms. Here the task is to recover women's experience expressed in their own words. A significant religious question is: to what extent does women's religious experience indicate that a struggle for self-affirmation, self-definition, and autonomous self-donation is intrinsic to women's conversion and progress in holiness.

A third phase is emerging in which women view themselves not as another minority but, more accurately, as the majority of humanity. Now the question becomes: what would history itself look like if seen through women's eyes and values?

Even the following modest survey of results in these three phases of tasks provides women with resources for praise, pride, and power to affirm their own religious history in the ongoing dialogue to promote the discipleship of equals.

Compensatory History: Documenting Patriarchy and its Effects

This approach to history documents the relationship of patriarchal religion both to feminine imagery and to the psychological and social self-images of women. It serves as a basis for suggestions of ways in which patriarchal religion must be reshaped to overcome its unjust and debilitating effects on women. The following survey is merely an enticing example of the results of this approach applied to the Hebrew and Christian scripture, to major periods of Christian history, and to a few individual persons and issues. Some of the positions cited here as having merit could well be debated by other feminist scholars.

Hebrew scripture is a collection of writings by males from a society dominated by males. Phyllis Bird, a Christian scholar of this literature, documents a wide range of images of women in the Old Testament, as she refers to this scripture.[8] In some texts the woman of ancient Israel is portrayed as property. In others she is depicted as possessing considerable freedom, initiative, power and respect.

The woman of the Old Testament, judged by economic criteria or in terms of interest in continuity of the male name, was deemed inferior to the man. In the realm of cult her activity was restricted and from the law's viewpoint she was a minor and dependent, whose rights were seldom protected. These roles and systems of status are the baseline for any discussion of woman's image; but they are not the whole picture.

In many situations the woman was, in fact or in theory, an equal despite pressures to treat her as an inferior. She was recognized as equal in certain kinds of knowledge and in religious sensibility. In love she might also be an equal, and could exploit as well as suffer exploitation. Man sees her as a partner in pleasure and labor, one whom he needs, and one who can deal him weal or woe. She completes him—but as one with a character of her own.

Genesis' two creation accounts suggest an original and intended equality and harmony in creation behind the present state of division and alienation. Some prophets see a renewed creation that would abolish exploitation based on distinctions of age, sex, and social status. That Israel rarely lived up to this vision does not deny its presence in Israel's scripture.

Synthesizing the best New Testament scholarship, Constance Parvey demonstrates that women were educated in the scriptures and assumed leadership roles of sufficient magnitude to attract many women in Christian congregations.[9] Their participation was, however, not problem-free. New Testament images of women reflect both theologically and socially a first-century male-centered religious culture. Nevertheless, Paul's theology of equivalence in Christ could support a new religious and social basis for women-men relationships in the future. The radically new theology of women, however, became obscured in the later epistles. What Paul had understood as a kind of temporary *status quo* ethics—in the context of the imminent end-time—became translated two generations later into moral guidelines for keeping things forever the way they are. Consequently, the church inherited two widely divergent messages: the theology of equivalence in Christ; the practice of women's subordination. In attempting to reconcile them it maintained the social *status quo* and affirmed women's equivalence by projecting it as a purely spiritual, otherworldly reality.

Bernadette Brooten concludes that Paul judges the morality of women's sexual relationship to other women entirely on the basis of culturally defined roles and the primacy of undisturbed order.[10] Lesbian relationships are morally wrong, for Paul, because in them women overstep the bounds of the role and status assigned by culture. That is, in them women exchange the passive, subordinate sexual role that Paul considers "natural" for them, for an active, autonomous role that could only be natural and, thus moral, for men. Lesbian women are condemned, in Paul's eyes, because they repeat the pattern of idolatry, that is, of refusal to defer to their head who is man, as man must defer to Christ who defers to his head who is God.

Christians, especially those who promote women's equality, commonly view the Fathers of the Church as ascetics and woman haters. It is true that they usually hated sex and often insulted women; but identifying the two themes obscures the issue. It tends to ignore the high praise of women, in their new role as virgins, in patristic theology. It also fails to explain the rise of that veneration of Mary that characterizes patristic thought in the fourth century C.E. Rosemary Radford Ruether judges that this ambivalence between misogynism and the praise of the virginal woman is not accidental.[11] One view is not more characteristic of the Fathers than the other. Both stand together as two sides of a dualistic psychology that was the basis of the patristic doctrine of humanity viewed as normatively male.

All the patristic traditions of feminine spiritual imagery were gathered together in their emerging theology of Mary. Mary became the epitome of all these images of spiritual womanhood, and the Fathers transferred to her the ancient titles of Queen of Heaven and Mother of God formerly given to the ancient Mediterranean Earth Goddess. They crowned Mary with the moon and stars of Isis, the turret crown of Magna Mater, and placed her enthroned with the divine child on her lap in an ancient image derived from the iconography of Isis and Horus. Patristic theology rededicated ancient temples of these Earth goddesses to Mary, and finally escorted her to the very throne of God to take her seat beside the Jewish Ancient of Days who, with his son Messiah, ruled the heavens in exclusive patriarchal splendor. The image of Mary's assumption emerged in popular piety in Egypt by the early fifth century C.E. The male ascetic devotees of the virginal woman saw her receiving the prize of heavenly glory. While these men were praising Mary, however, they were despising all real physical women, sex and fecundity, and wholly etherealizing women into spiritual love objects and warning against any physical expression of love with the dangerous daughters of Eve.

Ruether desires not only to decry the patristic tradition's defects. She wishes also to cherish the hard-won fruits of patristic theology: conclusions about transcendence and spiritual personhood won at the terrible price of men's denying their natural affections and fearing, or even hating, women's natural humanity.

While patristic theology developed in Christianity, Jewish tradition synthesized rabbinic legal tradition in the Talmud. Judith Hauptman presents three general conclusions about the images of women in the Talmud.[12] First, woman's role is well defined along traditional lines of caring for husband, children, and home in which she is always dependent upon a man. Given this framework, the rabbis tried to secure the greatest possible good for women, especially those least fortunate. Second, the rabbis guided their decisions by their ultimate goals. Since they defined Jewish commitment in terms of ongoing concern for the community and a quest for dialogue with God, they had to regulate family life in a way that would lead to optimum achievement of these goals. The easiest way to engage a man's help and his devotion to God was by keeping the woman at home so that her husband could fulfill his duties outside the home. Third, although Talmudic anecdotes taught a woman to accept a supportive role in life, there are numerous stories in which women buck the tradition, assert themselves, and speak their own minds. That Bruria, in many ways the antithesis of self-sacrificing Rachel, is recorded in the Talmud, even at the risk of her potentially subversive influence, is indicative of the fact that womankind was not monolithic nor was rabbinic legislation devoid of changing attitudes toward women.

Biblical, Talmudic, and Patristic scholarship is, of course, more complex than the previous summaries can convey. Ruether, for example, chooses to emphasize the pejorative interpretation of Church fathers, while Hauptman opts to demonstrate that the authors of the Talmud can be read as "moderates." There is more to the two situations than the emphases these authors feature.

Eleanor McLaughlin is amazed at the extent to which medieval assumptions about women remain effective today. Liberation from the misogyny of those assumptions can come only when the implications of that medieval past are made clear.

McLaughlin emphasizes three medieval assumptions.[13] First, for Thomas Aquinas there is in every aspect of the woman's life a tension and confusing ambiguity between her subordination in the order of creation and her equivalence in the order of salvation. This tension can be overcome only when the woman is able to renounce or escape (in heaven) that which has been considered essential to her femaleness, her reproductive function.

Second, these theories confront social reality in two institutions: marriage and monastic or virginal life. Here the church attempted to do justice to the equivalence of women and men while assuming and reinforcing their subordination. In marriage, for example, Thomas Aquinas, following Aristotle, speaks of a friendship between husband and wife, but it must be that of inferior to a superior, a hierarchical love comparable to the love of the soul for God.[14] In the virginal life, the religious equivalence of male and female is fundamentally undermined by the church's development of a rationale for the denial of Holy Orders to the woman. One aspect of this rationale is that ordination confers a superiority of rank that cannot be received by a woman who is by the order of creation in a state of subjection. Thus the woman, like the slave, may not validly receive Holy Orders. Another example is the refusal of Franciscan and Dominican men to give the female branches of their traditions the status of true membership in their respective orders. The rejection is explicit: both Dominican and Franciscan women wanted and struggled for equal membership with the Friars. Both groups of women wanted to receive pastoral care from the Friars rather than from local secular clergy; but the men refused, saying that care for these women (in whom their founders had taken such interest!) would interfere with their ability to preach, and other comments implied that association with women would endanger the health of their souls.[15]

Third, medieval theology of Mary has contradictory elements that have serious implications for women. Mary's role in Christ's work of redemption is both essential and characteristic of her sex:

secondary, passive, reflecting the male picture of the female as manip-
ulative and seductive. Bernardino of Siena describes Mary's relationship to God this way:

> . . . one Hebrew woman invaded the house of the eternal King.
> One girl, I do not know by what caresses, pledges or violence, se-
> duced, deceived, and if I may say so, wounded and enraptured
> the divine heart and ensnared the Wisdom of God . . . .[16]

For this theologian, it seems, the woman to whom God gives such
privilege and power could only have received it through seduction
and deception.

Calvin's reformation exegesis and pastoral advice continues the
patristic and medieval tradition of affirming the spiritual equality of
women and men while confirming the submission of women to men,
especially in Christian marriage.[17] For example, when advising
women who are suffering mental or physical abuse from their husbands, Calvin encourages silent acceptance and submission to what
God has sent them and wants to console them with the knowledge
that this kind of affliction is nothing compared with the spiritual infi-
delity of which their husbands are guilty. Mary Potter concludes that
although Calvin is not the first to use a double-sided argument for
male-female relationships, he is the first to place equal emphasis on
both sides of the argument. Calvin proposed a carefully contained
spiritual reformation for women in the sixteenth century; nevertheless, it was one that had little effect on social and political structures.

Compensatory history, as we see from these examples, has important implications. First, it demonstrates a pervasive tension between teachings about a new creation of equality between women and
men, and assumptions about women's different and inferior nature.
Then, it impels us to ask why and how this tension and inequality can
continue to shape the church and society tnousands of years later. It is
important to recognize that religious teachers in the past were deeply
and pervasively sexist; still, scholars agree that it is relatively impossible for anyone of any period, woman or man, to grasp any issue differently from the prevailing culture. It is another matter, entirely, to have
twentieth-century men and women resorting to these sexist traditions
as refuges from institutional change or personal conversion.

History That Recovers Women as Agents

The second phase of women's history asks the question: how did
women operate on their own terms in a male-defined world?[18] It
recovers women's experience as women interpreted and evaluated it,

often in their own words. It often reveals and reverses misconceptions about women, misconceptions rooted in male-centered assumption.

My own misconceptions about Margery Kempe, a fifteenth-century visionary, pilgrim, and mystic, were reversed by Clarissa W. Atkinson's historical scholarship.[19] I knew Margery Kempe as a middle-class English housewife called to weep and to pray for her fellow Christians and to adopt an unconventional way of life. Separating herself from her husband and many children, she became a pilgrim traveling around England and as far away as Jerusalem. In old age, she dictated to scribes an autobiography that recounts her extraordinary intimacy with Christ as well as her intense, commotion-filled life. To me, she did not seem very "saintly" in character or disposition, and her spiritual experiences had been conveyed to me as extreme or egotistical; indeed, she was usually presented to me as the opposite of her saintly contemporary, Julian of Norwich.

In order to appreciate and interpret properly Margery Kempe's life and spirituality, Atkinson demonstrates that one must go beyond conventional categories of social and religious history. One must examine six perspectives: the character of Margery's autobiography, her mysticism and pilgrim way of life, her social and family environment, her relations with her church and its clergy, the tradition that shaped her piety, and the context of medieval female sanctity.

Margery's *Book* was shaped by the writings of famous holy women and by pressures on memory and motivation that come with age. It is, nevertheless, an authentic autobiography: the story of a life told by its subject.

The vocation that called Margery to mysticism and pilgrimage made her unusual, and therefore, open to suspicion. It required her to leave her husband and children, to dress in white (a color usually reserved for virgins), to go on pilgrimage as a way to participate in Christ's earthly life and death. It graced her with a conspicuous gift: tears she could not control or resist. With the help of repeated assurance from Christ and her advisors, Margery was convinced her mystical gifts and tears were intended to make her a mirror of penitence, compassion, and God's love for sinners.

Margery's domestic and social background gave her the courage to persist in her strange vocation and unpopular way of life in spite of current norms about the behavior of married women. She was not deferential or quiet; she came from a powerful merchant family, so she spoke to her contemporaries (even priests and bishops) with straightforward language. She met scorn from most of her relatives, but found encouragement in Christ, the saints, and some representatives of the church.

During Margery's lifetime, the church displayed intense anxiety over the related issues of religious "feelings," discernment of spirits, and female visionaries. Margery consistently sought to have her religious "feelings" and way of life examined and approved. Many trustworthy persons, including Dame Julian of Norwich, advised Margery to accept what God sent her and judged her "feelings" to be "the work of the Holy Ghost."

Atkinson's most original and significant insights are in the area of Margery's spirituality. It is in the tradition of affective piety and of late medieval female sanctity that Margery's religious emotions and expressions can be best understood.

From Anselm of Canterbury in the eleventh century, to Prior Nicolas Love in the early fifteenth century, affective writers and preachers aimed to promote intense feelings. Principal among these were compassion, which enabled Christians to participate in the suffering of Jesus and his mother, and contrition which produced repentance and the emotive aspects of conversion. Margery incorporated these feelings in her own devotional life: identification with the human Christ, conspicuous humility inspired by Saint Francis of Assisi, "boistrous" emotion in sympathy with Mary grieving at the cross. Against this background, the religious life of Margery Kempe seems neither aberrant nor even unusual. Rather, it is her unique response to a tradition established by great saints.

Atkinson notices how Margery corresponds with the pattern of holiness in many medieval women such as Catherine of Siena, Birgitta of Sweden, Joan of Arc, and Julian of Norwich. They characteristically saw visions, communicated directly with God, found scribes or biographers who publicized their experiences. An increasing number of them were wives and mothers who struggled, like Margery, with the married state and eventually "transcended" it, becoming in effect "honorary" virgins through their humility and by God's special favor. Traveling widely, speaking publicly, departing from traditional women's roles, these women were a new creation of the late middle ages. Atkinson demonstrates how their lives and works form the only appropriate context in which to recognize and appreciate Margery Kempe's life and *Book*.

Not only does this approach to history correct misconceptions, such as those about Margery Kempe, but it also recovers the lost or neglected story of women's impact on society. A fascinating example of this recovery is the account of Quaker women's influence on American society.

In *Mothers of Feminism* Margaret Hope Bacon identifies the root of the conflict over women's roles that has plagued our country from the Puritans to the present.[20] What generates conflict is living according to the biblical revelation that every person has God's guiding spirit, so that each individual may and must trust her or his own religious experience. From its origin in the seventeenth century, the Society of Friends consistently acted on the belief that each person has an independent relationship to God, to "the inner Light," whether male or female, slave or free, educated or illiterate. Quakers were unique because they encouraged and expected women to participate equally in worship, to preach, organize, and administer the business of the community.

Other Protestants and Catholics found such Quaker attitudes not only dangerous but also blasphemous because they undermined "God-given" patriarchal authority in households, churches, and governments. In the name of social order, Puritans whipped, imprisoned and hung brave Quaker women who came into the Bay Colony as "traveling ministers." This fear of sexual equality remains, to this day, the root of conservative religious opposition to a discipleship of equals.

Bacon's description of the role of Quaker women in every major American reform movement, from abolition and universal suffrage to civil rights and disarmament, supports the conclusion that throughout our history there has been a "gender gap." On the one hand, in every era and reform effort there has been an exclusive, male-centered, authoritarian ethic in power; yet there has also been an inclusive, feminist, uncompetitive minority, incorporating Quaker values.[21]

Quakers were a feminist vanguard influencing other reformers to adopt such practices as shared leadership, consensus decisions and nonresistant protest. Quaker women were in the forefront. Women like Lucretia Mott, Susan B. Anthony, Alice Paul, M. Carey Thomas, and Grace Abbott led the struggle for prison reform, abolition, temperance, equal rights, coeducation, child welfare, peace and eventually disarmament. Quakers have participated out of all proportion to their numbers (never more than two percent of the population). Quaker women accounted for four out of five of the organizers of the first women's rights convention in 1848; five of the first eleven women doctors; and an estimated forty percent of the women abolitionists, thirty percent of the pioneer prison reformers, and fifteen percent of the suffragists born before 1830.

Quaker women's heroism not only offers women a "usable past" but also serves as a resource for feminist concept that is still applicable today in the quest for more humane social systems.

Historical Studies as a Copernican Shift in Consciousness

No man has been excluded from the historical record because of his sex, yet most women were. Gerda Lerner, a founding mother of

women's studies, reminds us that women have "made history" as ac-
tors and agents; however, they have been kept from contributing to
"history-making," that is, they have been barred from the task of officially interpreting the past of humankind as a whole.[22] They have not
been accepted as writers or teachers of what would be acknowledged
as the history of humanity.

This contradiction between women's central and active role in
creating society and their marginality in the meaning-giving process
of interpretation has been a force, causing women to struggle against
their subservient condition. When, in that process of struggle, at certain moments, the contradictions between the centrality of their action
and the marginality of their presence in the "official interpretation" of
that event are brought into women's consciousness, women's condition is perceived as a deprivation that is shared as a group. This consciousness raising becomes a force moving women into action to
change their condition and to enter into a new relationship to the
male-dominated society.

The most mature phase of women's history realizes that the
"event" which needs reinterpretation now is all of history, because
history has never yet been interpreted with women viewed as the majority that they are, rather than as a subordinate minority. Is the goal a
reverse discrimination? Exclude men the way they have excluded
women? Definitely not. As a temporary measure, civilization needs to
be reconceptualized from a women-centered perspective in order to
step outside of patriarchal thought and, thus, transform the whole system. The ultimate goal of most feminist historians, however, is a perspective on civilization that pays equal attention to women's and
men's experience.

Three metaphors help us capture the desired angle of vision.[23]
Feminist historians desire, first, a "doubled vision." Adding the female vision to the male in such a way that both eyes see together allows both a full range of vision and accurate depth perception. In another image, feminist historians picture men and women living on a
stage, on which they act out their assigned roles, equal in importance.
But the stage set is designed by men who have written the play, as-
signing themselves the most interesting parts. Realizing their disad-
vantage, women gradually negotiate for a contract that gives them co-
authorship of the play. We do not yet know what the new script will
be. A third metaphor imagines us removing the umbrella of male
dominance, stepping out under the free sky to observe a new universe
in which man is not the measure of all things, rather, women and men
are. This vision transforms *consciousness* as decisively as did Coperni-

cus' theory that the earth is not the center of the universe. We do not yet know what will emerge as we sail over the horizon of our current preconceptions. Feminist historians have begun and encourage us to follow. The process itself is the way, the goal.

Some scholars have begun to explore this new universe of consciousness and ask: if women were central to an issue in their scholarly field, how would it be defined? Gerda Lerner, for example, explores the question of the origins of class society and finds direct links with women and religion.[24]

Lerner raises and answers two difficult questions: How was class definition different for women than for men? Why did it take 3500 years for women to realize their subordination; that is, what could explain women's historical "complicity" in upholding the patriarchal system that subordinated them?

Through a series of brilliant and controversial judgments, Lerner concludes, regarding the first question, that men controlled women's sexual and reproductive capacity prior to the formation of private property and class society. Treating women's sexuality as a commodity is at the foundation of private property, rather than the other way around. Lerner's position, therefore, is the opposite of the standard Marxist interpretation of class which regards private property as the foundation, and only then turns to women as one example of men's property.

Women's sexual subordination was institutionalized in the earliest law codes and enforced by the full power of the state. Women's cooperation in this system was secured by various means: force, economic dependency on the male head of the family, class privileges bestowed upon conforming and dependent women of the upper classes, and the artificially created divisions of women into respectable (i.e., attached to one man) and not-respectable (i.e., not attached to one man or free of all men).

Feminist historians recognize that the later symbolic devaluing of women in relation to the divine imaged as male becomes one of the two founding metaphors of Western civilization. The other founding metaphor is supplied by Aristotelian philosophy, which assumes that women are incomplete and damaged human beings of an entirely different order than men. It is with the creation of these two metaphors, which are built into the very foundations of the symbol systems of Western civilization, that the subordination of women comes to be seen as "natural," and hence becomes invisible. Therefore, what is now called "women's complicity with patriarchy" was actually assimilation to the only meaning, that is, the only reality available to any-

one. As Lerner reminds us, when historical events allow new meaning
to emerge, and women perceive their situation as "deprivation," they
begin to act to change their condition.

It is this action, based on new meaning, that is the next topic for
discussion. "Present issues" are matters for urgent action.

II. PRESENT ISSUES

In my judgment, growth of the discipleship of equals requires action
in four areas. First, every Christian must participate in the ongoing
conversion of religious institutions. Second, we need prophetic insistence upon initial conversion of sinful structures. Third, theologians
should continue to enlarge the discipline of Christian feminist theology. Fourth, Christians must appropriate a feminist spirituality.

Participate in the Ongoing Conversion of Religious Institutions

Renewal of Religious Life.
I agree with Sandra Schneiders' claim that, as a group, women religious (and those assimilated to them educationally and culturally) are
the most creative element in the Catholic Church today. They are theologically well informed, have a variety of professional skills, have experience of ministry in many parts of the United States and the world,
and have been the most enthusiastic about implementing the renewal
of Vatican II in daily life. Therefore, it might be safe to claim: as
women religious go, so goes the church in the next decade.[25]

Mary Jo Weaver pinpoints the heart of their conversion as commitment to a discipleship of equals in the midst of misunderstanding
and opposition. Although the Vatican and the council originally encouraged the renewal of sisters, the Sacred Congregation for Religious
and Secular Institutes and the present pope are not supportive of the
directions taken by American "nuns." For Roman authorities, religious life is essentially a matter of dependence, hierarchical authority,
and separation from the world. For most sisters and many American
Catholics, on the other hand, religion is embodied precisely in the
struggles and opportunities of life in the world, and the gospel is best
expressed in feminist values of collective experience and collegial process. Each group espouses a different ecclesiology, and those operating out of feminist values believe that they have the stronger case to
claim that a discipleship of equals is truer to the gospel.[26]

The premier theologian of contemporary religious life, Sandra
Schneiders, specifies the meaning of the vows in terms related to the

discipleship of equals. Religious vows are a commitment to the transformation of all things and people in Christ through a life dedicated to mutuality of possessions, affectivity, and power. Through the vow of poverty, one responds to the world's staggering problems of selfishness and exploitation by sharing everything, by entering a relationship of sister to all in Christ. From this perspective, the task is to renounce artificial dependence on superiors or community for money, to abandon useless and unreal imitation of the destitute, and to devote one's energy to alleviating misery and building structures of solidarity. To vow celibacy is to enter the current cultural conversion from patriarchy to mutuality of women and men. Celibate women are in a favored position to challenge male domination because they have professional competency and social freedom. They are more likely to demonstrate the possibility of experiencing genuine intimacy in friendship free of violence and intolerance and marked by mutual acceptance and love that honors vulnerability. Vowed obedience aims at freedom for union with the will of God mediated not through hierarchical authority but through human events and persons which call for discernment of the appropriate loving response in particular circumstances. In this view, reliance on personal religious experience, which is the heart of discernment, is the only ground for confidence that one has found God's will. Here, cooperation is understood to be just as demanding as the older form of obedience.[27]

Religious life in this mode is a revelation of the biblical "eschatological community." By eschatological Schneiders means not so much what lies in the future as what acts as the focus of hope in the present. In the last twenty years, religious life, especially of American sisters, has emerged as an inclusive community bonded by shared love of Christ dedicated especially to God's reign of peace, justice, nonhierarchical authority, and egalitarian friendship.[28] American sisters understand that the root of the tension between them and the Vatican—evident in the mandated study of United States religious life—does not lie in the presumed dissent and defection of American sisters, but rather in the collision course of following two distinctly different and opposing models of authority based on different ecclesiologies: one is hierarchical, the other is the discipleship of equals.[29]

Spiritual Renewal in Women's Organizations.
Many Catholic women's organizations now equate spiritual renewal with espousal of feminist values. The contrast between the values promoted by the Grail and those of the National Council of Catholic Women highlights what I mean by the unity of feminism and renewal.[30]

The NCCW has consistently reflected the views of the American bishops. In their pamphlets defending their stand against the Equal Rights Amendment and in their case against the ordination of women, they maintain the traditional hierarchical view of women as different from and complementary to men, that is, women are best suited to roles which serve and support men. Here, they echo some medieval assumptions that were explained in the first section of this essay. As a women's organization, the NCCW supports women's issues, but never by way of structural analysis which would uncover the fact that their assumption that women are "different and complementary" works out, in practice, to being separate and unequal. The NCCW testimony at hearings for the forthcoming bishops' pastoral letter on women's issues, for example, assumes that women and men have different "natures" and thus, are suited to different roles in which women are the primary parent and the support for male leadership.

The Grail, founded to promote the lay apostolate of women, espoused the "traditional womanly role" until the 1960s when its members began to be more aware of the relations of domination and submission which are embedded in all social structures, including the church. Small and officially invisible, in contrast to the NCCW, the Grail is much more influential as a forum in which women's concerns are central to the task of a renewed theology and liturgy and search for a noncoercive model of authority.

Other organizations of Catholic women that work from within a feminist perspective do so because they believe that God's Spirit moves within the church today in the lives of the marginalized. Far from seeing the women's movement as a luxury in a world full of staggering problems, they perceive the real issue as the need to see the direct links between their own oppression and the problems that plague the disenfranchised people of the world. Since most of the world's poor are women and children, and since women have only secondary status in the Catholic Church, these groups see their inclusive Christian feminism as a most valid way to live the gospel in the modern world.[31]

The Womanchurch movement is another example of this fusion of feminism and Christian conversion. Womanchurch, begun in the 1980s, is a coalition of organizations founded in the 1970s around specific causes (e.g., Women's Ordination Conference, Center of Concern, Black Sisters, Las Hermanas, Women's Alliance for Theology, Ethics, and Ritual). Rather than focus just on the issue for which they were founded, these laywomen and sisters are bonding to form what Elisabeth Schüssler Fiorenza calls "the gathering of the ecclesia of women."

It is a forum for exchanging stories of women's experience, sharing spiritualities, celebrating liturgies, identifying issues and resources for future empowerment. In the midst of the hope that this sharing generates is an urgency based on the conviction that women are leaving the church in growing numbers because it has become irrelevant to their lives.[32]

The significance of Womanchurch is its claim to *be* church. Participants in the 1983 conference, Womanchurch Speaks, saw themselves not as exiles from the church but as in exodus from patriarchy. As Rosemary Radford Ruether later analyzed it, this community of liberation from patriarchy declares itself to be theologically church, that is, a community of redemption. Womanchurch makes no claim to "leave the church" or cut itself off from historical Christianity; rather, it is the beginning of a process of renewal which must include men and historical Christianity, but only when these, too, recognize that exodus from patriarchy is essential to the meaning and mission of the church.[33]

Since 1984 the original coalition has broadened to include newer and older groups of Catholic women and expects to become ecumenical. It provides political, spiritual, and liturgical possibilities for almost every Catholic feminist still trying to make sense of her tradition. Although the presence of Catholic lesbians and those favoring a pluralistic understanding of Catholic teaching on abortion may frighten conservative women, the inclusion of these groups makes Womanchurch a forum for those with different views to meet one another in dialogue and explore bonding possibilities that go beyond their immediate differences.[34]

Prophetically Denounce the Recent Creation of a Second Class "Alternate Christianity" for Women in the Catholic Church

Sandra Schneiders has called attention to a collection of events in the recent past that has had the effect of gradually creating what she calls an "alternate Christianity" for women in the Catholic Church.[35] Preaching is a good example. As women, especially those trained in theology and Scripture, began to emerge as excellent preachers, the Vatican ordered that women were not to preach the homily at the Eucharistic liturgy. While male deacons without even rudimentary formation in Scripture could give the homily, women with doctorates in Scripture could not. No doubt because the total exclusion of these women was patently absurd, an *alternative* form of preaching was developed for them. While they could not give the homily, they could give "reflections." And lest anyone conclude that the two were the same, reflections were not to be given after the reading of the gospel but at some other time before or after the liturgy.

Assistance at the altar is also a matter that is separate but not equal. Women may assist at the altar, but they may not be installed as acolytes. They may read the scriptures during liturgy but may not be installed as lectors. Even when women do exactly what men do their participation is to be understood as an *alternate* form of service rather than an official one.

Due to the increasing lack of ordained ministers in the Church, a situation which could be easily remedied by the ordination of already trained, experienced, and willing women, a number of women have assumed, with ecclesiastical approval, the role of community leadership in parishes without clergy. These women do many things including presiding at communion services. Yet their leadership cannot be acknowledged as pastoring and the services they lead are not the Liturgy of the Eucharist. Again, women are *alternate* pastors, *alternate* leaders of *alternate* worship.

The most serious example, from a theological point of view, of this gradual creation of an alternate Christianity for women was the declaration by the Bishop of Pittsburgh that the Holy Thursday footwashing service which Jesus explicitly commanded his disciples to do in imitation of him was to be carried out only with men because the liturgical instruction speaks of "*duodecim viros.*" In John's gospel, all biblical scholars note, the footwashing plays the role that the institution narrative plays in the synoptic gospels. Therefore, to exclude women from the footwashing is to symbolically declare them ineligible for Eucharist. The outrage of priests, women, and other laity at this sacramental discrimination drew from the Bishop what he considered a conciliatory gesture. He said that women could be included in some *alternate* rite expressing service in the church. Most recently this Bishop removed his original ban on women, but continues to favor the creation of alternate rites to include women.[36]

In summary, the increasing difficulty church officials are experiencing in maintaining women's exclusion from full participation in the Catholic community is gradually leading them to create an alternate and second class form of Christianity for women. While the various restrictions have occurred at different times and places and have differing official weight, women have not failed to notice the pattern of marginalization and exclusion by which the denial of their full Christian identity is made concrete in their daily experience, and they are beginning prophetically to renounce this abuse of pastoral authority.

Continue to Enlarge the Discipline of
Christian Feminist Theology

Christian feminist theology is participation in and critical reflection upon the religious faith of the Christian community by persons who are aware of the historical and cultural restriction of women in Christian tradition and who intend to reimagine and articulate Christian faith in such a way that it promotes mutuality and equality.[37] In order to give focus to the complex tasks of Christian feminist theologians, I will limit the discussion to Roman Catholic women and will use some of Mary Jo Weaver's synthesis and evaluation of their contributions.[38]

Christian feminist theologians admit from the outset that their tradition is relentlessly patriarchal in language, custom, practice, symbolism, memory, history, theological articulation, and ritual. They understand why some feminists judge that the tradition is so intrinsically sexist that it cannot be revised, or why others decide that the patriarchal religious structures are so entrenched that one's energy is better spent on other projects.

Mary Daly is perhaps the most famous feminist to make these decisions about the tradition. Of Roman Catholic background and education, she has parted company with the church and what she calls "American sado-society" because she finds them both to be unredeemably sexist. Because her first book, *The Church and the Second Sex* (1968), was a groundbreaking event for American Catholic feminists, I agree with Mary Jo Weaver's judgment that Daly must be considered in any discussion of Roman Catholic feminist theology. Weaver notices that, ironically, even now Daly exhibits some peculiarly Roman Catholic dynamics: her later work, especially, is characterized by dogmatic authoritarianism, a flight from and denigration of the world, a strong desire for transcendence, and an elitist understanding of the intellectual life, all hallmarks of preconciliar Catholicism.

Daly's second book, *Beyond God the Father* (1973), was a transitional one: it connected to the past by way of being a theological argument for a process God, dynamic revelation, and a realized eschatology; it mirrored the present because it was a feminist manifesto; it foreshadowed the future by being a book about language.

Most of Daly's subsequent work has aimed at a "transmogrification" of the language: she inverts and invents words, for example "gyn/ecology," in order to describe a new world of "radical feminist friendship and sisterhood."

If Daly is going to function as a prophet for feminism, Christian readers must weigh critically the alternatives she offers. Daly sees no

possibilities within the Christian community. Her choices are clear
and dogmatic: one must choose between the logic of radical feminism
and the logic of the Christian symbol system. She projects an image of
an all-female Utopia, but the identification of this place as "Other-
world" and the absolute exclusion of all men reinstates the divisive
dualisms other feminist theologians attempt to overcome.

Elisabeth Schüssler Fiorenza and Rosemary Radford Ruether exemplify the vision of these more inclusive feminists. They have decided to reinterpret the tradition in order to change its direction and
open it to the influence of women's religious experience.

Elisabeth Schüssler Fiorenza, a specialist in New Testament
studies, has produced an intense vision of feminist theology. German-
born and trained, the first woman in her diocese to study theology and
needing the bishop's permission to do so, Schüssler Fiorenza devoted
herself first to ecclesiological issues. Because of her long-standing
commitment to declericalization and structural change within Roman
Catholicism, she is wary of women seeking ordination within the present system without seeking significant structural change in the way
ministry is practiced and understood.

Schüssler Fiorenza's efforts to articulate a new interpretive
paradigm for New Testament study and to urge a new hermeneutics
that can prove that God is on the side of the oppressed are at the center of her book *In Memory of Her*.[39] Here she argues that an equalitarian
interpretive framework is the only one that can do justice to the dynamics of the Jesus movement, and the only one that has the power to
set free the egalitarian impulses of that movement both in the ancient
traditions and in contemporary practice. Her groundwork for a new
Church as been laid in grass-roots gatherings of women, as well as in
scholarly forums in the academy.

Schüssler Fiorenza works within a creative tension that is both
feminist and Christian: as a feminist, she criticizes Christianity for
being guilty of the structural sin of sexism, while, as a Christian, she
argues that the tradition is not inherently or necessarily sexist. To sustain this tension she focuses on the historical struggle of women and
other oppressed peoples, finding here the locus of God's liberating activity. She resists those outside the Christian tradition who have relin-
quished women's biblical heritage, and, at the same time, resists those
within the church who would judge a feminist reconstruction of the
New Testament period to be eccentric or marginal.

Schüssler Fiorenza establishes theoretically the task of feminist
theology, and she connects theory with practice by following the insight of liberation theology that "only active commitment to the oppressed and active involvement in their struggle for liberation enable

us to see our society and the world differently and give us a new perspective."[40]

Rosemary Radford Ruether is the most prolific writer in the Roman Catholic feminist community. Because her work has been directed by her own interests and because "social sin" has been a catalyst for her thinking and writing, Ruether's work is wide-ranging. She is equally at home in her area of academic specialization—the classics and early Christian writers—and in the ecclesiastical and social issues of the times: she has written articles on a spectrum of issues from birth control, divorce, the council and its aftermath, to civil rights, the Jewish-Christian dialogue, nuclear arms, and base communities. When asked about the many different causes she has espoused she says, "These issues were experienced by me not as a series of alternating commitments, but as an expanding consciousness of the present human social dilemma."[41] Refusing to hierarchicalize oppressions, she sees "sexism, racism, classism and other kinds of oppression as interconnected in an overall pattern of human alienation and sinfulness."[42]

Ruether (along with Daly) did pioneering work in grasping and communicating the basic issues of feminist theology. Her "Male Chauvinist Theology and the Anger of Women" (1971) and *Religion and Sexism* (1974) were challenging summaries of the issues at a time when very few people understood the dimensions of the problem of women in the church. Her book *Women of Spirit: Female Leadership in the Jewish and Christian Traditions* (1979), edited with Eleanor McLaughlin, and the new series she has edited with Rosemary Skinner Keller, *Women and Religion in America* (1982) make available views of female strength and greatness that have never been glimpsed until now.

Sexism and God-Talk .

Ruether's systematic theology, is at once a deconstruction of traditional categories, such as sin and redemption, and a reconstructive vision of theology from a feminist perspective.[43] Like much contemporary theology, she begins with experience rather than with deductive principles taken from Scripture or the teachings of the magisterium. What is unusual, however, is the weight she gives to *women's* experience and female cultural paradigms. The critical principle of this theology is: whatever denies or distorts the full humanity of women is appraised as not redemptive. The positive corollary maintains that whatever promotes the full humanity of women is "of the Holy." Feminist theology is not unique in claiming this principle, but women are firm in claiming it for themselves.

Ruether's liberationist theology, like biblical prophecy, is based on a concept of conversion and repentance. For her, prophecy is valid only as a form of self-criticism, not as a means of castigating communities and systems other than one's own. Her criticism of Catholicism and of aspects of American economic and political practice is, she believes, the legitimate task of an American Catholic. Feminism incorporates everything else. "For me," she says, "the commitment to feminism is fundamental to the commitment to justice, to authentic human life itself."[44]

In summary, pioneering feminist theologians have begun to enlarge the discipline of theology by changing its direction from one in which faith was considered primarily from a male-centered viewpoint to one which compensates for this imbalance by concentrating on women's experience as its starting point. Expansion of theology's perspective must continue in the direction of attending as faithfully to women's experience of faith as to men's, and articulating the new vision that emerges from the conversation and possible convergence of these commitments of faith. Some of this more inclusive theology comes from men who are feminists. Leonard Swidler, for example, has a distinguished record of attention to feminist issues in interreligious dialogue. With Arlene Swidler, he co-founded the *Journal of Ecumenical Studies* which incorporates feminist convictions.[45] John Carmody brings a feminist perspective to holistic spirituality and to theologies of peace and justice. In partnership with Denise Lardner Carmody, he has pioneered bringing a feminist viewpoint to textbooks on world religions.[46] William M. Thompson brings a feminist viewpoint into his Christology, and Matthew Fox does the same for creation-centered spirituality.[47]

Ongoing conversation will, no doubt, concentrate on such issues as inclusive language in worship and all prayer; prophetic action for conversion to an authority of service and mutuality; shared wealth; declericalization of ministry; renewal of theology to eliminate its use as an ideological support for denigrating women[48] and to enrich its possibilities of conveying revelation by incorporating women's religious insights.

Appropriate Christian Feminist Spirituality

Everything mentioned so far in this essay has been related to spirituality, for spirituality as life-experience and as a field of study is no longer identified simply with asceticism and mysticism, or with the practice of virtue and methods of prayer. Spirituality encompasses all of life from the perspective of the actualization of the human capacity to be spiritual; that is, to relate to self, others, and God in love, knowledge, and commitment. In relation to God, spirituality is who we really are, the deepest self, not entirely accessible to our comprehensive self-reflection. Spirituality is reflected in all we do; it is consciously cultivated, yet it is deeply informed by class, race, culture, sex, and by our time in history. We each live a personal story about the meaning of our life and the ultimate meaning of all life and death. Making this story explicit means that we have already gained perspective and made the story available for criticism.[49]

To realize that spiritual development is human development is to be aware of the problematic nature of women's spirituality. There are three reasons for this difficulty.[50] First, for women the possibilities for mature humanity, and thus for spirituality, are restricted. Models of human development universally recognize that movement away from conformity and predetermined role expectations and toward greater autonomy or self-direction is necessary for maturity. Yet, women's experience shows that most women are socialized into conformity to a passive role or are arrested at the threshold of autonomy. Second, Christian teaching and practice, instead of promoting women's maturity, has contributed significantly to this restriction. Especially sad is the fact that so many women are estranged from themselves by absorption of the Christian tradition's most common God-images: as male parent, as masculine spirit, as Lord who excludes women from representing him at the altar. Third, women's spirituality is problematic because the desire for spiritual maturity causes some religious women to separate from each other. Some women judge that spiritual maturity can really only be accomplished by rejecting biblical tradition, while others conclude that their spiritual development demands dedication to the challenging, exhausting, long-range task of reconstructing the entire Christian tradition because it is male-centered.

A reconstructed Christian tradition is slowly emerging as women and men become aware of the detrimental effects of patriarchy on everyone, and particularly on women. Women's spirituality can be promoted if all of us make progress in a two-fold process. To begin, we must reexamine presuppositions about human development, discover the history of women's experience and leadership that has not yet become common knowledge, and explicate the women-liberating insights implicit in biblical teaching about God.[51] As soon as these resources become available we must begin to incorporate them into every aspect of life and ministry: teaching, writing, celebrating, praying, counseling, reconciling, befriending, protesting. As long as this process remains "frontier territory," experienced as the unknown and fraught with risk, women's spirituality will continue to be very problematic.

I am particularly interested in supporting women's spirituality by demonstrating the compatibility of feminist psychology and Christian maturity. Contrary to common expectations, my primary inspiration comes not from contemporary psychology but from the classical tradition of Christian spirituality. Teresa of Avila and Catherine of Siena understood the primacy of adequate self-understanding before psychologists such as Carol Gilligan or Jean Baker Miller questioned the assumptions of the dominant psychology. While I regard the latter as valuable teachers, I have been drawn to them because I was already in the school of Teresa and Catherine.

In her *Life*, Teresa advises her readers: "This path of self knowledge must never be abandoned. . . . Along this path of prayer, self knowledge . . . is the bread with which all palates must be fed no matter how delicate they may be. . . ." Catherine, too, images self-knowledge as a basic food for spiritual growth. In *The Dialogue* she pictures God as saying, "So think of the soul as a tree made for love and living only by love. . . . The circle in which this tree's root, the soul's love, must grow is true knowledge of herself. . . ."[52]

I believe that feminist psychology is a necessary resource for this self-knowledge. This puzzles people who ask: How can feminism, which promotes self-fulfillment, be compatible with Christian spirituality which fosters self-denial?

The answer to this question lies in a critical examination of its assumptions. First, there is no need to assume conflicting goals. Both feminist psychology and Christian spiritual development aim at a common goal: maturity; both emphasize the balance between relationship and independence. Both spirituality and feminist psychology value vulnerability as a human quality capable of generating empathy for others; that is, when vulnerability is accepted as a normal human condition one can avoid the harmful defenses against having to admit it, and then one can be more sensitive to others.

The assumption that Christian spirituality and feminist psychology are incompatible assumes also that the self comes "ready made" with needs to be either fulfilled or denied. We must, however, ask deeper questions: How is one's self constructed? How can one avoid self-deception about what gives fulfillment and what should be denied?

Closer examination reveals that feminism and Christian spirituality have compatible goals and processes. Feminism teaches women a method of critical examination through which they come to recognize the way socialization in a patriarchal culture affects their self-understanding; it raises their consciousness to awareness and affirmation of themselves as authors of their own life-story. Christian spirituality promotes a parallel process: discernment. Experts on the subject, such as Teresa of Avila, Ignatius of Loyola, and Catherine of Siena advocate a process in which one examines one's feelings and thoughts, one's assumptions and actions in order to distinguish authentic religious experience from false projections, to separate illusion from honest self-assessment, to relinquish blind fear and egoism in favor of courageous adherence to truth and free commitment to love.

There are also similarities between the goal of Christian spirituality, which is union with God demonstrated by loving care for all persons, and the feminist goal of human development, maturity as understood by psychologists such as Carol Gilligan,[53] Robert Kegan,[54] and Jean Baker Miller.[55] Gilligan rejects autonomy as the only appropriate goal for human maturity in moral decisions and presents instead a goal which equally values relationships. Although she has not yet expanded the basic insights of her research into a full model of life-span development, her colleague, Robert Kegan, has done this. Kegan explicitly intends to present a model of maturity which listens as carefully to women's experience as it does to men's. Consequently, his model demonstrates how the qualities which have come to characterize men and women stereotypically—autonomy or relationship—are the focus of life-span tasks at every stage of everyone's development. Whereas Kegan contributes a complete developmental model, and Gilligan evaluates women's moral development, Miller presents characteristics of a whole new psychology of women. She explains that autonomy as the goal of maturity is a carry-over from men's experience and implies that one should be able to give up affiliations in order to become separate and self-directed. Women seek more than autonomy as was defined for men; indeed, they seek a fuller ability to encompass relationships *simultaneously* with the fullest development of themselves. Too often women are misinterpreted or penalized for affirming to men a basic truth: everyone's individual development proceeds only through affiliation as well as differentiation. And this development involves conflict as an inevitable fact of life which can be helpful if faced honestly and examined with mutuality.

According to feminist psychologists, then, the criterion for human maturity is an integration of both attachment and independence. Do traditional spiritual writers agree that both of these elements are part of the standard of religious maturity? They explicitly agree that the norm of religious maturity is relationship. The ability to sustain a wide range of loving relationships typifies the religiously mature person. I believe they agree also with the need for autonomy or self-direction, yet only contemporary authors use this language. Agreement in the classical sources is implicit, yet clear, I believe, when one examines their description of religious maturity as the fruit of a strenuous human process. Writers like Teresa, Ignatius, and Catherine speak of maturity as the result of developmental phases which require love even in darkness, loneliness, or misunderstanding. This lack of consolation which throws one back upon one's deepest inner resources is, I believe, the kind of experience which can promote what contemporary language calls autonomy, or what classical language calls perseverance or fidelity to one's inner calling, or discernment of the appropriate response to God's presence in a given situation.[56] Lack of consolation can also promote depression if one has not been helped to have deep inner resources such as a sense of identity as loved for oneself.

Nevertheless, this recognition of the importance of personal autonomy has seldom been taught to Christian women. Rather, women have been educated to find the meaning of themselves primarily in terms of relationships. At the same time as they have lacked sufficient encouragement in the direction of autonomy, they have not been helped to see the dangers inherent in a self that finds its meaning only in relationships. Religious models of development that idealize relationships are too often used to reinforce motifs of women's "self-sacrifice." This results in conformity to male-approved roles unless the praise for self-sacrifice is coupled with insistence on development of an independent self.

Exhortation to free choice and self-directed action are present, but not obvious, in classical discussion of discernment by writers such as Catherine of Siena and John of the Cross. These themes are implicit, I believe, in their meditation on fidelity in darkness, and on perseverance when one feels no consolation. For it is this struggle to sustain authentic love that forces one to question conventional wisdom and trust one's own religious experience. Discernment enables one to experience both ultimate dependence on God and personal empowerment by God.[57] This is what is important for women today, this conviction that God's Spirit affirms their self-direction as well as their surrender. What is essential for mature spirituality is the conviction that only an independent self can achieve authentic religious surrender.

In summary, the gospel call to a discipleship of equals urges us now to act simultaneously on at least four fronts. Participate in the ongoing conversion of institutions such as religious life and women's organizations. Insist on a reversal of the trend to create an alternative, second-class Christianity for Catholic women. Enlarge the discipline of feminist theology, and appropriate a feminist spirituality.

III. FUTURE ISSUES

Because Christianity believes that the future invites us to greater possibilities of God's reign of friendship, and liberation, we can speak with hope. Because the only way to risen life is through the mystery of the Passover of Jesus, we must set our face toward Jerusalem and prepare for suffering. As I pointed out in the last section of this essay, feminist spirituality values the self-direction and maturity that are the fruit of struggle and suffering. For this appropriate autonomy makes possible authentic religious surrender and the true discipleship of equals.

A theology for the future anticipates the likely experience of the future and discerns the Christian interpretation of that experience that might sustain us. We cannot live without meaning, so we try to anticipate or evaluate, in the light of past experience, what interpretation might sustain hope and reinforce the action we must undertake. Elie Wiesel, in a lecture at Villanova University (March 19, 1987), reminded us that when the unspeakable is spoken it then becomes possible. Referring to the Holocaust and to nuclear war, Wiesel noted that the ability to speak of these matters as though one were sane when doing so makes these outrages possible and perhaps likely. So too, he reminded us, we must speak words of hope in order to make hope possible. For example, in the Talmudic tradition it is said that the name of the Messiah was spoken even before creation. That is, the ultimate word of hope was spoken before Israel's long experience of struggle in order to sustain Jewish belief that human history is ultimately messianic.

The future holds more possibilities than I could mention or even imagine, but allow me to concentrate on one that I can imagine and then to suggest some theological words of hope that I believe we must develop in the future in order to sustain us in this experience.

Action or Experience in the Future

Completing the Exodus from Patriarchy: Adulthood.
I agree with those who interpret the signs of the times as indications that the church, especially the Roman Catholic community of the church, is moving to complete its exodus from patriarchal institutions.[58] Various segments are moving away from acceptance of the situation in which one male adult has absolute control over others who remain as children in relation to him. Whether this father figure be husband, work supervisor, parish priest, or pope, this person is no longer assumed to be the only one recognized as fully adult. The

future will bring stronger claims for adult status, for the discipleship of equal adults, from every segment of the Church. There are clear signs of this future experience, I believe.

For example, Sandra Schneiders notes six signs of demands for adulthood in the church.[59] First, the movement of women toward full and equal participation in the life and ministry of the Church is a demand for adult status. Second, the laity's insistence on their right to make responsible theological and moral decisions is a claim to adulthood. Third, there is the claim of theologians to the right to dissent from Vatican positions when their research and reflection reaches conclusions that differ from those presented by the Vatican. Fourth, various national hierarchies are emerging as genuine leadership groups which formulate teachings and even defend theologians, such as Leonardo Boff, who are under attack from the Vatican. Fifth, the emergence of spirituality as a central concern of all Catholics is the emergence of the desire to take personal responsibility for one's relationship to God. This attention to spirituality is bearing fruit in greater moral responsibility, ministerial commitment, and concern with justice. Sixth, the emergence of increasing pluralism of thought and practice is an indication of the exodus from patriarchy. Absolutism in doctrine and practice is possible only when the "father" thinks and plans and the "children" meekly follow and obey. Today all serious Catholics think, plan, and act.

All movement toward adulthood involves an uncomfortable shift from a need for certitude to a search for understanding, and, often, a struggle with parent-figures who exert pressure, try to manipulate, and abuse their authority. We must be prepared to interpret this experience with hope.

Words of Hope for Difficult Times to Come

Theological themes that have been used most often in the past to oppress women are now being reimagined in ways that make them capable of giving hope.

Anthropology.

Assuming that women are, by nature, subordinate to men, church officials have excluded women from ordination and leadership roles, demanded that they remain in abusive marriages, and restricted contemplative women in ways that do not effect contemplative men. Most disagreements between the bishops and representatives of the Women's Ordination Conference are rooted in this issue. Most bishops have a model of "two natures" in which they believe that women and men are different but equal and complementary. In practice, "complementary" means inferior and incapable of representing Christ at the altar. In the national hearings for the forthcoming pastoral letter on women's concerns in the church, the same "two nature" anthropology was used by conservative women's groups to bolster requests that only traditional roles be affirmed in the future.[60]

Now feminist theologians are reimagining this "two nature" anthropology according to a transformational model. They connect the transformation of gender stereotypes with the transformation of the social and cultural structures which promote and reinforce them. Any adequate understanding of the natures of women and men must have the power of social critique.[61]

Self-denial and the Cross.
Influenced by Constance FitzGerald's writing on impasse and the dark night,[62] Carolyn Osiek has begun to reformulate the theology of the cross.[63] This is one of the most difficult symbols to use in a feminist context. Under this sign, powerful men have identified their own cause with that of God and slaughtered "unbelievers," tortured "heretics" and "witches," and silenced dissidents. It has been used according to a double standard. Both women and men have embraced rejection and suffering in order to "die with Christ." Yet women's self-sacrifice was evaluated according to criteria set by men, and not vice versa; indeed, men set some standards which assumed that women should subordinate themselves to men. Women should "carry their cross," for example, by enduring an abusive husband or by accepting the rejection of their request for full participation in ministry. "The cross" has been manipulated by people who would submit others to it, but not themselves!

This double standard is most evident in its application to women of the notion of "bearing one's cross" in passive acceptance. Though seen as weaker by nature, women have been seen as capable of bearing greater suffering. For example, St. Bonaventure says, "It is for man to act, for woman to suffer";[64] that is, woman is naturally suited to endure, to be passive.

Osiek's theology of the cross aims to integrate feminist convictions about self-direction and free decision with traditional notions of the cross. To this end, she emphasizes the relationship of suffering, choice, vision, and redemption.

First, Christians must look to Jesus. He chose to devote his life to a vision and to the attempt to bring it about: the vision of the reign of God begun in this life. Jesus believed it was possible and was willing to give all for it. The suffering he experienced was not imposed but

came as a consequence of his choosing "with a passion" to remain
faithful to his vision.

So it is with the disciples of Jesus who envision the reign of God
as the discipleship of equals. We must prepare to live under the cross
of Jesus as a sign of contradiction. We choose to live coherently with a
perception of gospel life as that of the discipleship of equals; this much
is chosen. The contradiction results from the unexpected, irrational,
and sometimes violent opposition which such a choice attracts. Or,
even for those who expect suffering, the contradiction arises from the
fact that an opposing vision of the gospel generates a powerful deter-
mination to enflesh that dream in society. The ideal might be, for example, God's reign as the "order" of obedient unanimity in which
women "know their place"; or it might be the harmony that results
when women accept their complementary roles as "handmaid," and
"Martha." In her novel *A Handmaid's Tale* (which was on the *New York
Times* "bestseller" list for months in 1986-87), Margaret Atwood presents the harrowing story of a woman's life in the American society
that would result from a political takeover by Christian fundamental-
ists who have just such a vision of truth.[65] In any case, the contradiction which is the cross results from the violent reaction of opposition
that is aroused by a choice for the discipleship of equals.

The cross tears at us heart and soul, Osiek reminds us, because
we wish to have the vision without the cost. Women's affinity for harmony and peacemaking is violated; the feminine original sin of passivity lurks at the door as a tantalizing escape. There is no point in trying philosophically to see the conflict as "paradox," as only "seeming
contradiction." It is true contradiction, it is opposites which cannot be
reconciled, but which must be lived with in their intolerable conflict
and ambiguity as long as the vision is judged worth living for. There is
always the temptation to abandon the vision of a discipleship of
equals in order to have at least the peace of being left alone. But this
choice too, Osiek advises us, would take its toll in bitterness and disil-
lusionment, and thus is not really a viable option.[66]

The focus here is not on who is to blame or why we must suffer,
but on what happens to us in the process of suffering: we enter into
the suffering of God.[67] Contemporary theology describes this "pain of
God" as the result of the conflict between anger and love: God's anger
at human sinfulness is counteracted by the depth of love that is also an
integral aspect of the divine relationship with us. The result is forgiveness. Jeremiah, voicing the feelings of God imaged as a mother, cries:
"Is Ephraim not my favored son, the child in whom I delight? Often as
I threaten him I still remember him with favor. My womb stirs for
him, I must show him my mercy" (Jer 31:20). The only way in which

we can enter into that divine conflict, that suffering love of God, is to experience it within our own lives. The conflict is between anger at injustice in the Church and an abiding love of the Church that refuses to be killed by anger; the conflict is between a vision of the discipleship of equals and the price to be paid in individual lives—our lives, my life—to bring it about. This is how we enter into the mystery of the cross of Christ, into the suffering of God. This redemptive love is the only hope for the future of a discipleship of equals.

NOTES

1.   Elisabeth Schüssler Fiorenza, *In Memory of Her* (New York: Crossroad, 1983), p. 213.

2.   See, for example, Gerda Lerner, *The Creation of Patriarchy* (New York: Oxford University Press, 1986); Mary Briody Mahowald, ed., *Philosophy of Woman* (Indianapolis: Hackett, 1978); Alice S. Rossi, ed., *The Feminist Papers* (New York: Columbia University Press, 1973).

3.   Rosemary Radford Ruether, ed., *Religion and Sexism* (New York: Simon & Schuster, 1974), pp. 9-10.

4.   St. Teresa of Avila, "The Book of Her Life," in *The Collected Works*, 1, trans. Kieran Kavanaugh, O.C.D. and Otilio Rodriguez, O.C.D. (Washington, DC: Institute of Carmelite Studies, 1976), pp.68-69.

5.   Anne Carr, "On Feminist Spirituality," in *Women's Spirituality: Resources for Christian Development*, Joann Wolski Conn, ed. (New York: Paulist, 1986), pp. 53-55.

6.   Lerner, *Creation of Patriarchy*, p. 2.

7.   Gerda Lerner, *The Majority Finds Its Past* (New York: Oxford University Press, 1979), pp. 145-59.

8.   Phyllis Bird, "Images of Women in the Old Testament," in *Religion and Sexism*, Ruether, ed., pp. 41-88. See also, Phyllis Trible, *God and the Rhetoric of Sexuality* (Philadelphia: Fortress, 1978).

9.   Constance Parvey, "Theology and Leadership of Women in the New Testament," in *Religion and Sexism*, Ruether, ed., pp. 117-49. See also, Letty M. Russell, ed., *Feminist Interpretation of the Bible* (Philadelphia: Westminster, 1985).

10.   Bernadette J. Brooten, "Paul's Views on the Nature of Women and Female Homoeroticism," in *Immaculate and Powerful*, Clarrisa W. Atkinson, Constance H. Buchanan, and Margaret R. Miles, eds. (Boston: Beacon, 1985), pp. 61-87.

11.   Rosemary Radford Ruether, "Misogynism and Virginal Feminism in the Fathers of the Church," in *Religion and Sexism*, Ruether, ed., pp. 150-83.

12.   Judith Hauptman, "Images of Women in the Talmud," in *Religion and Sexism*, Ruether, ed., pp. 184-212.

13. Eleanor Commo McLaughlin, "Equality of Souls, Inequality of Sexes: Woman in Medieval Theology," in *Religion and Sexism*, Ruether, ed., pp. 213-66.

14. Thomas Aquinas, *Summa Theologica*, ed. English Dominican Province, 3 vols. (New York, 1947), II-II, 10, 1, ad 3, as referred to in McLaughlin, "Equality of Souls," p. 229.

15. Micheline de Fontette, *Les religieuses à l'âge classique du droit canon: Recherches sur les structures juridiques des branches feminines des ordres* (Paris, 1967), p. 116, as referred to in McLaughlin, "Equality of Souls," p. 242.

16. Hilda Graef, *Mary, A History of Doctrine and Devotion* (London, 1963), p. 317, as quoted in McLaughlin, "Equality of Souls," p. 249.

17. Mary Potter, "Gender Equality and Gender Hierarchy in Calvin's Theology," *Signs* 11 (Summer 1986), pp. 725-39.

18. Outstanding examples include: Carolyn Walker Bynum, *Jesus as Mother: Studies in the Spirituality of the High Middle Ages* (Berkeley: University of California Press, 1982); Rosemary Ruether and Eleanor McLaughlin, eds., *Women of Spirit* (New York: Simon & Schuster, 1979); William L. Andrews, ed., *Sisters of the Spirit: Three Black Women's Autobiographies of the Nineteenth Century* (Bloomington: Indiana University Press, 1986).

19. Clarissa W. Atkinson, *Mystic and Pilgrim: The "Book" and the World of Margery Kempe* (Ithaca, NY: Cornell University Press, 1983).

20. Margaret Hope Bacon, *Mothers of Feminism* (San Francisco: Harper & Row, 1986).

21. Elizabeth Griffith, "Friends Indeed," review of *Mothers of Feminism* by Margaret Hope Bacon, *New York Times*, 1 February 1986, p. 28.

22. Lerner, *Creation of Patriarchy*, p. 5.

23. *Ibid.*, pp. 11-14. See also, Joan Kelly, *Women, History, and Theory* (Chicago: University of Chicago Press, 1984).

24. *Ibid.*, pp. 123-230.

25. Sandra M. Schneiders, I.H.M., *New Wineskins* (New York: Paulist, 1986), p. ii.

26. Mary Jo Weaver, *New Catholic Women* (San Francisco: Harper & Row, 1986), pp. 105-06.

27. Schneiders, *New Wineskins*, pp. 95-113.

28. *Ibid.*, p. 263.

29. Weaver, *New Catholic Women*, p. 107.

30. *Ibid.*, pp. 118-27.

31. *Ibid.*, pp. 127-36.

32. Kevin Klose, *Washington Post*, 13 November 1983, as quoted in Weaver, *New Catholic Women*, p. 133.

33. Rosemary Radford Ruether, "Womanchurch Calls Men to Exodus from Patriarchy," *National Catholic Reporter*, 23 March 1984, p. 16, as quoted in Weaver, *New Catholic Women*, p. 133.

34. Weaver, *New Catholic Women*, p. 134.

35. What follows is a paraphrase of Sandra M. Schneiders, I.H.M., "New Skins: A Legacy for the Third Millennium," *Delta Epsilon Sigma Journal* 31 (October 1986), pp. 51-52.

36. This paragraph benefits from clarifications suggested by Gerard S. Sloyan, as do other sections of this essay.

37. This definition adapts John Macquarrie, *Principles of Christian Theology* (New York: Charles Scribners Sons, 1966), p. 1, to a feminist perspective.

38. This next section of the essay is a digest of material from Weaver, *New Catholic Women*, pp. 156-77.

39. See note 1.

40. Elisabeth Schüssler Fiorenza, "Toward a Feminist Biblical Hermeneutics: Biblical Interpretation and Liberation Theology," in *The Challenge of Liberation Theology*, Brian Mahan, ed. (Maryknoll, NY: Orbis, 1981), p. 100, as referred to in Weaver, *New Catholic Women*, p. 164.

41. Rosemary Radford Ruether, "Feminist Theology and Religion," unpublished paper presented at Lilly Endowment Seminar, March, 1983, p. 23, as quoted in Weaver, p. 164.

42. Rosemary Radford Ruether, "Of One Humanity," *Sojourners* 13 (January 1984), p. 17, as quoted in Weaver, *New Catholic Women*, p. 165.

43. Rosemary Radford Ruether, *Sexism and God-Talk* (Boston: Beacon, 1983).

44. Ruether, "Of One Humanity," p. 19, as quoted in Weaver, *New Catholic Women*, p. 170.

45. See, for example, Leonard Swidler, *Biblical Affirmations of Woman* (Philadelphia: Westminster, 1979).

46. See, for example, John Carmody, *Holistic Spirituality* (New York: Paulist, 1983) and *The Progressive Pilgrim* (Notre Dame, IN: Fides/Claretian, 1980); see also, Denise L. Carmody and John T. Carmody, *Ways to the Center* (Belmont, CA: Wadsworth, 1981).

47. See, for example, William M. Thompson, *The Jesus Debate* (New York: Paulist, 1985); and Matthew Fox, *Original Blessing: A Primer in Creation-Centered Spirituality* (Santa Fe, NM: Bear & Co., 1983).

48. See, for example, the use of St. Monica to reinforce stereotypical roles for women, as explained by Clarissa W. Atkinson, "'Your Servant, My Mother': The Figure of Saint Monica in the Ideology of Christian Motherhood," in *Immaculate and Powerful*, Atkinson, et al., eds., pp. 139-200.

49. See Joann Wolski Conn, "Women's Spirituality: Restriction and Reconstruction," in *Women's Spirituality*, Conn, ed., p. 9; Carr, "On Feminist Spirituality," pp. 49-50.

50. See essays in my *Women's Spirituality*, pp. 3-5, 9-57.

51. See, for example, Susan Cady, Marian Ronan, and Hal Taussig, *Sophia: The Future of Feminist Spirituality* (San Francisco: Harper & Row, 1986). The authors demonstrate how the image of God as Sophia (wisdom) is less likely to be coopted by the white race or the upper class.

52. Pertinent texts from Teresa and Catherine are reprinted in my *Women's Spirituality*, pp. 177-200.

53. Carol Gilligan, *In a Different Voice* (Cambridge: Harvard University Press, 1982). See also, the critique of Gilligan by a panel of feminist scholars and Gilligan's reply in *Signs* 11 (Winter 1986), pp. 304-33.

54. Robert Kegan, *The Evolving Self: Problem and Process in Human De-*

velopment (Cambridge: Harvard University Press, 1982).

55. Jean Baker Miller, *Toward a New Psychology of Women* (Boston: Beacon, 1976).

56. Saint Thérèse of Lisieux, for example, developed an independent, original vision of holiness by struggling with spiritual darkness and reevaluating the tradition common in her nineteenth-century French Carmel. See my "Thérèse of Lisieux from a Feminist Perspective," *Spiritual Life* 28 (Winter 1982), 233-39.

57. This theme is developed in Constance FitzGerald, O.C.D., "Impasse and Dark Night," in *Women's Spirituality*, Conn, ed., pp. 287-311.

58. See, for example, Richard A. McCormick, S.J., "Dissent in Moral Theology and Its Implications," *Theological Studies* 48 (March 1987), 87-105, esp. 104; Madonna Kolbenschlag, *Authority, Community and Conflict* (Kansas City, MO: Sheed & Ward, 1986).

59. Schneiders, "New Skins," pp. 50-60.

60. *Origins* 14 (21 March 1985), pp. 652-66; 15 (3 October 1985), pp. 242-56. See also, Sidney Callahan, Sally Cunneen, Monika Hellwig, Margaret Brennan, and Doris Smith, "The Pastoral on Women: What Should the Bishops Say?" *America*, 18 May 1985, pp. 404-13.

61. See, for example, Anne Carr, "Theological Anthropology and the Experience of Women," *Chicago Studies* 19 (Summer 1980). 113-28; report of Mary Ann Donovan's presentation on this theme in *Proceedings of the Catholic Theological Society of America* 41 (1986), pp. 151-52; Mary J. Buckley, "The Rising of the Woman is the Rising of the Race," *Proceedings of the Catholic Theological Society of America* 34 (1979), pp. 48-63; Mary Ann Hinsdale, "Women's Experience and Christian Anthropology," as reported in *Proceedings of the Catholic Theological Society of America* 42 (1987), pp. 164-65.

62. See note 57.

63. Carolyn Osiek, R.S.C.J., *Beyond Anger: On Being a Feminist in the Church* (New York: Paulist, 1986).

64. *III Sententiae*, d. 12, a. 3, q. 1, as noted in Osiek, *Beyond Anger*, p. 91, footnote 2.

65. Margaret Atwood, *A Handmaid's Tale* (Boston: Houghton Mifflin, 1986).

66. Osiek, *Beyond Anger*, pp. 73-74.

67. *Ibid.*, pp. 75-76.

2

The Challenge of
Feminist Theology

Georgia Masters Keightley*

ABSTRACT

The feminist critique of theology is a radical and extensive one. This chapter examines contemporary feminist scholarship as it relates to three strategic issues in theological anthropology: (1) traditional interpretations of woman's nature; (2) the long-standing tendency to justify woman's social inferiority on the grounds of her "natural" inferiority; and (3) the complete oversight of the area of woman's experience. It will then be shown that this particular critique comes to a point of convergence in theological method, thus creating fundamental questions about accepted principles now directing the theologian's work.

Feminist theology offers a radical critique of fundamental Christian positions. It is *critical* in that it challenges the presuppositions and methodology according to which the classic treatises have been developed. It is *radical* in that it calls for a thorough recasting of the basic evidence upon which the theologian must reflect.[1] My purpose here is to indicate the nature of this critique and to show just how deep-rooted and extensive it is. I propose to do this by highlighting some of the issues relative to theological anthropology that have been raised by a growing body of work produced by feminist scholars and theologians.

According to this developing consensus, it is imperative that contemporary theologians formulate a more adequate anthropology.

*Georgia M. Keightley (Ph.D., Catholic University of America) is Assistant Professor of Theology at Trinity College (Washington, DC 20017). She participated in the NEH Seminar for College Teachers, "Early Christianity from a Sociological Perspective," directed by Howard Kee of Boston University. Her review of the draft of the U.S. Catholic Bishops' Pastoral Letter on Women was recently published in *Theological Reflections*.

This requires an understanding of human being that not only draws upon the substantial achievements of the scientific and humanistic disciplines; more to the point, it must be one that deliberately includes the original intuitions that accrue from women's lived experience. Additional questions concerning the inherent appropriateness of the categories used to elaborate the essential Christian meanings have also been raised. Feminists increasingly charge that these interpretive schemes incorporate a definite bias and that, in many respects, the Christian account of salvation speaks more directly, more meaningfully to the life-experience of men than of women.

While such questions pertain to theological anthropology, feminist theologians quite accurately observe that assumptions about the human condition as well as understandings of human beings and their experience are also relevant to such other areas as theological method, ethics, spirituality, and pastoral ministry. They would further agree that theorists in these fields tend to presume rather than define a concept of person. As a result, this work may be distorted either by assumptions that reveal a narrowly masculine frame of reference or that unthinkingly reiterate the traditional prejudices against women. Because of the breadth and depth of their criticisms, theologians cannot afford to ignore the feminist observations.

Prior to examining some of these issues at length, however, it is essential to recognize that the challenge feminists present Christian theology is neither an anomaly nor an aberrance. To the contrary, their criticism is firmly grounded in the achievement of the Enlightenment and rises out of the cumulative insights of the western philosophic tradition.

For instance, feminist criticism may appropriately be described as an exercise in modern epistemology. It originates in the Kantian attempt to establish in the subject the grounds for the conditions of knowing. It also rests on that more modest assessment of the historian's effort offered by Wilhelm Dilthey. Thus presuming the valuable insights of nineteenth-century historiography, feminist scholars are very much aware that human experience is eminently historical, that the data of history must be dealt with contextually, and that one can never lose sight of the historian's own irreversible, historically conditioned stance. It has since become an axiom of feminist methodology that western history has been conceived and written from the standpoint of male interests and that therefore to acquire a more adequate reading of any period—as well as to recover the history of women themselves—a substitution of both interpretive categories and sources is requisite.

From Nietzsche, women scholars have learned to respect the sheer power of the idea.[2] From the Marxist tradition, women scholars have come to appreciate the function of knowledge, that is, the way in which ideas have been made to serve the interests of the dominant social group. At the same time, Marxist analysis reveals that an individual's self-understanding is shaped and conditioned by one's social experience. Engels' thesis that a system of patriarchy has supplied the supporting framework of social organization in the West goes a long way towards explaining why women traditionally have been relegated to—and have had to accept—a lot inferior to that of men.

Finally, feminist scholars are just now beginning to see the utility of a sociology of knowledge approach. Building on the thesis that all thought has a definite social matrix, feminists find the categories of social theory to be a viable means of setting out and exploring the dialectic between what a society holds to be true and the unique social conditions out of which this body of knowledge is the outgrowth. This type of analysis holds great promise for theology because it permits a better apprehension of the ecclesial context within which the historical growth of doctrine and praxis may be viewed. For feminist interests it promises to underscore the clearly political aspect of many conventional Christian attitudes towards woman. At the same time, use of this type of methodology provides criteria by which to judge the degree to which the Church of the present has been faithful to its Founder's intentions.

A review of the literature shows that feminist criticism addresses theological anthropology at three strategic points: (1) the traditional assumptions about woman's nature; (2) the long-standing tendency to justify woman's social inferiority on the grounds of her natural inferiority; and (3) the complete neglect of the area of women's experience. My aim is to specify the content of this critique and to consider the main elements of the feminist argument in each instance.

I. DEFINITIONS OF WOMAN'S NATURE

Considerable attention has been given to examining definitions of woman's nature, especially those that have been operative in the past. Feminist scholars are generally suspicious of all attempts to explain what woman *by nature* is; the evidence is that such definitions invariably become valuational, placing woman in the category of "Other," as representing that which is completely antithetical to what is male,

and of course, as antithetical to that which society views as norma-
tive/constitutive.[3] Summary review of the tradition discloses that
Christian anthropology has by no means been immune to such a development.

In fact, survey of the literature shows that a presupposition of
woman's natural inferiority has been normative theology for centuries.[4] Indeed, as the anthropological argument was developed by the
shapers of the tradition (the early fathers, Augustine, Aquinas) one
discovers here the implicit assumption that woman is an incomplete
being. While Genesis 1:27 confirms that man and woman alike are
made in the image of God with an essential equivalence between
them, there is abundant evidence that it has been exceedingly difficult
for the church's theologians to keep this constantly in view.[5] Under
the influence of Greek thought, it was natural for the early fathers—
even as Philo had done before them—to describe the character of the
imago Dei imprinted in individuals in terms of soul or reason. Similarly, it was natural to them to assimilate the male/female dyad to the
body/soul dualism of philosophy.

Such thinking stands behind Augustine's statement that man
alone is God's image "fully and completely," that woman is only insofar as "the totality of this human substance forms a single image."[6]
Besides this incapacity to mirror God in her own right, woman's inferiority manifests itself in other ways. Because "there is a kind of
congruity between the male body and the asexual soul," Augustine
considered the human being of male sex as being the exemplar to
which woman must be compared.[7] That sin originates with her, of
course, attests to an innate moral incapacity. While Augustine would
not deny that woman's rational soul is identical to man's, Eve's deception by the serpent suggested to him that there was an inherent mental
weakness in the female sex as well. On these grounds he argues that
because of the superiority of man's reason, his authority over woman
is entirely justified.[8]

Aquinas re-pristinates the patriarchal anthropology of Augustine, providing it a biological basis by means of the Aristotelian thesis
that woman is a "misbegotten male," so confirming what by then had
become traditional theology. He states that woman's inferior estate
was integral to God's original creation, and was not, as some had
suggested,[9] simply a product of the fall. He too believes Adam to be
superior on the grounds of his creation; Adam was not only the first in
time and the founder of the human race but his body provided the
matter out of which the first woman was made.[10] Secondly, Aquinas
argues that Adam alone displays the peculiar end and essence of
human nature (intellectual activity) while Eve's finality (as an aid to

reproduction) is purely auxiliary and summed up in her bodily, gen-
erative function.[11]

Not only did the early fathers hold woman to be an inferior
being; because she so thoroughly represented carnality (i.e., sexuality,
the lusts of the flesh, the downfall of rationality when confronted by
desire), there was an irresistible tendency to denigrate her body and
its functions, primarily those associated with the female life cycle,
with marriage and childbearing. For instance, in advising a correspon-
dent about her daughter's upbringing, Jerome recommends against allowing the girl to frequent the public baths whenever married women
are present. Not only will she find the pregnant bodies of these
women to be utterly disgusting, but such sight might well arouse
thoughts as to the potential of her own body which could prove injuri-
ous to her Christian vocation. To avoid seeing her own unclothed
body, he even suggests that the girl forswear bathing entirely![12] In the
Exhortation to Chastity, Tertullian rather crudely describes marriage in
terms of "the belly, breasts and babies."[13] And, of course, it was cus-
tomary in some places to forbid women to enter church buildings at
the time of their menses. As was true for the Jewish community, this
disposition of nature was believed to create a spiritual impurity in
Christian women: according to the *Canonical Epistle of Dionysius of
Alexandria*, "The one who is not entirely pure in soul and body must
be stopped from entering the Holy of Holies."[14] Thus he advises that
women who are so indisposed should stay outside the gate and ab-
stain from communion.

While this misogynist tendency was rooted in the dualistic tension between spirit and flesh, it continued to be nourished over time
by the ascetic ideal of virginity. The "powerful aversion of Christian
male thinkers to female sexuality gave additional impetus to the honoring of Mary. . ."; as a woman who was both asexual and passively
obedient, the Mother of God represented the "ideal of the good feminine"; above all, she was an image of woman completely untroubling
to the celibate male psyche.[15] As a result, the cult of Mary permitted
"men to love and respect their ideal of woman in her." At the same
time, it allowed them to belittle those women who used their sexuality, it enabled them "to ignore or dominate concrete real women with
impunity and with immunity."[16]

While today one is not likely to find theologians describing
women as tantalizing sources of sin or as incomplete beings, feminists
argue that similar assumptions nonetheless continue on in the minds
of some theologians. For instance, they suggest that a presumption of
woman's inferiority underlies all those claims to the effect that by
nature or disposition she is not suited to certain pursuits. While few

theologians would be as bold as Louis Bouyer ("Femininity is a sign of the essential incompleteness of the creature"),[17] many do not hesitate to attribute certain natural infirmities to women. According to the teaching of the Roman Catholic Church's magisterium, for instance, woman possesses an extreme sensibility, one that affects the quality of her decision making.[18] Not only is a basic naiveté and a lack of discernment intrinsic to her character,[19] there seems abundant evidence that a woman's intellect can readily be swayed by an appeal to the emotions. Leo XIII, author of the great social encyclicals, held that "women are not suited for certain occupations" because "by nature" they are fitted for home work.[20] Pius XI argued against an equal education for women for the reason that "there is not in nature itself . . . anything to suggest that there can be or ought to be" equality in the training of the two sexes.[21] And while Vatican II's *Declaration on Christian Education* prescinds from this view, it still compromises its proposals when it suggests that teachers "should pay due regard. . . to sexual differences and to the special role which divine providence allots to each sex in family life and in society."[22]

Feminist criticism of theologians and their treatment of the category "nature" is of three sorts. First, in the light of the latest scientific evidence, they would argue that claims about woman's natural weakness now appear indefensible. To the contrary, a good deal of biological evidence demonstrates that women have a more durable physical constitution than men.[23]

Secondly, women scholars also point out the extent to which the belief that women are naturally inferior makes classic explanations of the divine economy logically inconsistent. For instance, if woman's inferiority is held to be a product of the fall, why is it the case that the consequences of original sin prove far graver for her than for Adam? That is to say, while sin is presented as having corrupted human nature at its core, theologians' descriptions suggest that after sin, woman's mental and moral incapacity exceeds that of man; in fact, it is this that contributes to her inferiority, it is for this that she is fated to a life of subordination. On the other hand, if woman is inferior to Adam even in the order of creation, this raises questions about her very freedom to act, the extent to which she can/ought be held to the same level of responsibility. It asks whether the theory of original justice even has application here.

Likewise, feminists suggest that in terms of results achieved, theologians have unwittingly presented Jesus as being a less effective savior for women than for men. That is to say, if before sin there is an original equality between man and woman, the grace of Christ seems powerless to restore woman to a condition equal to, or at least comparable to, that of redeemed man. As our historical survey shows, even Christian woman, woman redeemed, continued to be identified with the material order no less than her unbelieving, unbaptized sister.[24] Feminists additionally argue that despite the fact that life within the church is supposed to provide a foretaste of the Kingdom, even at this moment, possession of grace and the Spirit prove insufficient to bring Christian women an equality with men within the *ecclesia*; even within the eschatological community itself, incorporation into Christ cannot bring about the demise of those structures that permit women only a marginal, passive role.

In the face of mounting criticism, some theologians have begun to emphasize the complementarity of the sexes; one thus finds contemporary church documents affirming particular feminine attributes and extolling woman's unique place and function in church and society.[25] The problem is, however, that in most cases the distinctions between male and female are so tightly made as to to suggest that humanity is actually comprised of two independent natures, one masculine, one feminine. This, of course, not only undercuts past explanations of sin, grace, and redemption which presupposed but a single human nature; it raises new, perplexing questions. Specifically, in articulating its argument against the ordination of women, the Vatican Declaration of 1976 so tightly linked the maleness of the priest with the maleness of Christ that it suddenly became imperative to ask: "Can a male savior save women?"[26] In the attempt to establish a point of absolute discontinuity between Jesus and women (for the purpose of disqualifying the latter from sacramental ordination), the undue emphasis given to Jesus' maleness appeared to destroy a vital connection that made women beneficiaries of the redemption effected by him. What is more, the Vatican position seemed a clear reiteration of Augustine's belief that, of herself, woman can in no way represent the image of God.

Finally, feminist theologians, in concert with other feminists, call for a redefinition of the category "nature" because they find that many traditional presuppositions about it no longer hold. For example, they observe that this term has consistently been construed in a biological way.[27] While these scholars would not disagree that the idea "nature" can have an important explanatory function (it denotes the underlying structure of things that explains their behavior) they also argue that a biological interpretation does little more than confirm that there are two distinct kinds of humanity, one male, one female. Such an approach, however, is hardly able to explain what men and women as human beings with a history actually are or why they act as they do. As Charles Curran suggests, the reduction of the human to a matter of mere biology in Christian ethics leads to physicalism ("the tendency to identify the moral act with the physical structure of the act"), thus providing a distorted view of the moral life.[28] Feminists argue that to grasp reality's human side, one must think of nature as a social phenomenon, as an entity that is "socially constituted and historically evolving."[29]

Also central to past understandings has been the presumption that human nature in its essential structure is immutable. By this means, theologians could conclude that nature gave to woman certain dispositions, that these in turn predestined her to the performance of specific roles. Today, however, scientists recognize that the capacity for change (adaptation) is actually built into nature; they are aware that biological facts "can be changed or their results affected by social conditions and by deliberate human action."[30] On this account, feminists not only emphasize the centrality of environment and social factors in the creation of nature/gender differences; they also conclude that it is more meaningful to define nature in terms of a cluster concept. By this means, men and women are shown to possess distinct natures (genders). Thus in speaking of woman's nature, one would refer to that cluster of psychological traits that women tend to have more than men, traits which are systematically related to one another and which are instrumental in explaining a wide range of feminine behavior. An advantage of this approach is that it recognizes that natures are flexible and subject to continual modification; it also allows for the fact that "women of different cultures or subcultures [may] have different subsets of this common core of traits."[31] More importantly, while such a definition serves the purpose of explanation, it is in no way evaluative; that is, nothing follows therefrom about how women ought or ought not to live or how society ought to be structured.[32]

A third invalid presupposition concerns the thesis that the biological differences between male and female are the source of important psychological differences that in turn provide a basis for determining male and female stereotypes.[33] Once again, feminist research shows that "the *significance* of biological differences depends on social, historical facts, and moreover, is maintained in every society by complicated social practices."[34] According to Marxist analysis, "the differing forms of human labor (and the resultant social practices and institutions) change the mental and physical capacities of human beings," thus generating psycho-physical structures that "constitute the nature of human beings *qua* social beings."[35] Hence, because women do different sorts of labor than men, different "behavioral dispositions reflective of specific cognitive/affective structures" appear that "generate the different sets of traits" which serve to constitute the distinctive natures of women as social beings.[36]

Feminists would argue that not only does the construal of nature in social terms yield a far more meaningful analysis of human beings, one having considerable advantages for theology, it also requires that the theological anthropologist consider anew the following questions: In the light of revelation, to what extent ought sexual differences be recognized theologically? To what extent are these differences theologically meaningful?

II. WOMAN'S SOCIAL INFERIORITY

As women well know, the presumption that theirs is an inferiority prescribed by "the nature of things" has had profound implications in relation to what has been allowed them socially and culturally. Historically, the theological argument has worked to establish and justify woman's role and status for both church and society. It has become a truism that a woman's anatomy determines her destiny. Whether theologians have held that woman's subordination to man can be directly related to Eve's disobedience and Sin,[37] or whether they have believed the Genesis 2 account of creation that presents a God-given order of creation in which women were subjected to men right from the beginning,[38] women have continually discovered just how potent, even insidious, this argument actually is. Time and again in history, women have found the Scriptures used against them whenever they have tried to attain liberation or equality.[39] Even today the Reverend Jerry Falwell can with confidence assert: "A definite violation of holy Scripture, ERA defies the mandate that 'the husband is the head of the wife, even as Christ is the head of the church' (Eph 5:23). In 1 Peter 3:7 we read that husbands are to give their wives honor as unto the weaker vessel."[40] Similarly, on the same suppositions, Phyllis Schlafly, head of the "Stop ERA" movement, insists that the amendment represents "an attack on God's plan for the family."[41]

While the work of determining to what extent contemporary theologies reiterate the misogynism of the past has barely begun, the belief that socially woman is necessarily limited to the "nature" roles of wife and mother continues to be a fundamental part of the theology of clerical, episcopal, and papal pronouncements.[42] Homilies are commonplace that encourage women to be "fruitful vines who are a credit to their husband's homes," as Gudorf puts it, and that assume that "women and children are natural pairs and belong together at home."[43] Official statements continue to be made to the effect that "true" women's liberation does not lie in "formalistic or materialistic equality with the other sex, but in the recognition of that specific thing in the feminine personality—the vocation of a woman to become a mother."[44] While a recent encyclical on the subject of the family admits that all women have a "right of access to public functions," it urges that society be "structured in such a way that wives and mothers are not in practice compelled to work outside the home. . . ." To this is added the statement: "true advancement of women requires that clear recognition be given to the value of their maternal and family role, by comparison with all other public roles and all other professions."[45]

Feminists point out that the supposition that woman's physical being determines her social being is a correlate of the essentialist conception of human nature described above. The same shift in thinking that results in a new understanding of human nature also requires that the roles of wife and mother be seen differently as well. When recognized to be social products, these same roles—heretofore taken as absolutes—are now revealed to be but culturally defined and arbitrarily given. For the theologian in particular this means that she or he must consider again revelation and its historical interpretations. The question is: In view of the modern shift of horizon, what is one to do with the fact that revelation appears to ordain the roles of wife and mother as essential ones for women?

Certainly in this day and time, exciting new possibilities have opened up for women. For one thing, women need be subject no longer to the control or authority of their nearest male relative. Having won the right to legal and economic freedom, women in western countries may choose whether or not to be wives. This newfound freedom, of course, has not been without effect, and one significant result has been that traditional relationships between men and women continue to be reshaped and redefined. The point however is this: In light of all that has come to pass, it would be exceedingly difficult to continue to maintain that woman's reality must be defined completely in terms of her relationships to men/children. To the contrary, her present experience is that her self-understanding, her self-worth derives from what she has achieved through her own efforts, just as is and has always been the case for men.

While the church's magisterium now grudgingly accepts that women have the right to opt for life in the public square, it steadfastly refuses to accept the desire of many women that they be able to exercise a similar freedom of choice with respect to motherhood. On this issue the Catholic Church is unyielding. It permits a woman to bypass motherhood only if she be willing to deny her sexual being. In the past, and in exchange for a vow of perpetual virginity, ecclesial society did give women another option. As members of religious houses, women could not only avoid the demands of husband and children by means of vows but they also had opportunities for education and some measure of personal freedom. Even now the church continues to offer contemporary women the same narrow gate. For the single woman, the official church demands that she either take a vow of virginity or postpone all sexual activity until she marries; for the married woman, periodic continence is the only acceptable means of avoiding pregnancy. Whatever choice she makes, each requires that a woman deny her sexual self.

While the church defends its stance with arguments taken from revelation and natural law, feminists question that the teaching on birth control is actually of divine origin or whether in fact it represents an attempt on the part of misogynist male celibates to control the church's women. By means of their painstaking survey of the tradition, scholars like Ruether and Daly show that despite the fact that the marital relation has been raised to the level of a sacrament, the sexually active woman has hardly been dealt with positively by churchmen and theologians. One only need recall the long-standing practice in the church of extolling and promoting the celibate life at the expense of marriage. One feminist critic, Carol Christ, observes that while pregnancy and birth are traditionally occasions of joyful celebration, Christian rituals that enable a woman "to celebrate the process of birth as a spiritual experience" are completely nonexistent.[46] And while religious iconography may well lionize the soldier, the monk, the theologian, the virgin, the martyr, it "does not celebrate the birthgiver."[47] Clearly, the pregnant woman's swollen body is an all too obvious reminder of her deliberate choice to affirm, even enjoy, her sexuality.

A critical element in the theological defense of birth control has been the assumption that a woman's body absolutely intends her for motherhood. But, for a first time ever, women now have the capacity to control their own reproduction; for a first time, the argument that motherhood is intrinsic to being a woman is far less compelling or convincing. To the contrary, motherhood is now shown to be but one of several possible life-styles. For this reason, Catholic women claim the right to choose when, even whether, they are to be mothers. As modern women they have come to realize that an indispensable part of their achievement of selfhood necessarily involves the question: "What am I to do about the procreative choice that is mine by virtue of being born female?"[48] Feminist ethicists defend women's right to make this claim by citing the impropriety of male churchmen having excluded women from taking any part in the process of formulating Christian moral norms. Women scholars also observe that where male interests are at stake, a lenient interpretation of the moral law has usually prevailed; stringency, however, tends to be the case wherever female interests are concerned. Not only have women not been heard on an issue that concerns them vitally, intimately, but feminists also argue that over the centuries theologians have treated women as though they were incapable of competent moral agency, assuming that critical decisions about pregnancy and birth had to be made for them.[49]

At the same time, feminists observe that the new approach to nature also serves to compromise the church's argument. Discussions of motherhood and birth control now take place within a social frame of reference. While the word "mother" continues to have undisputed biological meaning, emphasis is now placed on its social ramifications, something which the essentialist/natural law perspective tended to ignore. Modern societies have discovered that while giving birth is a relatively simple, thoroughly natural act, the task of responsible parenting is not. Every woman who can give birth to a child may not have the resources—personal, psychic, economic, or otherwise—to be a parent. The truth is, mothering is a vocation, one to which not every woman feels herself called. Contemporary society daily learns the serious problems created when there are no loving, caring parents willing to commit themselves to the long-term process of socializing their offspring into the community's established meanings, values, and traditions. Even in America there daily grows an underclass of unparented children who live at society's edge ignorant of the community's mores and who prove disruptive to its functioning. Contemporary experience would seriously dispute that responsible parenting involves allowing each sexual encounter to be open to procreation; to the contrary, in society's view, good parenting involves the individual's reflection and deliberation that takes into account the good of the parent, the child, and the well-being of the community at large.

III. WOMAN'S EXPERIENCE:
THE DISCUSSION OF SIN AND GRACE

Much feminist criticism has been directed at the interpretive categories that have been used to articulate essential Christian meanings. For example, a survey of recently published articles and books would show that not one of the treatises of systematic theology has escaped scrutiny or comment.[50]

Examination of some of the more substantive analysis being done in conjunction with the topics of sin and grace shows just how pervasive the feminist project actually is. Because the questions that are being raised in this particular area are not so well known—and yet deserve to be—attention will now be given to a consideration of the feminist claim that traditional explanations of sin and grace are insufficient because they universalize as well as make normative male experience alone.[51]

One of the first to make such a judgment was Valerie Saiving Goldstein in a 1960 article entitled "The Human Situation: A Feminine View."[52] In summary form, Goldstein's argument is as follows: (1) the estimate of the human situation made by theologians reflects a singularly male perspective; (2) such theological interpretations do not provide an adequate interpretation of the situation of women; (3) despite the claim to comprehensiveness, because they are unable to provide an adequate interpretation for the whole of the human situation, these theologies must be judged to be inadequate.

In the introduction to her dissertation work published in 1980, Judith Plaskow announced her intention "to carry forward the analysis begun by Valerie Saiving."[53] Here she attempts to show that although the theologies of Reinhold Niebuhr and Paul Tillich purport to speak universally about the realities of sin and grace, those particular experiences that they cite as having been "judged and transformed by the work of God in Jesus Christ" are "more likely to be associated with men in our society," while those experiences they either regard as secondary or else ignore are those likely to be associated with women.[54]

For example, Plaskow notes that both Tillich and Niebuhr, following tradition, identify sin with pride; for both theologians, sin takes the form of an egoistic self-assertion and the misuse of personal freedom. While this may well describe the situation as men know it, Plaskow argues that because women have been socialized to accept subordinate roles, their "original" sin is more apt to be that of self-abnegation and the refusal of transcendence. Thus, if in Niebuhr's view the sin of sensuality involves losing oneself in the world, woman's offense does not lie in the same excessive love of things; according to the testimony of women themselves, the irresistible temptation is to continue on in a state of dependency, thus avoiding the effort and risk that comes with accepting responsibility for self. In short, woman's "mortal" sin lies in her willing acceptance of all the socially imposed definitions that confine her to the life of man's secondary and companion. In her acquiescence, woman hence becomes a willing accomplice to her own oppression. Above all, Plaskow wishes to make the point that neither Niebuhr nor Tillich consider the failure to make use of one's God-given freedom as great a sin as its misuse.

Insofar as the themes of sin and grace are correlates, both theologians describe grace in terms of that which overcomes and supplants human weakness. For Niebuhr, God's grace shatters the prideful self that stands in the way of achieving mutuality with God and with others.[55] The self-sacrificing love of Christ acts as both remedy and model. But as Plaskow observes, the norm of self-sacrifice presumes a self that is constantly tempted to self-assertion; mainly, it presumes a self that has already been reconstituted in responsibility before God.[56] In the case of women for whom the basic struggle is becoming "a centered self," achieving "full independent selfhood," this theology appears irrelevant. At worst, the theology of self-sacrifice can present an insurmountable barrier to women's efforts to become self-sufficient since it both encourages and justifies a life of continuing servitude.[57] Beyond this, women know from experience that generous self-giving does not necessarily lead to or inevitably contribute to self-realization. "Unless the self is continually replenished through the mutuality of its relations, it can give and give until it is depleted."[58] Since her relationships tend to be those that are not fully reciprocal, a woman may easily "become an emptiness, almost a zero, without value to her self, to her fellowmen, or perhaps even to God."[59] As Plaskow reiterates, for the norm of self-sacrifice to be a positive or meaningful one, there must first exist an independent self, one that is capable of making a deliberate but responsible gift of self-denial.[60]

While Tillich is more concerned with the problem of the self's constitution than Niebuhr, Plaskow criticizes the way Tillich interprets the experience of justification, i.e., God's merciful forgiveness and acceptance of the sinner. Plaskow observes that for Tillich, one's acceptance of justification obliges the self to surrender itself in its entirety, in all of its goodness, to the sole activity of God. "Not only can no moral, intellectual, or other work secure the self's acceptance—this is of course the meaning of justification—but no work need follow from it. The self must simply accept the fact that it is accepted.[61] In questioning the feasibility of such a static response, Plaskow goes on to ask:

> Is this an appropriate response to the self whose sin is the failure to become a self? . . . Where sin is perverse inaction rather than self-assertion, does the message that the self is forgiven despite persistence in sin foster a passivity which is women's real problem?"[62]

On this basis, she concludes that an interpretation of the doctrine of justification is called for that is just as critical of the individual's failure to become a self and to open up into a process of self-actualization.[63] A doctrine of grace is needed that not only acknowledges the indispensability of the divine activity but one which also perceives it in and identifies it with those "moments of self-creation which point toward a future in which all persons can become whole."[64]

The Goldstein-Plaskow argument rests on the thesis that women experience reality in ways fundamentally different than men, and its validity hinges on the authors' ability to establish the truth of this claim. To do this, Goldstein looks to the cultural anthropologists whose research she cites as confirming that "every distinction between the sexes above the biological level is purely arbitrary"; on the strength of such studies she thus concludes that definitions of masculinity and femininity are socially assigned.[65] In the ensuing years, mounting evidence from the areas of biology, psychology, and sociology provide strong reinforcement for her position.[66] For her part, Plaskow suggests that one of the inherent difficulties in dealing with the category "women's experience" and why it seems so elusive is that one must first distinguish between what has been said about women (mostly by men) and women's own experience of themselves.[67] As she so convincingly argues, the fundamental dilemma of Everywoman is in finding that male society's definitions of who she is and what she ought to be are usually in conflict with her own lived reality; in other words, woman's experience is essentially the struggle of trying to live out this contradiction. Plaskow's presentation suggests that it is mainly in the modern period and in the appearance of a growing body of feminist literature that the heretofore silent voice of woman has at last begun to be heard.

If Goldstein and Plaskow are correct, Christian theologians, because they have neglected to take into account the experience of women and have failed to speak to women's situation, must commit themselves to a thorough reassessment of all of theology's classical positions and undertake a careful reconstruction wherever necessary.

IV. THEOLOGICAL METHOD:
THE CONVERGENCE OF THE FEMINIST CRITIQUE

Feminists are just now beginning to recognize that their analyses of past standpoints on woman's nature and experience come to convergence, now challenging and creating fundamental questions about the very methodological principles that direct the theologian's work. A brief examination of the way in which feminist thought impacts here underscores once again just how penetrating this contemporary critique proves to be.

Today, a plurality of contexts and categories makes it essential that theologians be able to articulate and defend a select mode of inquiry. A method of critical correlation—a refinement of that originally proposed by Paul Tillich[68]—set forth by David Tracy in *Blessed Rage for Order*[69] conceives the basic theological task as involving (1) an analysis of common human experience and language, (2) an investigation of the basic Christian experience spoken of by the New Testament and subsequent Christian tradition, and (3) a critical relating of these two sources.[70] While most feminist theologians would not argue with Tracy's basic proposal,[71] they would insist that theology's two sources need to be approached more carefully and critically than has been done to date.

As far as theology's first source is concerned, feminists would question that it is possible to speak of "common human experience." Such a view too readily dismisses the social and cultural conditionedness—and thus the unique particularity—of human experience; feminist scholars are agreed that one of their primary tasks is to thematize and make public for a first time the rich panoply of woman's experience that heretofore has remained hidden and silenced. For example, in defining a methodology for Christian feminist ethics, Barbara Andolsen, Christine Gudorf, and Mary Pellauer observe that while "feminist ethics begins with female experience," "women's own voices and insights" have rarely been recognized or incorporated into classical systems. This is because women have had "few opportunities to examine [their] lives in the common world where social definitions of reality are articulated";[72] but even more significantly, "the patriarchal legacy of the West has hidden women's experience from ethical view, covering the lives, voices and insights of women with darkness, hedging them about with fences, falsifying landmarks, forbidding exploration altogether, or more often, simply ignoring reports."[73] Consequently, an integral part of the ethicist's work must be an explication of the moral questions arising in connection with women's lives. Issues respecting the distribution of housework and child-care responsibilities, violence against their persons, consideration of the special economic problems of women workers, the situation of minority women who are doubly oppressed prove to be ones about which most ethics books, courses, discussions have been remarkably silent.[74]

More importantly, the phrase "common human experience" pre-supposes that beneath the specificities of individual experience there exists a single human nature. As we have seen, feminists have good reason to be wary of this kind of assumption. Accordingly, women have been understood either as lacking the more important human traits (e.g., rationality) or else those traits more true of men than women (e.g., participating in politics) are designated as being para-digmatic of the human.[75] Even recent efforts to establish that male and female are the necessary, complementary correlatives of a single an-drogynous nature fail to win broad feminist support. As indicated in Section I above, feminist scholars have begun to pay increasing atten-tion to the distinction made between gender (a social construct) and sex (a biological given).[76] Because of the clear evidence that the human organism adapts to pressures exerted on it by socio-cultural factors, they argue that it is more appropriate/meaningful to define human nature in essentially social terms. On this basis, they conclude that for purposes of analysis, there is not one, but two distinct human natures—one masculine, one feminine.

While Tracy appears unaware of the feminist discussion and hence gives no indication as to why he finds it an acceptable thesis, the assumption that there is a common human nature and thus a common human experience is nonetheless indispensable to his argument for re-ligion. That is, Tracy wants to establish that there is a religious dimen-sion to existence and that this is available to all indiscriminately. He does this by proposing that it is in the universal experience of limit that one confronts the conditions for the possibility of the divine.[77] For example, in peak moments of ecstasy such as love and joy, individuals find themselves able to transcend the realm of the everyday; at these times "we experience a reality simply given, gifted, happened."[78] Neg-atively, the "limit-to" the human condition is experienced in terms of the apprehension of finitude and contingency.[79] In this instance, there are certain moments during which we are obliged to acknowledge that "the final dimension or horizon of our own situation is neither one of our making nor one under our control."[80]

Feminist research suggests that while experiences of this sort may well be constitutive of male experience and derive from the in-fantile experience of having to separate from the primary care-giver in order to acquire gender identity, women's formative encounter with the world is quite different.[81] In contrast, a woman's basic experience is that of an ongoing relationship with the mother, "thus fusing the ex-perience of attachment with the process of identity formation,"[82] as a result of which "girls come to experience themselves as less differentiated than boys, as more continuous with and related to the external object-world, and as differently oriented to their inner object-world as well."[83] Unlike boys for whom the world becomes "a place of dangerous confrontation and explosive connection"[84] because personal identity has to be created and maintained by an explicit act of separation and isolation,[85] girls tend to identify themselves in relation to the world, a world made coherent by a network of nurturing relations and hence regarded as a place of care and protection.[86]

On these grounds, the feminist theologian wants to argue that the category of limit may not be as fundamental an experience as her male counterpart believes; moreover she would suggest that a more meaningful way to thematize the reality of a gracious ground of being is to do so in terms of woman's primordial experience of connectedness, in terms of the existential continuum "relation-alienation." Certainly this option has strong New Testament support. In contrast to Tracy who must rely upon a sophisticated hermeneutic to identify the biblical language with the category of limit,[87] one needs no special interpretive tool to discern the language of relationship. It thoroughly pervades the pages of the New Testament.

The sharpest critique of the method of critical correlation comes from Rosemary Ruether.[88] She would accuse scholars like Tracy of being unfaithful to their own methodological canons since they fail to take seriously the social rootedness of their own thought. That is, while the revisionist method requires the theologian to effect the critical turn, most scholars do not really attend to the fact that their own view of reality is also a limited, particular one. As Ruether observes, "there are very different contemporary experiences" and these "depend on one's class situation and consciousness." It is obvious that "people who view contemporary experience primarily in terms of the conflicts of secularity, scientific methodology, and the problems of boredom and meaninglessness in an affluent society think out of a very different social base than those whose contemporary experience is primarily that of life-and-death struggle of the poor of the world for survival." Thus for Tracy *et al.* to presume that the "common human experience" of the white male academic has an essential commonality with the majority of the world's men and women is not just an unthinking act of hubris; it is an intensely political act. "The theology of the academy expresses a perspective that privatizes religious commitment" and in so doing makes normative "an ideology of neutrality."[89] In contrast to liberation theology which conceives a self-conscious partisanship on behalf of the oppressed to be normative, academic theology prefers to limit the theologian's role to that of disinterested interpreter, arguing that an advocacy stance undermines one's capacity to be critical.

V. CONCLUSION

My intent has been to show that the feminist critique of Christian theology is radical in the strictest sense of the word. It challenges the methods and presuppositions heretofore found acceptable and approved by centuries of theologians. Pointedly, it argues for a thorough reassessment of theology's interpretive categories as well as for a new valuation of its traditional formulations, all from the feminist vantage point.

In particular, feminist analysis of the complex of issues touching theological anthropology as well as those areas dependent upon definitions of personhood and experience must be taken seriously. The distorted views of woman's nature mediated by Augustine and Aquinas must be dispensed with; theologians need a new understanding of human being, one that allows for the vital distinctions of sex and gender but one which in no way presumes or makes these differences valuational. Credence must be given to the feminist thesis that one simply cannot understand what it is to be human if one has not also considered what it is to be woman. While men and women together represent human nature, attention must be paid to the different ways in which each of them embodies and engages reality.

To this end, scholars must concern themselves with the category of feminine experience. Above all, they must be ready to see the truth of the feminist charge that throughout history, the experience of womanly existence has been little heard from or explored. Now for a first time, the theologian must carefully attend to the voices of women, both past and present; in so doing, a myriad of heretofore unexamined standpoints on existence open up to reflection. Theologians also need to discover new categories for use in expounding the Christian meanings. These must be ones that, on the one hand, critically appropriate the role and place of women in Christian tradition and that, on the other, take into account woman's unique construal of reality—religious and otherwise.

While feminist criticism does indeed seem to require a dismantling of the theological edifice, it would be wrong to assume that its intent is essentially destructive. To the contrary, and as Judith Plaskow herself suggests, the feminist project is ultimately constructive. It not only points the way to a more meaningful appropriation of the realities of faith, it makes possible a better understanding of persons and their experience. Feminist analysis opens the way to a better apprehension of the ways of being human and makes possible a more authentic Christian existence.

NOTES

1.   See Pauline Turner and Bernard Cooke, "Feminist Thought and Systematic Theology," *Horizons* 11/1 (Spring 1984), pp. 125-35.

2.   See Elisabeth Schüssler Fiorenza, "Breaking the Silence—Becoming Invisible" in Elisabeth Schüssler Fiorenza and Mary Collins, eds., *Women: Invisible in Church and Theology* (Edinburgh: T.T. Clark, 1985), p. 9.

3.   Nancy Holmstrom, "Do Women Have a Distinct Nature?" in Marilyn Pearsall, ed., *Women and Values: Readings in Recent Feminist Philosophy* (Belmont, CA: Wadsworth, 1986), p. 51.

4.   For many Catholic women, awareness of just how misogynist the Church's theological tradition has been began with a reading of studies which included detailed historical summaries, e.g., Mary Daly, *The Church and the Second Sex* (New York: Harper and Row, 1968), George Tavard, *Woman in Christian Tradition* (Notre Dame, IN: University of Notre Dame Press, 1973), and Rosemary Radford Ruether, ed., *Religion and Sexism* (New York: Simon & Schuster, 1974).

5.   The matter of the *imago Dei* is an exceedingly important one, and one that deserves in-depth study. The idea that man and woman in some way share in the divine nature is absolutely fundamental to the whole Christian economy. While today it is presumed that men and women equally possess the image of God, a survey of the earliest centuries shows there has been an obvious difference of opinion about this. Some of the Antiochene fathers (e.g., Diodore of Tarsus, Ambrosiaster) held that woman did not possess the image at all. There were also those who, following Paul (1 Cor 11:3ff.), believed that the image in women was different than that in Adam because while "Adam was formed immediately to the image of God, the female was formed immediately to the image of man . . . therefore to the image of God mediately, through the image of God that is the male," cited in Walter J. Burghardt, S.J., *The Image of God in Man According to Cyril of Alexandria* (Woodstock, MD: Woodstock College Press, 1957), pp. 134-35. And, of course, Aquinas's own Aristotelian categories seem to commit him to the view that God's image in woman is different, i.e., less, than it is in man. Since the rational soul is proportioned to the body, and woman's body is inferior to man's, the feminine rational soul is consequently less perfect than the masculine. See Kari Elisabeth Borresen, *Subordination and Equivalence: The Nature and Role of Woman in Augustine and Thomas Aquinas* (Washington: University Press of America, 1981), pp. 315-16.

6.   "Man is the image of God by being solely what he is, an image so perfect, so whole, that when woman is joined with him it makes only one image," *De trin.* XII, 7, 10.

7. Borresen, p. 29.

8. *Quaestiones in Heptateuchum* 419; *Gen. c. Manich.* II, 13, 18; *De mor. eccl. cath.* I, 30, 63. Augustine speculates that this may be due to the fact that because Adam was formed first, he enjoyed intellectual superiority as far as knowledge is concerned, *De Gen. ad litt.* XI, 42.

9. E.g., Gregory Nyssa, *De Opif. Hom.* 16.

10. *Summa Theologiae* I, 92,2,c.; also see I, 93,4, ad 1; see Borresen, pp. 162-63.

11. See Eleanor C. McLaughlin, "Equality of Souls, Inequality of Sexes: Woman in Medieval Theology" in Ruether, ed., *Religion and Sexism*, pp. 217-18.

12. *Ep. 107, to Laeta*; see Ruether, "Misogynism and Virginal Feminism in the Fathers of the Church," in her *Religion and Sexism*, p. 170.

13. *De exhortatione castitatis*, p. 9.

14. "Cited in Tavard, *Woman in Christian Tradition*, p. 95.

15. Elizabeth A. Johnson, "The Marian Tradition and the Reality of Women," *Horizons* 12/1 (Spring 1985), p. 123.

16. *Ibid.*, p. 124.

17. Louis Bouyer, *The Seat of Wisdom* (New York: Pantheon, 1962), p. 87.

18. Pius XII, October 21, 1945, address to Italian Women.

19. Pius XII, September 21, 1948, speech to International Association for the Protection of the Girl.

20. Leo XIII, Encyclical Letter, *Rerum Novarum*, 15 May 1891.

21. Pius XI, Encyclical Letter, *Divini Illius Magistri*, 31 December 1929.

22. *Declaration on Christian Education*, n. 8.

23. For instance, see Jo Durden-Smith and Diane Desimone, *Sex and the Brain* (New York: Arbor House, 1983), pp. 102-03, 114, 121-22.

24. It is also true that for generations, theologians used the metaphor, "becoming male," to define the religious ideal for woman; such usage reflects the belief that only by a life of virginal asceticism could a woman hope to overcome the inherent debilities of feminine nature and achieve holiness; see Kari Vogt, "'Becoming Male': One Aspect of an Early Christian Anthropology" in Fiorenza and Collins, pp. 72-83. As several other scholars observe, this type of thinking ultimately led to the suggestion that at history's end, every resurrection body would be male.

25. Anne Carr, "Theological Anthropology and the Experience of Women," *Chicago Studies* 19 (1980), p. 114. Karol Wojtyla takes such a position in *Love and Responsibility* (New York: Farrar, Straus, Giroux, 1981).

26. Rosemary R. Ruether provides a helpful summary of this question in a chapter entitled "Christology and Feminism: Can A Male Savior Save Women?" in her *To Change the World: Christology and Cultural Criticism* (New York: Crossroad, 1985), pp. 45-56.

27. Aristotle, for example, conceived the distinction between male and female natures to lie in woman's lack of an appropriate degree of soul heat: because she is "unable to concoct, or cook her menstrual blood to the final state of refinement, i.e., semen," the philosopher concluded that woman represents only partial humanity; see Caroline Whitbeck, "Theories of Sex Difference," *Philosophical Forum* 5 (1973-74), p. 56.

28. Charles E. Curran, *Directions in Fundamental Moral Theology* (Notre Dame, IN: University of Notre Dame Press, 1986), p. 186.

29. Holmstrom, p. 57.

30. *Ibid.*, p. 56.

31. *Ibid.*, p. 59.

32. *Ibid.*

33. *Ibid.*, p. 53.

34. *Ibid.*, p. 56.

35. *Ibid.*, p. 58.

36. *Ibid.*

37. E.g., John Chrysostom, *Discourse 4 on Genesis.*

38. Elizabeth Clark, *Women in the Early Church* (Wilmington, DE: Michael Glazier, 1983). Augustine and Aquinas are among those who argue that with the fall, that subordination was merely increased.

39. In the nineteenth century, Elizabeth Cady Stanton proposed to publish a corrective feminist interpretation of the Bible when she realized that rather than being an ally, Scripture became a potent political weapon against women's struggle for liberation; see Elisabeth Schüssler Fiorenza, *In Memory of Her* (New York: Crossroad, 1983), pp. 7-8.

40. Cited in Charlene Spretnak, "Christian Right's 'Holy War'" in Charlene Spretnak, ed., *The Politics of Women's Spirituality* (Garden City, NY: Doubleday Anchor, 1982), p. 472.

41. *Ibid.*

42. Kari Borreson finds that the emphasis given to the complementarity of male and female merely masks the belief that "male and female roles are not interchangeable" ("Male/female Typology in the Church," *Theology Digest* 31 [1984], p. 25).

43. Christine Gudorf, "Renewal or Repatriarchalization?," *Horizons* 10/2 (Fall 1983), p. 250.

44. Paul VI quoted in Mary Daly, *Beyond God the Father* (Boston: Beacon, 1973), p. 3.

45. John Paul II, *Familiaris Consortio*, December 15, 1981.

46. Carol Christ, "Why Women Need the Goddess" in Spretnak, ed., *The Politics of Women's Spirituality*, p. 78.

47. *Ibid.*

48. Beverly Harrison, *Our Right to Choose* (Boston: Beacon, 1983), p. 9.

49. *Ibid.*, p. 8.

50. In addition to Rosemary Ruether's substantial body of work, one should consult Daly, *Beyond God the Father*; Letty Russell, *Human Liberation in a Feminist Perspective: A Theology* (Philadelphia: Westminster, 1974); Patricia Wilson-Kastner, *Faith, Feminism, and the Christ* (Philadelphia: Fortress, 1983).

51. While there is a growing body of work reflecting feminist efforts to restate the basic Christian meanings in more inclusive terms, I will limit my discussion here to the specific points of critique developed in what I consider to be classics of feminist theological analysis, i.e., the works of Valerie Saiving Goldstein and Judith Plaskow. At the same time, Paul Tillich and Reinhold

Niebuhr, the subjects of Plaskow's study, represent the mainstream of modern Protestant theological interpretation.

52. Valerie Saiving Goldstein, "The Human Situation: A Feminine View," *Journal of Religion* 40 (1960), pp. 100-12.

53. Judith Plaskow, *Sex, Sin and Grace: Women's Experience and the Theologies of Reinhold Niebuhr and Paul Tillich* (Lanham, MD: University Press of America, p. 2.

54. *Ibid.*, p. 3.

55. *Ibid.*, pp. 83-94.

56. *Ibid.*, pp. 84-86.

57. *Ibid.*, p. 87.

58. *Ibid.*, p. 89.

59. Goldstein, quoted in Plaskow, pp. 87-88.

60. Plaskow, p. 90.

61. *Ibid.*, p. 157.

62. *Ibid.*

63. *Ibid.*

64. *Ibid.*, p. 175; at one point, Plaskow suggests that perhaps "one must be a bit Pelagian to be faithful to women's experience!"

65. Goldstein, p. 102.

66. In the area of psychology, one of the most important studies is that of Carol Gilligan, *In a Different Voice* (Cambridge: Harvard University Press, 1982), who argues that women tend to have a more positive view of the world than men because of their earliest experiences. Gilligan also insists that this helps to explain why women also construe problems of morality differently. A significant new work on the subject of women's experience is Mary Field Belenky, Blythe McVicker Clinchy, Nancy Rule Goldberger, and Jill Mattock Tarule, *Women's Ways of Knowing: The Development of Self, Voice, and Mind* (New York: Basic Books, Inc., 1986). A basic thesis here is that while men regularly use the metaphor of sight to describe the experience of knowing, of discovering truth, women are more likely to explain this in terms of speaking/hearing, of "gaining a voice."

67. Plaskow, p. 9.

68. Paul Tillich, *Systematic Theology*, 3 vols. (Chicago: University of Chicago Press, 1975 ed.), 1: pp. 59-66.

69. David Tracy, *Blessed Rage for Order* (New York: Seabury, 1975).

70. In his "Particular Questions with General Consensus" in Leonard Swidler, ed., *Consensus in Theology: A Dialogue with Hans Küng and Edward Schillebeeckx* (Philadelphia: Westminster, 1980), pp. 33-39. Tracy observes that he finds Schillebeeckx and Küng to be in substantial methodological agreement with this proposal (p. 34).

71. Mary Daly, however, suggests that under the patriarchal system of the academy, "Method has wiped out women's questions so totally that even women have not been able to hear and formulate our own questions to meet our own experiences" (*Beyond God the Father*, pp. 11-12).

72. Barbara Andolsen, Christine Gudorf, and Mary Pellauer, eds.,

Women's Consciousness, Women's Conscience, (New York: Winston, 1985), p. xiii.

73. *Ibid.,* p. xii.

74. *Ibid.,* p. xxiv.

75. Careful analysis of these theories can be found in Whitbeck, "Theories of Sex Difference," pp. 54-80.

76. For an analysis of the current state of the question, see Barbara Andolsen, "Gender and Sex Roles in Recent Religious Ethics Literature," *Religious Studies Review* 11 (July 1985), pp. 217-23; and Richard Kahoe, "Social Science of Gender Differences: Ideological Battleground," *Religious Studies Review* 11 (July 1985), pp. 223-28.

77. My contention will be that all significant explicitly religious language and experience (the 'religions') and all significant implicitly religious characteristics of our common experience (the 'religious dimension') will bear at least the 'family resemblance' of articulating or implying a limit-experience, a limit-language, or a limit-dimension" (Tracy, p. 93).

78. *Ibid.,* p. 106.

79. *Ibid.,* p. 107.

80. *Ibid.*

81. See, e.g., Gilligan, pp. 7-8.

82. *Ibid.,* p. 8.

83. Nancy Chodorow, *The Reproduction of Mothering* (Berkeley: University of California Press, 1978), p. 167.

84. *Ibid.,* p. 38.

85. Gilligan, p. 29.

86. *Ibid.*

87. See Tracy, pp. 119-45.

88. Rosemary Ruether, "Is a New Consensus Possible?" in Swidler, ed., *Consensus in Theology?,* pp. 63-68.

89. *Ibid.,* p. 67.

3

Renewal or Repatriarchalization? Responses of the Roman Catholic Church to the Feminization of Religion

Christine E. Gudorf*

ABSTRACT

This chapter will outline a feminist interpretation for responses of the Roman Catholic Church to particular events in modern history, and sketch feminist proposals for solving the resulting problems of the church today. The first section interprets the church's initial response to scientific and philosophic discoveries and movements of the late Renaissance and the Enlightenment period as responsible for the feminization of the image of Roman Catholicism in the secular mind. The second section interprets the church's response to liberalism in the nineteenth and early twentieth centuries as confirming for the secular, and increasingly popular, mind this feminine image of Catholicism. The third section depicts Vatican II as a contemporary attempt to create a more masculine image for the faith by moving the church's sphere of action from the feminized private sector to the public world characterized by masculine rationality and technology. The final section sketches some ways in which modern feminist scholarship and its perspective can be a major and necessary contributor to the eradication of this feminine view of religion through the elimination of public/private dualism.

*Christine E. Gudorf (Ph.D., Columbia University) is Professor of Theology at Xavier University (Cincinnati, OH 45207). She is the author of *Catholic Social Teaching on Liberation Themes* (Washington, DC: University Press of America, 1980), and *Victimization: Examining Christian Complicity* (Philadelphia: Trinity Press International, 1992).

I. THE RATIONALIST ATTACK
ON THE CHURCH: ITS RESPONSE

In the western world since Hellenic times, rationality has been considered essentially masculine, that is, characteristic of males.[1] Rationality was understood as the ground of truth and virtue, for only through reason could one discover what was good and true and then abide by it. Order and civilization were similarly understood as dependent upon rationality and so were also masculine. Rationality was supreme, but irrationality was recognized as indirectly necessary for society, for women were understood as irrational but essential for procreation. Woman's purpose was seen as limited to procreation which did not require, and to some extent, excluded, rationality; so specially designed for their carnal purpose were women's bodies that they had proportionally less capacity for other, especially non-carnal, tasks. Thus, women were not understood to have public functions; their role was a domestic one. Women and their domestic realm were characterized by irrationality, emotionality, and intuition.

Christianity understood itself to be both rational and spiritual, as would be expected considering the strong influence of Hellenic culture throughout the Roman Empire. But beginning in the sixteenth century, the common understanding of rationality began to shift due to scientific discoveries. Discoveries in astronomy, and later in biology, genetics, evolution, and chemistry, challenged the more primitive understandings of the Scholastics regarding the structures of the physical world, understandings which had become a respected part of church teaching. The problem for the church arose from the growing identification in the European mind of scientific method with reason. Beginning with Galileo's case and continuing through Pius XII's condemnation of evolutionary polygenism in *Humani generis*, the church disavowed many of the discoveries of science.[2] Thus, to the extent that science embodied reason for many Europeans, it was commonly believed that the church could no longer make the claim that faith, hence religion itself, was rational. This problem became more and more acute for the church as the discoveries and prestige of science increased through the centuries. That is not to say that the perceived opposition between science and religion was accurate, or that the newer understanding of rationality was superior to that with which the church was accustomed to reflect. But it is important that proponents and adherents of the secular culture beginning in Europe came to see faith as irrational—that is, not capable of scientific proof—because a side effect of this belief was that within the battle between religion and secularism religion acquired a more feminine image and thereby lost status.

The trend begun by the scientific revolution continued as the new approach toward and understanding of rationality as critical rationality was developed by Enlightenment thinkers into political philosophy. If rationality could dissect and understand the physical world, then why could it not direct societies, making social and political decisions? Human nature came to be understood almost completely in terms of rationality, and from thence it was a short step to see human beings as responsible for constructing the society which their rationality could envision. This view was opposed by the church much more strongly than the discoveries of science had ever been, not because the church denied the existence or usefulness of reason, but because it did not regard reason alone as sufficient for the discovery of the religious and moral truth should be reflected in society. Thus the *Syllabus of Errors*, issued in 1864 by Pope Pius IX, not only condemned the ideas that the truths of religion are derived from reason, that human reason is the sole judge of truth and falsehood, that faith contradicts reason, and that Christian dogmas can be arrived at through reason alone, but went on to attack the idea of the civil power deriving its authority from the support of rational human beings. The *Syllabus* insisted that the survival of religious and moral truth in society required that church and state not be separated, that other religions not be recognized by the state, and that civil powers not regulate education, marriage, or church offices.[3] Six years later the first Vatican Council affirmed that, while reason confirmed and did not contradict faith, it was not sufficient for faith.

This position was not well understood. When added to the church's political alignment against the French Revolution and national democratic movements such as Italian unification, this position on the insufficiency of reason suggested to many outside the church that the church accepted the view that religion and human beings were both irrational. For purposes of history, what was believed to be said was perhaps more significant than what was actually said.

By the mid-nineteenth century, the church had suffered a stunning series of losses and crises: the loss of church members and property engendered by the Reformation, the French Revolution and its resulting anticlericalism, the spread of democratic liberalism and socialism, the loss of the Papal States, and not least, the hostile intellectual climate of the Enlightenment and post-Enlightenment. The church's responses to these crises was the standard response of institutions to crisis, one which might be characterized today as macho: it tightened its belt, lifted its chin, and stepped forth fighting. Specifically, it accelerated the historical trend to centralize authority at the top, demanded increased loyalty and obedience from the ranks, and vociferously attacked its enemies, both internal and external. It is important to note that this response was not just a papal response; it was supported by the majority of the hierarchy and stirred no mutiny in the ranks of the laity, due to a common perception of the crisis.

Examples of this reaction are clear. Centralization of authority in the Vatican is perhaps best illustrated by Vatican I, which asserted the supremacy of the pope over the church and papal infallibility in defining faith and morals. The power of bishops over the laity was increased through church pronouncements such as that of Pius X in 1911, which gave bishops complete authority over all Catholic organizations; Pius XI and Pius XII continued to assert episcopal control over all forms of Catholic Action.[4] Doctrinal loyalty and obedience were mandated during the Modernist controversy under Pius X and Cardinal Merry del Val: a 1907 encyclical, *Pascendi gregis*, and a decree, *Lamentabili*, condemned the modernists and then ordered all teaching or pastoral clergy to take a strict anti-Modernist oath. It was thus made clear that orthodoxy would be enforced, and that questioning or innovative thinking in theology or Biblical studies would be discouraged.

The effect of this ecclesial response was to further feminize religion's image in the eyes of its opponents and thus to allow them a powerful weapon in the battle for the popular mind. All of the attempts to make the church a strong instrument wielded by the hierarchy in the modern world drained the ranks of the laity of any independence of either thought or act and of any participation save unquestioning obedience. The church's response to its series of crises was to make loyalty to the institutional church the litmus test of Christianity, and to evaluate that loyalty in terms of exclusivity and obedience. The church *hierarchy* continued to be viewed as masculine in secular culture due to its authoritarianism and political machinations. But the image of the church *member* which emerged as a result of this emphasis was one characterized not only by a lack of rationality, but also by subservience, thus augmenting the feminity of the image. Thus the body of the church appeared much more feminine as a result of the church's attempt to create a more masculine image through authoritarianism.

II. THE CHURCH FURTHER
CONFIRMS RELIGION AS FEMININE

The church unwittingly contributed even further to religion's feminine image through its teachings in two ways. First, as the church lost ground to liberalism in attempting to retain its former niche in the world, it shifted the grounds of religion's defense from the public political sphere to the private domestic sphere. This reinforced religion's feminine image by suggesting that there was indeed a special connection between religion and the feminine domestic sphere. Second, by the twentieth century, the church couched its arguments in defense of the traditional sexual division of labor in the Victorian language of the pedestal. While the language of sexual complementarity had long been standard within the church and society, two distinctive changes are noticeable in church teaching in the twentieth century. We begin to find references to the religious and moral superiority of women over men (impossible earlier when virtue and faith had been linked to reason). And the masculine world of rationality, efficiency, technology, and self-interest comes to be portrayed in very negative, depressing terms as a harsh, mechanistic, and unloving world.

In its depiction of women as naturally religious and moral, the home as the font of religion in the world, and the world and the home as in some ways opposed to each other, the church affirmed the very charges it had combated for centuries—that religion is primarily a private occupation for irrational creatures, divorced from the reality of social and political life. The twentieth-century church did not entirely capitulate to this view. However, it became very difficult for the church to combat effectively the forces attempting to cast religion as socially and politically irrelevant when the church in parts of its own teaching seemed to view religion as a domestic matter natural only for women.

The Retreat to Marriage and the Family

The church's emphasis on a defense of marriage, family and parental rights was dictated by the political climate in which the church was confronted with liberal governments not open to church views on political questions. These liberal governments were the heirs of the secular culture with which the church had repeatedly clashed in the past. The church's interest in marriage was not new; it had historically addressed the issue. But beginning with the French Revolution, a two-step shift occurred in church teaching on marriage. Before this time church pronouncements on marriage focused on either isolated cases of judges in church courts too readily granting marital nullity,[5] laxity in granting dispensations for degrees of affinity and consanguinity,[6] clerical laxity in requiring proper form in marriages,[7] or laxity in allowing mixed marriages.[8] In the first step of the shift soon after the French Revolution, the church attempted to defeat civil attempts to wrest control of marriage from the church. Beginning with the condemnation of the Jansenist ideas that the civil power can regulate a betrothal and establish diriment impediments to marriage,[9] the church issued a constant stream of documents denying that the civil power can regulate marriage, witness it, restrict some from entering it, or nullify it on any grounds.[10] The second step to the shift occurred in the 1930s, when papal documents on marriage began to focus less on the presumption of civil regulations on marriage.[11]

The significance of the shift was that the church moved from a demand that the state respect the *church's* right to regulate marriage to a demand that the *state*, in regulating marriage, respect the rights of *individuals* involved in marriage and family life.[12] This latter line of teaching, begun by Pius XI and Pius XII, continued and was expanded in the teaching of John XXIII and Paul VI and is still strong today.[13] Since the above shift in the 1930s, the church came to see both the family as the basic social unit which underpinned the stability and determined the character of society, as well as the church as the defender of the family, guiding society through the family.

One of the effects of this concentration on marriage, sexuality, and parental rights in the education of children was to convey the idea to many Catholics that religion was essentially a domestic affair, and to confirm the suspicions of anticlerical liberals. Even within the church, many persons came to understand their faith solely in terms of contracting marriages according to canon law, attending Sunday Mass, abstaining from adultery, contraception, and abortion, and raising children who received a Catholic education. Likewise, many both within and without the church came to see societies as "Christian" if they allowed the free exercise of the sacraments and the establishment of Catholic schools, and as "Catholic" if they also prohibited divorce, abortion, sterilization, or other forms of contraception. This is not to say that the church did not develop social teaching in other areas, especially in economic affairs. But the social teaching in other areas did not permeate the consciousness of ordinary Catholics, much less that of non-Catholics, to the extent of the teaching on marriage and family. The Catholic masses were much more likely to know of the warnings against public education, mixed marriage, divorce, artificial contraception, and abortion than to have heard of the just wage and the principle of subsidiarity. The clergy was much more likely to know of and preach on the former than the latter. Moreover, the church was much more likely to exert pressure, both diplomatic and political, on societies trespassing on the marriage and family teachings than on those engaged in massive offensive armaments buildups or those in which workers were not adequately housed or fed, or in which other human rights were violated. A major reason for this state of affairs was that church pronouncements on social, as opposed to domestic matters, were addressed to a different audience. The church aimed the social teaching very explicitly at the powerful whom it considered able to affect social problems, not at the laity who filled the pews at Sunday Mass. The laity learned church teachings on subjects in which they were considered responsible for action—Mass attendance, religious education of children, sacramental marriage, birth control. The teaching on non-domestic subjects fell into a void—the laity never heard them, and the powerful paid them no heed. The social teaching of the church has been the province of scholars and bureaucrats alone. It was, and is, no wonder that religion has been considered by many as irrelevant to public affairs, but as important only within the personal domestic circle.

Direct Confirmation of Religion as Feminine

The papal teaching on men and women, their differences and roles, provides more support for those who associate religion with feminine domestic concerns rather than with the masculine world of work and government. Within the context of this teaching, the popes of the twentieth-century have described women in stereotypic ways, and the home as the realm of women. Furthermore, they have depicted men's realm as one lacking not only the Christian virtues, but even humaneness.

Leo XIII, who was pope until 1903, built the foundation for much of twentieth-century social teaching in the area of sexuality and marriage just as he did in economics and church-state relations. Leo described man both as provider of maintenance, health, and education for the family,[14] and as the authority over the dependent submissive wife.[15] Man was the provider because he, through his work, engaged in the public world. In this public world he represented Christ in the marital analogy of Christ and the church because woman was, according to Genesis, derived from and dependent upon man, just as the church is derived from and dependent upon Christ. With Benedict XV, the Victorian rhetoric became stronger. He described woman as the "soul of society," the superior spiritual and moral force, and the social source of religion.[16] Women, he said, are the binding force of the home and are naturally home centered: "In the home she is queen, and even when she is far away from home, like a wise governor, her maternal affection and all of her thoughts must be centered therein...."[17] Moreover, in keeping with the stereotype, Benedict did not think that women were rationally capable of sound decision-making;

they needed the "watchful care" of fathers and husbands to keep them from evil,[18] and were both unconscious and ultimately ignorant of the evil within their power.[19]

Pius XI's marriage encyclical, *Casti connubii*, 1930, describes the "order of love" which must reign in the home as implying "the primacy of husband over wife and children and the ready submission and willing obedience of the wife." In an attack on the emancipation of women in the same encyclical, Pius defended the inequality of the sexes as necessary for the "welfare of the family" and "the unity and ordered stability which must reign in the home."[20] Furthermore, Pius paints the public world as a jungle; he echoes Leo XIII's *Arcanum* when he says that:

> If she [woman] abdicates the royal throne upon which the Gospel has set her in the home, to follow her own bent, and engage in business and even in public affairs, she will soon find herself reduced, in reality if not in appearance, to the slavery of ancient days, and will become what she was among the heathen, nothing more than the tool of her husband.[21]

The same argument was used not only by Leo and Pius XI, but also by Pius XII.[22]

In Pius XI's 1937 condemnation of communism, *Divini Redemptoris*, the question of the proper sphere of women arose. Pius condemned communism because, among other things, it was:

> ... characterized by the rejection of any link that binds women to the family and the home, and her emancipation from the tutorship of man is proclaimed as a basic principle. She is withdrawn from the home and the care of the children, to be thrust, instead, into public life and collective production under the same condition as man."[23]

The contrast drawn between the domestic and the public spheres is startling. Christian teaching has been effective in the home, where woman is accorded respect and protection because of the Gospel; but Christian teaching has been so ineffective in the public world of male production that women risk slavery upon entering it.

Pius XII concurred with the view of Pius XI that thrusting women into public affairs was detrimental both to women and to the domestic scene. At the same time he saw that because of the imbalance in the numbers of men and women following World War II many women were forced to work to support themselves. Also, he felt that the greater religiosity of women could be beneficial to the church and to the moral tone of society in general if women took a more active, but still limited, role in public affairs.

Pius XII described women in terms of extreme sensibility,[24] natural piety and innate abhorrence of war,[25] naivete and a lack of discernment.[26] Here again is the link between piety and a lack of rationality. Woman is good but needs to be protected because she does not comprehend real dangers: "The illusion of solidity and strength, the illusion of experience and prudence, both of them nourish a presumption to which her nature, even if well trained, is only too prone."[27]

Pius XII's thought becomes clearest when one looks at his speeches on working women. He understood the domestic hearth as a refuge, a place of religion, compassion and nurturance, in the midst of a hostile world. Women were the creators and caretakers of these refuges; their job was to humanize their husbands and children, to support the victims of the harsh public world. Thus Pius said:

> Both sexes have the right and the duty to work together for the good of society, for the good of the nation. But it is clear that while man by temperament is more suited to deal with external affairs and public business, generally speaking the woman has a deeper insight for understanding the delicate problems of domestic and family life, and a surer touch in solving them. . . . The sensibility and delicacy which are so characteristic of the woman may perhaps bias her judgements in the direction of her impressions, and so tend to the prejudice of wide and clear vision, cool decision or farsighted prudence; but on the other hand they are most valuable aids in discerning the needs, aspirations and dangers proper to the sphere of domestic life, public assistance, and religion.[28]

Here again the religious-domestic/rationalized-public split in reality is explicit.

Perhaps Pius XII's most explicit speech on the private/public split and the sexes was a 1942 speech in which he said:

> . . . the truth is that it is the woman who must mold and nourish the family hearth, and that in this, her place can never be taken by her husband. . . . [T]he material fireside is not enough to form the spiritual edifice of happiness. . . . Who will create then, little by little, day by day, the true spiritual fireside, if not the action par excellence of her who has become a 'housewife,' of her to whom the heart of her husband trusts? Whether her husband be a laborer or a farmer, professional or literary man, scientist or artist or clerk or official, it is inevitable that his work will carry him for the most part outside the home. Or if in the home, it will

confine him for long hours in his study, out of the current of family life. For him, the family hearth will become the place where, at the end of his working day, he will restore his physical and moral powers in rest, peace and intimate enjoyment.[29]

In Pius' mind, the world was clearly not a humane place. He concentrated a great deal of energy in teaching the proper role of women because he saw modern trends in women's roles threatening the refuge of the home, and thereby morality and religion. No longer were rationality and religion allied in the papal mind. Rationality characterized both men, who make "cool decisions" with "clear vision," and the masculine world of public affairs. The seat of religion, on the other hand, was the feminine world of the domestic hearth. Religion was a central concern of women by virtue of both nature and role; women were the natural caretakers of religion in the world. Rationality's sole religious task in this framework is to see that women are kept in the home or other domestic refuges in order that they not be corrupted and their necessary gifts of moral and spiritual maintenance thereby lost to the world.

John XXIII concurred in this vision, and completed the picture of the public world as unhealthy when he urged women who feel they must work not to neglect their duties to the domestic refuge:

> Everyone knows that outside work, as you might naturally expect, makes a person tired, and may even dull the personality; sometimes it is humiliating and mortifying besides. When a man comes back to his home after being away for long hours and sometimes after having completely spent his energies, is he going to find in it a refuge and a source for restoring his energies and the reward that will make up for the dry, mechanical nature of the things that have surrounded him?

> Here again, there is a great task waiting for women: let them promise themselves that they will not let their contacts with the harsh realities of outside work dry up the richness of their inner life, the resources of their sensitivity, of their open and delicate spirit; that they will not forget those spiritual values that are the only defense of their nobility; last of all that they will not fail to go to the fonts of prayer and sacramental life for the strength to maintain themselves on a level with their matchless mission.[30]

Since John, we do not have such clear papal statements on the split between public and private world, though the sexes are still understood in terms of complementarity. Church authorities still see the world divided into two spheres, one masculine, the other feminine.

III. VATICAN II AND
THE FEMINIZATION OF RELIGION

The changes wrought in the church since Vatican II have been aimed, I suggest, at moving the church from the feminine, private side of the public/private split to the masculine public side. Pope John XXIII in calling the Council was not constrained by any significant internal crisis. Rather he said he called the Council to examine the modern world outside the church in order that the church be better able to serve the world.[31] This was perhaps nowhere clearer than in the Pastoral Constitution *Gaudium et Spes*, parts of which read today as if written by European political theologians attacking privatization:

> Therefore let there be no false opposition between professional and social activities on the one part, and religious life on the other. The Christian who neglects his temporal duties neglects his duties toward his neighbor and even God, and jeopardizes his eternal salvation. Christians should rather rejoice that they can follow the example of Christ, who worked as a artisan. In the exercise of all their earthly activities, they can thereby gather their humane, domestic, professional, social and technical enterprises into one vital synthesis with religious values, under whose supreme direction all things are harmonized unto God's glory.[32]

The move toward the public sector has caused crisis in both spheres. The authorities in the public sphere resent the intrusion of what they regard as a feminine, domestic, irrational private life concern (religion) into their realm through pronouncements on poverty, human rights, disarmament, land use, energy, racism and other issues. At the same time they recognize that papal and episcopal *figures* are not easily dismissed as softhearted, unrealistic, feminine and naive. After all, these figures function as a rationalized masculine authoritarian elite presiding over a feminized (because subordinated) mass membership. The public storm over the hierarchy's attempt to jump the church over the public/private barrier therefore centers on the question of the appropriateness of mixing soft sentimental religion with practical, technical, self-interested politics, rather than on the ability of religious leaders to function in leadership roles in the public realm.

The crisis *within* the church over the hierarchy's attempt to scale the public/private fence since Vatican II is relatively rare in church history, and not well examined from this perspective. The attempt of the hierarchy to restore to the church the public role it lost in the modern world creates crisis because neither hierarchy nor laity really understand their roles and situations. They are divided. There are those who hope to regain for the church the same public role it lost at the hands of Enlightenment liberalism; they fail to understand, however, that liberalism not only transformed the church's place in the world, but also transformed the world. These persons do not see that though the church can move with some difficulty into the public realm, it must act a role different from any it has held in the past. This different role requires certain internal changes.

The majority of the hierarchy, and many laity, are more aware that the new role of the church in the public sphere is dependent upon the church's ability to internally transform its own functioning. The hierarchy can neither rule the laity and the world, nor manipulate the world through commands to its lay troops.[33] Even if the troops are willing to be commanded, such action is rejected by the public sphere as characteristic of dangerous fanatical organizations. The public sphere now demands evidence of critical rationality as the basis of corporate action. The public sphere begins to demand that the church take a consistent stand on issues such as critical reason, the human person, individual freedom, and responsible authority. The church has only lived up to Vatican II goals in a very limited way. The church as an *institution* has made a strong claim to a place in the public world. But the church as a *community of persons* has not done the synthesis of public and private, social and religious called for by the Council. In fact, much of the church community reacts to the hierarchy's attempts to interest it in the public world with not only disinterest but suspicion.

This suspicion is not based merely on *attraction* to the privatized model of religion as liberals tend to assert. It is much more complicated than that. For some there is a fear of losing the social and political autonomy which the restriction of church authority to the private allowed them to develop. They fear the church's move into the public sphere includes the extension of hierarchical control over their political life as well as their "spiritual" life. Such people are wont to ask how a church that is not without a need to change internally on religious issues (as evinced in Vatican II) can claim to speak with authority on social, political issues.[34] In others, long-standing acceptance of hierarchical authority in the privatized sphere of family and religion has given them an image of themselves as incapable of agency, incapable of action in the public sphere. For these, the calls to involvement in the evangelization of the world are largely incomprehensible. They cling to privatized religion as the source of meaning in their lives, and often resent Vatican II for its disruption of the devotions which nourished their religious lives. They tend to feel that since Vatican II the church has been so intent on the development of a masculinized public role that it has slighted the feminine, nurturing, intuitional activities which had come to characterize the privatized church. Some of the attractions of the old church were the beauty of the traditional worship, the unassuming homiletic style (which, though often deplorable, did at its low key, pastoral best, present, as if from confessor to penitent, the wisdom acquired through years of struggle for individual virtue) and the private devotions like novenas, rosary, and forty hours which provided an atmosphere for both meditative communion with the divine and critical assessment of one's life and faith. Likewise, prominence of Marian devotion in the pre-Vatican II church was the result of a commonly felt attraction to feminine, essentially private mediation of the God/human encounter. It was these feminine attractions in the pre-Vatican church, rather than the authoritarianism of the lack of community, which nourished the laity.

Yet these nurturing activities, and the individualistic interpretations of the sacraments which accompanied them, were marginalized or eliminated after Vatican II. In the attempt to become a public community, privatization was attacked within the church as well as in the church's understanding of its relationship with the world. The internal crisis in the church is that the old attractions are largely gone but their replacements are incomplete.

Real community was supposed to replace the traditional forms of nurture. Unfortunately, we are in some ways further from real community than before Vatican II. What used to pass for community in the large ethnic, urban parishes of the United States was shared experiences of urban ghettos and clerical and religious domination begun in parochial school and extended through the reception of Extreme Unction before death. Mobility, lay education, and the effects of Vatican II verbiage have lessened authoritarianism, inclined laity to be more active, and ended the phenomenon of the local ethnic church where everybody knows everybody. Thus the old basis of community is lost. The new community in which individuals share themselves at all levels with others, where all take responsibility for the community has not yet arrived. The church does not seem to have realized that real community cannot be mandated. Moreover, since it is voluntary it requires autonomy both for participating members and for the communities they create.

That autonomy is not possible yet within the church. Power to choose pastors and bishops, to dispose of community property, to hire and fire staff, to veto lay decisions, is still vested in the bishops and pastors.[35] Lay autonomy exists—where it does—solely at the whim of the pastor/bishop. Vatican II itself was a series of reforms chosen for the laity by the hierarchy. Vatican II never realized that the laity of the church cannot fulfill the Vatican II goal of evangelizing the world unless the laity is allowed the autonomy required to form community capable of supporting such a crusade. The laity cannot be expected both to function in the public world of critical rationality and autonomy and to uncritically follow the dictates of the hierarchy. Herein lies the inconsistency of Vatican II, and of the church's reform efforts ever since.

IV. THE FEMINIST PERSPECTIVE AND THE CHURCH'S DILEMMA

Eliminating the contradictions in present church operations requires a feminist perspective. The church will not be able to embody both masculine and feminine aspects, nor to address both public and private areas effectively, until it heals the division between them. The masculine/feminine dualism, and its offspring the public/private dualism, preceded the church. But when the church decided that women could be Christians, did have souls, and could be saved,[36] it took on a task which entailed a mission to be relevant to both sides of the dualism. That is a task beyond the abilities of any institution to do well. For in a world characterized by such dualism, the institution itself is relegated to one side of the dualism or the other. To escape such a fate the institution must abolish the dualism itself. Feminism can be useful at this task.

The major focus of feminist scholarship has been succinctly summed up in the phrase "the personal is political." Feminism is the belief that men and women are equal. Feminism has arisen precisely because the division and the rationale for the division between the public and private realms of reality have developed chinks in modern society. The chinks are most easily perceived by those who are forced by circumstances or personal drive to straddle the fence between the masculine public and the feminized private domains. The fence provides a new vantage point, which leads not only to belief in the equality of the sexes, but to new ways of perceiving reality as a whole.

Feminist scholarship is leading the way in demonstrating through the use of history, psychology, economics and sociology that the political world has always influenced (some would say determined) the structure of personal life. Self-consciously feminist writers have traced domestic concepts which popes took for granted as natural—the social institution of childhood, the character of women, the nuclear family, the division of labor inside and outside the home, the educative role of women, and home as the center of "real" life— and demonstrated that these concepts are the result of widespread social patterns in the economy and the political arena.[37]

In fact, the social and the domestic are inseparable. We are whole persons, inevitably involved in both areas. Compartmentalization works well for desks; it is not a successful strategy for people. The lack of integration of the two areas for many people causes intense stress, and is suspected of being a contributing cause not only of depression and mental illness, but also of physical ailments.[38]

The home cannot be isolated from the currents sweeping society; it cannot be a refuge either for human beings or for religion. To retreat to the home is naive; at most it buys a little time until the threats must be faced. Investing the domestic sphere with the rank of "real world"—the place where we are really ourselves, where self-creation is possible and happiness and fulfillment are found—is simplistic. Whatever we are fleeing, whether alienating, boring work, low status, irreverence for religion, divorce, drugs, materialism or anything else, follows us into the home, if only in our fear. Moreover, our private lives and relationships cannot stand the pressure of having to compensate for the part (often the larger part) of our lives that is not fulfilling. Thus there arises what many today call the crisis of the family. Social problems are echoed in family problems.

This is the argument of feminist scholarship, which investigated the family only to be led from it to social problems. Rigid sexual stereotyping and sexism in the working class compared to the middle class suggest something about the relationship between self-image and class location.[39] Correlations between rates of spouse and child abuse and rates of unemployment suggest even more about the connection between public and private realms.[40] Studies of the effect of public assistance on family structure and self-perception push the social/private connection; examinations of the effects of white racist attitudes on black sexual relations and family life break open yet new avenues of investigation.[41]

This attack on the social/private split by feminist scholarship is crucial to the attempt to change the church's understanding of its mission of evangelization. Evangelization had been commonly understood to mean converting new members to profess belief in the doctrine of the church. Since Vatican II the trend has been to widen the meaning of evangelization to include the conversion of the world to Christian values and lifestyles, to humanize the world. The humanization of the world requires the reconciling of the public and private aspects of reality. If warmth, compassion, forgiveness and love continue to be understood as natural to and appropriate for only the domestic sphere of personal relations, then the Good News does not have much chance of a serious hearing in the world.

The release of women from exclusively domestic concerns, contrary to much nineteenth-century feminist thinking,[42] is not enough to liberate women or to improve the social sphere. Though the split in reality *originated* with the exclusion of women from the public sphere, we see today that the inclusion of women in the public sphere is insufficient to eliminate the split. Both sexes do participate in both realms, but the public/private split and the stereotypic views of the sexes are preserved by the insistence that women accept primary responsibility for maintaining the domestic refuges, and a secondary, supportive public role as breadwinner. (One may doubt that this is a stable situation, however entrenched it seems. Sooner or later women carrying the double burden of full domestic responsibility and shared public responsibility begin to question their role.)

Women are not more naturally good, loving, gentle, tactful, and all the other Christian adjectives for virtue. If women seem to be virtuous, it is because they have been denied power and autonomy, and have had to develop sensitivity, tact, and other endearing qualities as tactics for surviving and thriving. If their environment changes, so will their characterological response to it. We can only evangelize the world by seeing that all of us, men and women alike, develop Christian virtues and practice them in all areas of our lives. The home and private life has only the virtue we attribute to it and the healing and restorative power we invest in it.

If we are to bring the world to worship of God, we cannot hope to succeed with all those who doubt the existence of, and feel unworthy of, a loving God until we couple the preaching of God's love with real evidence of that love working through the church community to end their alienation and victimization. The warmth which has characterized the natural family must be extended to all God's family. The Spirit does not restrict its communication of God's love to those in the family, but spreads it through the public sphere in social and political events also. So should we. The domestic sphere is neither naturally separate from the public domain, nor does it enjoy any kind of Christian privilege. Certainly Jesus did not elevate the domestic sphere:

neither in his treatment of his own family,[43] nor in speaking to his disciples about theirs.[44] In fact, the early church invested singleness with importance in order to free people from the exclusive claims of domestic life so that Christians could evangelize by carrying the love and example of Jesus to others in the world. The church *itself* was to embody in the world all the virtues of the natural family—love, loyalty, compassion, obedience.[45]

If the church is to succeed in the public agenda it has set for itself, it must address itself to healing the public/private split. The split is real, and cannot be ignored. It is through ignoring the split that the church has allowed itself to support an internal dualism which has the potential to divide the church. This dualism consists of two different and contradictory messages concerning human nature, humanization, the nature of the Kingdom, and the work of the church. One message, the public one, stresses autonomy, responsibility, community conscience, the presence of the Spirit, and proportional consequentialism as the appropriate moral methodology. The other, internal, message contains an imposed, absolutist moral code (especially in sexuality and church law) and a method of decision-making which is remote from the person, hierarchical, and non-communal in the extreme. This internal message mandates the nurture of individuals by women, and orders the formation of community and conscience in the structured absence of either possible role models or real freedom to experiment and learn. In this message there is little reference to the presence of the Spirit in the here and now, but much is made of the role of the Spirit in the establishment of authority and past tradition.

Some feminist suggestions for the healing of the public/private dualism in the church follow. It is important to note that these suggestions are linked. Should the institutional church try to implement only those most palatable, the split may again be altered, but it probably will not be eliminated.

1. Ordain women, make celibacy voluntary, and open some governance positions (at synods, Councils and in the Curia) to male and female laity. This would separate the clerical/lay division from the male/female division, from the celibate/sexually active division, as well as prevent these three from coinciding with the powerful/powerless division. Internal power constellations might become more open to creative new combinations.

2. Much more consultation needs to be done before the magisterium speaks. The consultation process for the Midwest bishops' statement *Strangers and Guests: Toward Community in the Heartland*[46]—a series of open meetings—seems a good step in this direction. The consultation process should prevent bishops from speaking out of

ignorance on important lay concerns (such as sexuality), as well as provide a setting where bishops can stimulate a lay thought on important issues such as nuclear war or farm policy. The bishops' statements will sometimes lag behind the general stance of the laity, but the distance should be minimized. Neither is it good for bishops to be far in advance of the laity, for their teaching authority is equally weakened then. Prophetic voices, however courageous and principled they appear when unheeded by the many, are most *effective* when operating just two steps ahead of the masses.

3. Authoritarianism must be rooted out and replaced by some steps toward democratic representation. This does not necessarily mean election of bishops, cardinals, and popes. But we need to recapture the original role of the local community in calling priests to ordination, and reflect that important role in the relationships canon law structures between parish and pastor, parish and bishop, and parish and seminary. Experimentation is in order here, and a pluralism of models may well be necessary. But if the community which all the liturgical reforms claim to call forth is really desired, it must be given a *function* in the church. The most concrete manifestation of community is the local parish. It needs to be other-oriented, to have a task, a responsibility, a mission. It should not be an end in itself. The parish must be trusted to be Christian in the fullest sense of the word.

4. The church must end its moral dualism. It must approach moral issues in the private sphere with the same ethical method it uses in the public sphere. Proportional consequentialism must replace traditional method in the private sphere not only in order to end the prevailing methodological recognition of two realms, but also because traditional method's absolutist propensities are incompatible with the decentralization of power which accompanies the end of authoritarianism.[47]

The church must also provide support for those seeking to form and to act on individual conscience. Bishops' statements in this country have of necessity begun to acknowledge that they are advisory, to be considered seriously, but not binding on decisions of conscience.[48] There have been a very few papal intimations of such approach, especially under Paul VI.[49] The present instrument for Examination of U.S. Seminaries, drawn up at the request of John Paul II, contains a section asking seminaries to describe their teaching on conscience and magisterium, and uses language which presumes that even the informed conscience is an insignificant moral authority, especially compared to the presumed authority of the magisterium. Moral dependence makes any form of authentic communal responsibility impossible.

5. The church must forgo or redefine some of its most traditional language and imagery—among them, the use of the feminine for church,[50] including the analogy of church as bride of Christ. References to all Christians as brothers, sons of Christ, men, must be made inclusive. Individual episcopates must be allowed to reselect Mass readings from Scripture, or the readings should be changed for the entire church. Every set of readings is selective according to the values of its agents; the agents who selected Old Testament and New Testament readings for our A, B and C liturgical cycles shared some different values than we do today. Readings should be chosen primarily for their teaching value. There is no excuse to be reading either "Wives, be submissive to your husbands" or the story of the sacrifice of Isaac in an age when the church publicly refers to the equality of men and women and to the parental love of God for all of us—even children like Isaac.

The analogy between Christ and church (and Israel as the bride of Yahweh) is a difficult one. It will lend support to sexism and public/private dualism so long as our concept of God is so masculine.[51] The feminist question of whether Christianity can be other than patriarchal when both God and the Incarnated offspring of God are masculine is important. Perhaps this masculinity of the divine is one reason why even Vatican II reforms aimed supposedly at creating a human community of faith have taken on such a strong masculine tone of domination. Is it too late for us to go back and discover and lift up in God's interaction with our ancestors feminine qualities also? Is it too late for God to be androgynous? We can only eliminate the public/private split by eliminating the perceived split between masculine and feminine. This in turn may depend upon our ability to deny superiority to the masculine based upon its being characteristic of divinity.

6. The church must stop teaching traditional sex roles in sermons, documents, and parochial schools, colleges, and seminaries. Catholic schools should be coed and assume that all persons should be capable of earning a living; taking care of personal needs like cooking, sewing, driving, and car repair; and participating in athletics. Both sexes should be represented on pastoral and teaching staffs from parish through seminary. Let us have no more sermons on women as fruitful vines who are a credit to their husband's homes, or on the seductive power of women exemplified in Eve. No more assuming that all men—and only men—are spiritually and morally bankrupt and dependent because they work hard to fill their role as sole family breadwinner in a harsh world. No more assuming that women and children are natural pairs and belong together at home. The church's

concern for the care of children and the establishment and maintenance of domestic life should be addressed to both parents. Neither
should the church presume that the home is an oasis in the desert of
society, for this is to deny the possibility of real community in the
church or in society in general.

7. Lastly, the church must somehow reverse the *feeling* labels it
has attached to both private religious life and life in the world. Joy is
not only present in the personal encounters with the divine in liturgy
and prayer. Nor is it restricted to religion and domestic events such as
marriage, childbirth, and sticky children's kisses. Joy is also found in
our social experiences, in the steps groups take toward community
and peace, in small victories over injustice. There is no corner of our
lives that is not open to joy, just as there is no corner immune to suffering. Perhaps if we celebrated the social joys more we could move beyond the common understanding that our private, religious joys support us in the depressing obligation of working in the world.

V. CONCLUSION

Religion suffered both from the discoveries of science and from the
Enlightenment philosophy and politics they accompanied in that, due
to church opposition to scientific and philosophical innovation, religion in the popular mind became increasingly divorced from reason
as represented by scientific method.

The church fought the labels of irrationality, intuition, and femininity, but because of a series of defeats at the hands of secular and
anti-clerical liberalism, by the twentieth century the church had been
pushed out of the public realm as a principal actor. The church's
acceptance of a new role on the feminized domestic side of the
public/private dualism reinforced the conviction in the public mind
that religion is a private life interest of irrational, subordinate creatures.

Vatican II was an attempt on the part of the hierarchy to move
the church back over to the masculine, public side of the public/pri-
vate split. Feminist analysis suggests both a way of explaining the internal and external crises engendered by this attempt on the part of
the hierarchy, and steps which can solve these crises through a process eliminating the public/private distinction completely. The elimination of the public/private split seems, within feminist analysis, necessary if the church is to be effective in satisfying the demands of the
Gospel to evangelize all areas of our lives.

NOTES

1.   Short surveys of patristic and medieval attitudes toward and understandings of women can be found in Rosemary Ruether, "Virginal Feminism in the Fathers of the Church" and Eleanor McLaughlin, "Women in Medieval Theology" in Ruether, ed., *Religion and Sexism* (New York: Simon & Schuster, 1974).

2.   Kenneth Latourette, *A History of Christianity*, Vol. II (New York: Harper and Row, 1975), pp. 692-93, 982-87.

3.   *Ibid.*, pp. 1099-1101.

4.   Latourette, p. 1105; *Chers fils, Acta Apostolicae Sedis* 42 (1950), p. 639; *Dequelle consolation, Acta Apostolicae Sedis* 43 (1951), p. 784; *Se a tempere, Acta Apostolicae Sedis* 32 (1940), p. 362; *Divini Redemptoris, Acta Apostolicae Sedis* 29 (1937), p. 100.

5.   *Encyclical Matrimonii*, 1741 to Polish bishops; letter *Deessemius Nos*, 1788 to the Bishop of Mottola; Apostolic Constitution, *Dei miseratione*, 1741; Apostolic Constitution, *Apostolicii ministerii*, 1747. Sources of translations of papal documents not otherwise identified: *Papal Teachings: Matrimony*, Benedictine Monks of Solesmes, eds. tr. Michael J. Byrnes (Boston: St. Paul Editions, 1963); *Papal Teachings: Woman in the Modern World*, Benedictine Monks of Solesmes, eds. (Boston: St. Paul Editions, 1958).

6.   Apostolic Constitution, *Ad Apostolics servitutis*, 1742.

7.   Encyclical *Satis vobis*, 1741; encyclical *inter omnigenas*, 1743 to the Bishop and people of Serbia.

8.   Encyclical *Magnae nobis*, 1748, to Polish Bishops; Apostolic letter *Quantopere*, 1763; letter to Archbishop of Malines, *Exequendo nunc*, 1782; letter, *Gravissimam*, 1789, to Archbishop of Prague; letter, *Litteris tuis*, 1789, to Bishop of Agra.

9.   Apostolic constitution, *Auctorem fidei*, 1794.

10.   Letter, *Etsi fraternitatis*, 1803, to Bishop of Mainz; encyclical *Traditi humilitati*, 1829; encyclical *Commissum divinitus*, 1835, to clergy of Switzerland; Apostolic letter, *Ad Apostolicae Sedis*, 1851; letter, *La littera, 1852, to King Victor Emmanuel; Consistorial allocution September 27, 1852, on civil matrimony in New Granada; the Syllabus of Errors* #65-74; letter *Tuae litterae*, 1875 to Bishop of Ghent; encyclical *Inscrutabili*, 1878; encyclical Quod apostolici, 1878; letter *Ci siamo*, 1879, to episcopate of Turin, Vercelli, and Genoa; encyclical *Arcanum*, 1880; letter *Les evenements*, 1883, to President of French Republic: encyclical *Humanum genus*, 1884; encyclical *Quod multum*, 1886 to Bishops of Hungary; encyclical *Dall'alto*, 1890, to Italian episcopate; encyclical *Rerum novarum*, 1891; letter *Il divisamento*, 1893, to Italian episcopate; letter *Quam religiosa*, 1898, to Bishops of Peru; encyclical *Annum ingressi sumus*, 1902; letter *Dum multa*, 1902, to Bishops of Ecuador; letter *Afflictum propioribus*, 1906, to Bishops of Bolivia; encyclical *Ubi arcano*, 1922; letter *Ci si e domandato*, 1929, to Cardinal Gaspari.

11.   Encyclical *Casti connubii*, 1930; *Dilectissima nobis*, 1933, to Spanish episcopate; encyclical *Divini Redemptoris*, 1937; Apostolic letter *Con singular*

complacencia, 1939, to Phillippine episcopate.

12. *Casti connubii*, 1930; encyclical *Summi Pontificatus*, 1939; 1941 allocution to Sacred Roman Rota; Radio Message to the World, May 13, 1943; allocution to Biological-Medical Union of St. Luke, 1944; allocution to French journalists, April 17, 1946; radio message to Swiss people, 1946; allocution to Congress on European Unity, 1948; allocution to Bureau International du Travail, 1949; speech to International Union of Family Organizations, 1949; speech to International Congress of Catholic Doctors, 1949; speech to Cardinals, Archbishops and Bishops, November 2, 1950; speech to Fathers of Families, 1951; speech to midwives, 1951; speech to Association of Large Families, 1951; allocution to First Symposium on Genetic Medicine, 1953; speech to 26th Congress on Urology, 1953; speech to 2nd World Conference on Fertility and Sterility, 1956; allocution to 7th Congress on Hematology, 1958.

13. John in *Mater et Magistra*, #188-195; Paul VI in *Humanae Vitae*, #17,23; John Paul II in January 28, 1979, address at Puebla, III, 5.

14. *Immortale Dei*, 1885, *Acta Sanctae Sedis*, 18: pp. 167-68.

15. *Arcanum*, 1880, *Acta Sanctae Sedis* 12: p. 389.

16. *Natalis trecentesimi*, December 27, 1917, *Acta Apostolicae Sedis* 10 (1918), p. 57.

17. October 21, 1919, speech.

18. *Bonum sane*, June 25, 1920.

19. October 21, 1919, speech.

20. *Casti Connubii*, 1930.

21. *Ibid.*

22. September 10, 1941, speech to newlyweds.

23. *Divini Redemptoris*, 1937.

24. October 21, 1945, address to Italian Women.

25. October 24, 1955, speech to Italian Education Association.

26. September 21, 1948, speech to International Association for the Protection of the Girl.

27. *Ibid.*

28. October 21, 1945, address to Italian women.

29. February 25, 1942, speech to newlyweds.

30. *Ci e gradito, Osservatore Romano*, December 8, 1960.

31. Thomas Shannon and David O'Brien, "Introduction to the Pastoral Constitution on the Church in the Modern World" in *Renewing the Earth: Catholic Documents on Peace, Justice and Liberation* (Garden City, NY: Doubleday, 1977), pp. 171-72.

32. *Gaudium et Spes*, 43 in Joseph Gremillion, ed., *The Gospel of Peace and Justice: Catholic Social Teaching Since Pope John* (Maryknoll, NY: Orbis, 1976), p. 278.

33. The second draft of the U.S. Bishops' pastoral letter on war and peace, for example, oscillates between old style demands ("Catholics must..." to men and women in the military) to more basic recognition of basic autonomy in conscience.

34. Much of the opposition to the U.S. bishops' letter on war and peace both at the local level (as seen in newspapers and heard on radio talkshows) and at the national level (the formation of the American Catholic Committee) comes from people who still resent Vatican II as a disruption of their religious certainty and consequent security.

35. The New Code of Canon Law continues this situation virtually unchanged—as is to be expected since it was drawn up within the present center of power.

36. These decisions were not, of course, finally made until the late Middle Ages. The fact that Thomas Aquinas felt obliged to deal with such questions in the *Summa* attests to their real presence in the Church of his time.

37. See, for example, Carolyn Merchant, *The Death of Nature: Women, Ecology, and the Scientific Revolution* (San Francisco: Harper & Row, 1980); Eli Zaretsky, *Capitalism, the Family and Personal Life* (New York: Harper & Row, 1976); Dorothy Dinnerstein, *The Mermaid and the Minotaur: Sexual Arrangements and the Human Malaise* (New York: Harper & Row, 1976); Del Martin, *Battered Wives* (San Francisco: Glide Publications, 1976); Joseph Pleck and Jack Sawyer, *Men and Masculinity* (Englewood Cliffs, NJ: Prentice-Hall, 1974) and Joseph H. Pleck, *The Myth of Masculinity* (Cambridge, MA: The MIT Press, 1981); Jacques Donzelot, *The Policing of Families* (New York: Random House, 1979); and Hilda Scott, *Does Socialism Liberate Women? Experiences from Eastern Europe* (Boston: Beacon, 1974).

38. Especially of heart attack and stroke. Many corporations are offering workshops for their employees on ways of integrating work and family to cut down on the costly medical effects of job-related stress and its pressures on the home and health.

39. Lillian Breslow Rubin, *Worlds of Pain: Life in the Working Class Family* (New York: Basic Books, 1976).

40. Martin, *Battered Wives*, pp. 54-55.

41. Frances Fox Piven and Richard A. Cloward, *Regulating the Poor: The Functions of Public Welfare* (New York: Random House, 1971); Michele Wallace, *Black Macho and the Myth of the Superwoman* (New York: Dial, 1978).

42. Many feminists advocated suffrage on the grounds that the greater morality of women would eliminate corruption and evils (such as war) in the public sphere when women were granted political power.

43. Lk 2:49; Mt 12:46-50; Lk 8:19-21; Mk 3:31-35.

44. Lk 14:25-29; Mt 10:37-38; Lk 9:59-62; Mt 8:19-22.

45. See Stanley Hauerwas, *A Community of Character: Toward the Construction of a Christian Social Ethics* (Notre Dame, IN: University of Notre Dame Press, 1981), p. 190.

46. *Strangers and Guests*, National Catholic Rural Life Conference, 4625 N.W. Beaver Drive, Des Moines, Iowa 50322.

47. Timothy O'Connell's treatment of traditional moral method and the revisionist position in *Principles for a Catholic Morality* (New York: Seabury, 1978) makes this point well.

48. The second draft of the U.S. Bishops pastoral letter on nuclear war ends with this acknowledgment.

49. *Octogesima adveniens*, pp. 3-4

50. Letty Russell, "Changing Language and the Church" in Letty Russell, ed., *The Liberating Word* (Philadelphia: Westminster, 1976), pp. 87-88.

51. See *ibid.*, pp. 92-94.

4

The Marian Tradition and the Reality of Women

Elizabeth A. Johnson, C.S.J.*

ABSTRACT

After a brief explanation of the feminist theological perspective, this chapter explores three critiques from that perspective of the marian tradition, highlighting ways in which the symbol of Mary has been used to the detriment of the full humanity and dignity of women. A reinterpretive move then examines three parallel possibilities for a new naming of Mary which would cohere with the full liberation of all human beings. No definitive resting point is arrived at, the conclusion being that a renewed theology of Mary will emerge only with renewed attitude and praxis regarding women in the churches.

I. INTRODUCTION

The Catholic marian tradition in its complex relationship to theory and practice regarding women in the church and in societies influenced by the church has come under increasing scrutiny in recent theological reflection. This issue concerning both Mary and women has arisen at a time when the post-Tridentine symbolization and synthesis of thought about Mary, called "Mariology," has for all practical

*Elizabeth A. Johnson, C.S.J., Associate Professor of Theology at Fordham University (Bronx, NY 10458), received the Ph.D. from Catholic University of America. In addition to articles in *Theological Studies, Thomist, Heythrop Journal, Eglise et Théologie,* and *Horizons,* she is the author of *Consider Jesus: Waves of Renewal in Christology* (New York: Crossroad, 1990) and *She Who Is: The Mystery of God in Feminist Theological Perspective* (New York: Crossroad, 1992).

purposes shattered under the impact of the Second Vatican Council's decisions regarding the place and emphases of marian teaching.[1] Accordingly, thought about Mary is now being reassembled in the light of biblical, patristic, and liturgical renewals, ecumenical discussions, and developments taking place in systematic theology, most pertinently in the areas of the theology of God, christology, pneumatology, theology of grace, ecclesiology, and eschatology. A theology of Mary for the present and future church is slowly taking shape in line with advances made in these other areas of post-conciliar development. But concomitant with these theological shifts, there is a sea change occurring in our society in the self-perception and self-definition of women, and consequently in the understanding of women's nature, capabilities, role, status, and relationship to men and male-created structures. These changes on the anthropological, psychological, economic, and social-political levels are affecting the way the marian tradition is being perceived and evaluated, at least by those who are aware of this portentous turning of the tide. It is from this point of view that the marian tradition is reflected upon here. It goes without saying that men are as affected by this issue as are women, for the two sexes as a whole make up the human race, and redefinition of the nature and role of one draws into its purview by implication the reenvisionment of the shape of the other.[2]

An example will serve to indicate the depth of the change in perception which accompanies the new awareness of women's reality. To the question "What is Mariology?," the noted Mariologist Juniper Carol answered in the 1950's:

> By its very definition, Mariology is the study of Mary. More precisely, it is that part of the science of theology which treats of the Mother of God in her singular mission, prerogatives and cult.[3]

His book's development of each of these stated aspects makes clear that Mary's singular mission includes its preparation through Old Testament prophecies, its fulfillment in divine maternity, and its consequences in her universal mediation and universal queenship. Her prerogatives include the Immaculate Conception, perpetual virginity, and Assumption; the legitimacy of her cult is an obvious corollary. To the same question, "What is Mariology?," Rosemary Radford Ruether responded twenty years later that Mariology has been a creation by male human beings which

> . . . sanctifies the image of the female as the principle of passive receptivity to the transcendent activity of male gods and their

> agents, the clergy. . . . (It) is the exaltation of the principle of sub-
> mission and receptivity, purified of any relation to sexual fe-
> maleness. . . . Mariology exalts the virginal, obedient, spiritual
> feminine and fears all real women in the flesh.[4]

Her development of this theme argues that Mariology comes into
being and grows as an exercise of male projection of idealized femininity. As such it is dissociated from the reality of women and functions as a tool of repression, an instrument of male power over
women. Only if reflection on Mary is freed from its androcentric presuppositions can Mary emerge as a true sign of redemption, a sign of
God's liberating favor on those who are broken and have nothing.

The change in perspective is startling. Rosemary Radford
Ruether is, of course, a feminist theologian and her writing as a whole
embodies the feminist perspective. A brief word about that theological stance is in order before exploring its critique of the traditional
marian symbol.

II. THE FEMINIST PERSPECTIVE

The feminist theological perspective is an orientation to theology as a
whole which has as its critical principle the promotion of the full humanity of women, up to now marginalized in theory as well as fact.
According to this critical principle, whatever promotes the full humanity of women is judged to reflect a true and right relation to the divine; whatever distorts or diminishes the full humanity of women is
appraised as non-redemptive and non-reflective of the Holy. The
uniqueness of feminist theology is not the critical principle of full humanity, for this operated as a principle in classical Christian theology.
What is new is that rather than allow men alone to consider themselves as norms of authentic humanity, women claim this principle
also for themselves. "Women name themselves as subjects of authentic and full humanity."[5]

The working out of feminist theology utilizes a complex of
sources: the human experience of women as a primary source, and
dialogue with usable tradition from Scripture, classical Christian theology, alternative though suppressed Christian movements, ancient
non-Christian religions, and critical post-Christian philosophies. In
this effort several theological themes come to the fore as particularly
valuable. These include the priestly writer's vision of creation in
which both male and female are created in the divine image; the
prophetic insistence on the holiness of justice for the poor and

oppressed; the teaching of Jesus of Nazareth about the approaching reign of God as well as Jesus' characteristic behavior which, in the power of that reign, was inclusive of the marginalized even to the point (dramatic in a patriarchal society) of choosing women as disciples; early Christian praxis which baptized women and men alike, breaking out in song which proclaimed that in the light of the new creation there is "neither Jew nor Greek, slave nor free, male nor female, for all are one in Christ Jesus" (Gal 3:38); and the eschatological vision of redeemed humanity before God, a humanity redeemed in *all* its dimensions.

These and other elements of usable tradition are faced with the now conscious experience of the dehumanizing subordination of women, in theory and practice, throughout the Christian tradition.[6] This situation, judged to be sinful injustice, prevents the fullness of creation/redemption from being victoriously fulfilled in individual persons and in the human community. Those who theologize from a feminist perspective seek first of all to unmask the massive distortion of those aspects of the Christian tradition which have systematically subordinated women on the basis of their gender; to name such discrimination as the sin of sexism blocking the reign of God, which it is; to critique the supposed divine sanctions which are adduced in support of it; and ultimately to move the church toward change, away from patterns of domination/subordination toward the ideal of freedom and the possibility of self-actualization for all persons. This involves equivalence in the valuation of women and men as persons, genuine mutuality in their relationships, and the correlative reshaping of institutional structures. From the feminist perspective it is not enough just to interpret the tradition in the light of today's questions. Rather, it is necessary to engage in radical critique of the tradition insofar as it has abetted a situation of oppression. The critical interpretation which then results intends to serve the full emancipation of women as persons in their own right and, not incidentally, the emancipation of men, also freed from being cast into preset, gender-determined roles.

Thought from the feminist perspective, then, is both critical and hopeful. It is critical, protesting in the power of the Spirit the radical distortion of the Christian tradition regarding women. It is also hopeful, drawn by the power of the same Spirit to believe in the eschatological promise, that what exists in the present is not all there is, that God's deepest hope for humanity is the liberation of all people and indeed of the whole universe. The Christian feminist perspective fundamentally demands conversion, and leads to a transformation of values in every dimension.

When this perspective is brought to bear on the Christian tradition about Mary, a distinctly different judgment is made about the blessing that Mariology, with its glorification of a single woman, has been for women as a whole. Prevailing wisdom would have it that "the dignity of woman was raised in her,"[7] that is, the dignity of Our Lady in being the Mother of God is for Christians the measure of women's dignity which is modeled on hers. While there is some truth to this insight, it is not without ambiguity and in effect states only half the story, omitting consideration of the ways in which the marian tradition has functioned to block the self-realization of women as persons. A sampling of judgments by women religious writers makes this clear:

> Patricia Noone: It is a question whether Mary is really there for women or is not rather a Trojan horse raised to ambush women's aspirations for personhood, human dignity, and corresponsibility for the church and society.[8]

> Kari Børresen: The figure of Mary is a patriarchal construct: virgin, wife, mother, and adjunct to the male. She embodies the essential connection between femininity and subordination forged by the patriarchal mind-set. To make her the model for free women is absurd, until that connection is broken.[9]

> Mary Daly: Women are enslaved symbolically in the cult of the Virgin Mary, who is glorified only insofar as she accepts the subordinate role assigned to her.[10]

> Elisabeth Schüssler Fiorenza: Mary has almost never functioned as a symbol of women's equality and capacity to lead; adherence to her can deter women from becoming whole persons.[11]

> Mary Gordon: It is necessary to reject the traditional image of Mary in order to hold onto any hope for one's own intellectual achievement, independence, and sexual fulfillment.[12]

> Marina Warner: Mariology is a weapon in the armory of male chauvinism and an effective instrument of female subjugation. Clothed in theology legitimation, it is the instrument of a dynamic argument from the Catholic Church about the male-dominated structure of society and of the church, presented as a God-given order.[13]

The list could go on and on. Notice that the charge is not that of irrelevance, heard from other quarters about the marian tradition. It is rather that of complicity in the oppression of women. Mariology has legitimated women's subordination, has presided over the evil rather than challenging it.

Ten years ago, in his apostolic exhortation *Marialis Cultus*, Pope Paul VI took note of what he termed this "alienation" of women from the marian tradition, suggesting that traditional, culturally conditioned images of Mary were at the root of the problem. His solution was to replace timid, submissive images of Mary with the picture of one who gave active and responsible consent, one who proclaimed God's vindication of the humble and oppressed.[14] Similarly, the bishops of the United States in their pastoral letter *Behold Your Mother: Woman of Faith* proposed that Mary be envisioned as intelligent, apostolic, inquiring, creative, courageous, a woman of faith, indeed, the "model of all real feminine freedom."[15] While these are worthy suggestions which have the possibility of making a contribution, they have not led women to flock back in large numbers to the honoring of Mary. Women have developed what Patricia Noone describes as the "painful habit" of laying church documents and rhetoric about Mary side by side with the actual condition of women in the church, a habit which gives rise to clear perception of contradictions.[16] Thus, the critique from the feminist perspective has grown stronger rather than weaker. It is simply not enough to replace one set of virtues with another more suited to our present value system and to propose this new Mary as worthy of emulation. The basic structures which give rise simultaneously to the glorification of Mary and the subordination of women, the root attitudes which generate this pattern, need to be exposed and corrected. There is too much deep prejudice involved in the marian tradition for the simple strategy of a redescription of Mary's virtues to resolve.

And thus the two questions which focus this consideration of the subject: First, in what ways has the marian tradition functioned to the detriment of women, aiding and abetting a system which has kept women in an inferior position because of their gender? Second, in what ways might this tradition be critically reinterpreted in such a way that it would serve the goal of liberation and true mutuality between women and men? Three distinct but interrelated considerations are proposed under each question.

III. DETRIMENTAL ASPECTS

Critique I: The marian tradition has been intrinsically associated with the denigration of the nature of women as a group.

An overview of the history of early Christian thought about Mary and about the nature of women gives evidence of this paradox: that the exaltation of the one woman, Mary, grew in direct proportion to disparaging theory and vituperative rhetoric regarding the rest of womankind. The growing honor paid to Mary in theology and cult redounded to her benefit to the exclusion of other women, and this because of one fundamental assumption: that Mary was not a type (*typose*), exemplifying the capacity of redeemed humanity including women, but the great exception. Her glorious precedence prevented any analogy between herself and other women, all of whom fell short by comparison.

This is particularly evident in the Mary-Eve symbolism introduced by Justin in the second century and developed by Irenaeus and others with great embellishment. Just as the woman Eve was the disobedient one responsible for the fall of humankind and all of its attendant misery, so the woman Mary, the new Eve, was the one who through her obedience brought forth the conqueror of death, the Savior. "Death through Eve, life through Mary" became the axiom, with the accent on the contrast between the two. Occasionally in the poetry and hymns of the East the opposition is mitigated and the two women are placed in positive relationship. A hymn of Ephrem envisions Mary rejoicing in the redemption that has come to the first mother, who can now experience peace because her daughter has paid her debt; a Syrian poem pictures Mary as a child comforting Eve, stretching out her hand to the downcast ancestress and raising her up. But more usually a sharp opposition is built between the two. Mary is the obedient and faithful woman, Eve the temptress and sinner. Since no other woman is as obedient or pure or holy as Mary, no other woman can resemble her. Rather, all other women have more in common with Eve and share her sinful character. Typical of this pattern of thought, Tertullian addresses women and alleges,

> Do you not realize that you are each an Eve? The curse of God on this sex of yours lives on even in our times. Guilty, you must bear its hardships. You are the devil's gateway; you desecrated the fatal tree; you first betrayed the law of God; you softened up with your cajoling words the one against whom the devil could not prevail by force. All too easily you destroyed the image of God, Adam. *You* are the one who deserved death, and it was the Son of God who had to die.[17]

Woman is the cause of the fall, the accomplice of Satan, the destroyer of humankind. Indeed, the fury unleashed against Eve and other women is almost flattering, so exaggerated is the picture of woman's fatal and all-powerful charms and man's incapacity to resist.[18]

Chrysostom, Jerome, Augustine, and others operated within the same fundamental dynamic, projecting responsibility for the sinful condition of humankind onto Eve and all other women who are in solidarity with her, instead of perceiving clearly the solidarity of the whole human race, both men and women, in sin and grace. Mary *alone of all her sex* is exempt from this condition, being the door through which the Savior arrived. Her uniqueness sets her apart from all other women. Thus, not necessarily but by a certain logic, denigration of women became the shadow side of the glorification of Mary in the early centuries of the church.

Adding to the complexity of this development was the fact that the prevalent intellectual tradition of these early Christian centuries gave credence to the kind of dualism which posited undying tension between the spirit and the flesh, prizing spiritual detachment from the world as of the highest value. In the battle which the aspiring male waged between the spirit and the flesh, women were placed on the side of the flesh due to their obvious appeal to sexual males as well as their connection with pregnancy and childbirth. Correlatively, in the light of the growing ascetic ideal of virginity also related at this time to an anti-flesh bias, the evils of sex were particularly identified with the female. The resulting powerful aversion of Christian male thinkers to female sexuality gave added impetus to the honoring of Mary for her uniqueness in having conceived virginally, that is, for the non-use of her sexuality vis-à-vis a man, and to the corresponding belittling of women who exercised their sexuality.[19]

Throughout most of the history of the Christian tradition, this early pattern is repeated. Mary is the great exception rather than the type. The influential writings of Thomas Aquinas provide an interesting illustration of the logical gaps embraced under the rule of that assumption. To counterpose his texts which describe women as defective and misbegotten males, inferior not just because of the state of sin into which human beings have fallen but originally and by nature, with his texts on Mary which describe her as exalted above all creatures, even above the angels, is to expose a real inconsistency in his thought which he at least never resolved.[20]

Those who approach this issue from a contemporary psychological point of view have noted that the marian tradition, having been created primarily by male minds and hearts, bears an overload of male projection. Men have divided women's reality into good and evil elements, projecting the good onto Mary in an idealized fashion and the evil onto the rest of women who are then to be kept subject due to their low estate. The ideal of the good feminine which is projected onto Mary reflects the desire for a woman who is untroubling to the celibate male psyche, with asexuality and passive obedience being the most notable elements which characterize her image. The "Madonna-whore syndrome," of which this issue is a classic example, enables men to love and respect their ideal of woman in Mary but to ignore or dominate concrete real women with impunity and with immunity even from the searchings of their own conscience.

To claim, as official rhetoric does, that the dignity of woman is raised in Mary is at best a half truth. In its root dynamic, the marian tradition has persisted in idealizing the one to the detriment of the many. Instead of seeing Mary as a type, a symbol of the capacity of women, it has exalted Mary as the great exception in comparison to whom all other women are denigrated. Further evidence for this judgment is provided by sociological observation. In those countries where the cult of Mary still flourishes strongly, women have not emerged in a significant way toward involvement in public and political life. The same is true of those churches which have the strongest official attachment to Mary: they are the least likely to be open to full participation of women in ecclesial public life and ministries.

Critique II: The marian tradition has dichotomized the being and roles of women and men in the community of disciples following Christ.

As with the first criticism, the subject of this second also results from a fundamental and false assumption, namely, that the relationship between Jesus Christ and Mary in theological interpretation should serve as the model for the relationship between concrete historical men and women in the sociological and interpersonal spheres. On the basis of such an assumption, despite heroic efforts to the contrary, it is inevitable that women are relegated to a hopelessly inferior position. God takes initiative and Mary responds. Her son is the Messiah of God, and she is caught up in the mystery of salvation centered in him. This is, of course, theologically sound. But then, God is envisioned as male: *he* took the initiative and *she* responded. Jesus' undoubted maleness is brought to the fore and interpreted in naive fashion: he is Messiah and *she* is oriented to *him*. The pattern is translated into normative social mores which shape relationships and structures on the premise that men are active, women passive; men take initiative, women respond; men are slated for the public sphere, women for the private; men exercise power, women are supportive of them.

Within this pattern the question of how men and women are related to each other is usually answered by the concept of complementarity. According to this concept each of the sexes is identified with a

distinct role supposedly supplementary to one another, but roles
which in actuality give the lion's share of influence to the male and re-
serve for women the stance of passive receptivity to and support of
the primary male role. For example, the argument has been mounted
that since Christ "operated" while Mary, totally dependent upon him,
"cooperated," in her cooperation is revealed the intention of the divine plan concerning the whole of femininity (rather than the whole of
humanity). From this divinely revealed pattern, a conclusion is drawn
regarding the proper roles of women and men in the church, namely,
that man preaches the word and woman receives it; her role is her listening silence by which she renders service to the man who speaks.[21]
Beyond the debatability of the role definitions, the point to note is that
the argument is being mounted from the marian symbol in relation to
Christ, applied sociologically in direct fashion. It is a form of argu-
mentation frequently heard. Another more recent example: man is the
icon of Christ, woman the icon of the church which images Mary. As
Christ is the head of the church which in turn is loved by him while he
remains head (Eph 5), so the fatherhood exercised by the priest is not
abrogated but complemented by the spiritual motherhood of women
in the church. Likewise, the husband as head of the domestic church is
complemented by the mothering role of the wife. The conclusion is
drawn that "as Mary fulfills her complementary role we can see how
the beautiful complementarity of man and woman, Christ and the
Church, enriches the human race and the new people of God."[22]

    Suffice it to say that from a feminist perspective, complementar-
ity conceived of in this way is far from beautiful. It is a mask for an
ideology which places woman in a stereotyped role because of her
gender, a role where she is praised for living at less than full capacity.
(We might also note that it does the same for men, with the difference
that the preordained role of the male is that of the superior.) The marian tradition has been used to legitimate this conception of the relationship between the sexes, for Mary the woman is exalted precisely
for accepting the secondary role assigned to her in view of the priority
of Christ the man. A true theological affirmation has become a destructive and oppressive symbol by being applied in naive analogical
fashion to personal and sociological relationships. As Simone de Beauvoir critiqued the effect of the Christmas crib scene:

> For the first time in human history the mother kneels before her
> son; she freely accepts her inferiority. This is the supreme mascu-
> line victory, consummated in the cult of the Virgin—it is the
> rehabilitation of woman through the accomplishment of her
> defeat.[23]

The marian tradition has provided justification for a dichotomization of the being and roles of the sexes, casting woman in an auxiliary, receptive mold complementary to the dominative male.

Critique III: The marian tradition has truncated the ideal of feminine fulfillment and wholeness.

This effect of the tradition has resulted from several coalescing assumptions: that Mary is the model for the behavior of women; that the particularities of her life should therefore be directly imitated by women; and that these particularities are accessible to our knowledge through a literal reading of the Scriptures. Although even with regard to Jesus, the concept of "following" is replacing that of "imitation," since the historically conditioned character of his life makes a literal imitation impossible in later ages, the tenacity of the imitative idea persists with regard to Mary. As Cahal Daly expressed it with unintended irony:

> Some of the resentments occasionally expressed by women about motherhood and child-bearing would hardly be expected to come from people who had reflected seriously upon the privilege and grace of Christian motherhood as this is revealed preeminently in Mary. Some of the more strident formulae of some exponents of "women's liberation" are very far removed from the understanding of women's vocation which is given to us in the example of the Mother of Jesus Christ.[24]

Precisely! It is particularly the aspects of the image of Mary which portray her as handmaid, virgin, and mother which have defined the shape of the feminine ideal for centuries of believing women, curtailing the exploration of the full range of possibilities of human wholeness.

Handmaid.
Luke's narrative of the Annunciation (1:26-38) presents a powerful image of a human *fiat* to the invitation of the transcendent mystery operating within history. But Mary's *fiat*, far from being seen as the radical autonomous decision of a young woman to risk her life on a messianic venture, and more fundamentally as a free human act of faith in God, has (especially in the Counter-Reformation centuries) been interpreted as an act of submissiveness to the will of God, who is imaged furthermore as male. In preaching and spiritual writing, Mary has stood forth as a model of dependence upon this male God's initiative, a model of humility understood as a lack of possession of a personal

ego, a model of obedience understood as acquiescence: "I'll do whatever you say." The overwhelming passivity connected with the marian image has rendered Mary "a psychological model of a perpetual minor,"[25] hidden and enclosed, timid and sweet, taking direction from others with no inner purpose of her own. Since she is held up as the feminine ideal, women learn that they find their true vocation in being submissive, self-sacrificing, silent, deferential.

Even when women as members of the laity are actively engaged in church ministries, the image of Mary still haunts them with the passive ideal. One theologian in the 1950's described the virtues which the blessed Virgin models for the apostolate of the laity, including in his list

> . . . her silence, her subordination to the legally prescribed religious life of her people, her self-effacement in the public life of her Son, . . . her unpretentious membership of the community at Pentecost, when she is in herself the central point yet in no way detracts from the official rights of Peter and the Twelve. . . .

It was Karl Rahner who wrote that,[26] demonstrating the powerful pervasiveness of the passive ideal, accepted without examination by him at a time when he was critically revising other foundational concepts (although to his credit he has since written about Mary and the image of woman admitting that an ambiguity now exists on the question).[27] The marian tradition with its emphasis on Mary the handmaid has legitimated the image of woman as a vessel of passive receptivity, a receptivity moreover to the primary activity of males, be they divine or human, God, fathers, husbands, or priests. Note how the problem is compounded by the thoroughly masculine character of the deity.

Virgin.
As already noted, emphasis on Mary's virginity grew in an environment which was innately suspicious of the body and of the exercise of sexuality. Mary has been idealized as the Virgin *par excellence* from whom any trace of human sexuality has been exorcised, while the value of feminine sexuality has been correlatively undermined. The usual perception is well phrased by Cahal Daly, who asserted that "Mary's virginity is the highest peak of the history of the female sex."[28] The highest peak of the history of female sexuality is its non-use. In an age when women are discovering their own sexuality and becoming comfortable with the gift which it indeed is, such an ideal embodied in Mary is emphatically rejected. The ideal is furthermore critiqued for having divided the women in the Roman Catholic Church, because it

carries the implication that women who live a life of virginity are closer to the ideal than those who actively exercise their sexuality. It is a regrettable deficiency that nowhere in the Christian tradition is there a highly honored symbol of the exercise of female sexuality—nor of male sexuality, for that matter. The need for a Christian theology of sexuality and a theology of marriage to counteract the influences of our ever more secular culture is not filled by the tradition of Mary's asexuality. Rather, the image of her virginity has functioned to impede the integration of women's sexuality into the goal of wholeness.

Mother.
Historically Mary was indeed the mother of Jesus and, no doubt, can be assumed to have had influence on the kind of man he became. However, concentration on Mary's motherhood in the tradition has served to reinforce the perception that motherhood is the *raison d'etre* of a woman's life, the one divinely approved accomplishment, rather than the gospel proclamation that Mary's blessedness consists in hearing the Word of God and keeping it. It has thereby legitimated domesticity as the primary vocation for women.

In the history of the marian tradition, emphasis on Mary's motherhood gave rise rather early to the practice of intercession (the *Sub tuum praesidium* can be dated to the late third or early fourth century). Implicitly prerequisite for the practice as it developed was the projection of the patriarchal model of the human family into the heavenly sphere. One of the key roles of the mother in the patriarchal family is intercession or merciful influence with the male head. Such a role is now attributed to Mary, a move which also created the possibility for the later medieval aberrations which envisioned Mary as the zone of mercy over and against Christ or God the Father, angry and just judges needing to be placated.[29] More to the point here, the mother's role vis-à-vis the children is presumed to be total dedication and service. In a linguistic study of 216 marian hymns done at the Institute Catholique in Paris, one researcher discovered that the word "mother" was used 85% of the time, usually linked with the imperative mode of the verb.[30] The supplicant requests, pleads, gives orders for the fulfillment of needs to which Mary the Mother is supposed to respond. What image of woman is assumed here? One always at the beck and call of her children? Perpetually available? Is she ever thought of as an independent individual, someone with a right to a room of her own, in Virginia Woolf's memorable phrase? The thought is never entertained. The connotation is rather that the natural order of things for a woman is motherhood, expressed in total devotion to the needs of the children. The other side of that relationship, as

Laurentin has pointed out, is that too frequently the devotees are kept in a state of perpetual childhood, narcissistically looking to the mother for the satisfaction of needs, a state which is the antithesis of adult responsibility for the world.[31]

To sum up: Being responsive to the inspiration of the Spirit, being virginal, and caring for the needs of one's children are not bad things—in fact they are quite excellent values in themselves. But when in the tradition about Mary they are set within an androcentric framework, so that the ideal of woman becomes the passively obedient handmaiden, the asexual virgin, and the domestically all-absorbed mother, then the tradition implicitly and explicitly supports the truncation of woman's fulfillment and is vigorously contested in the interest of greater wholeness.

IV. REINTERPRETATIONS

Is there any hope? Is there any possibility of retrieval of the marian tradition such that it would serve rather than hinder the cause of liberation/salvation for the *whole* of the human race? A number of feminist theologians are negative on this point, judging the interconnectedness of the cult of Mary and the oppression of women so intricate that the effort to save something from it is scarcely worthwhile. On the other hand, it can be argued that it is important to set Mary free from the image that has been made of her and from projections attached to her by male theologians and priestly hierarchy. Out of a deep sense of solidarity or sisterhood some feminist theologians do not want simply to let go of Mary.[32]

In addition, as critical analysis of the marian tradition brings to light the mechanisms used to make Mary an impossible model detrimental to women, in no way critical of men, and legitimating of the gap which persists between (female) sexuality and the mediation of holiness, the effort toward resymbolization can aid in the creation of new patterns of thought and relationship within those communities where that tradition is strong. Again, the marian tradition did keep alive the memory of a woman closely associated with the saving action of God on our behalf, a memory which some theologians in the churches of the Reformation have recently been seeking to rediscover for their own tradition.[33] An area coming under increasing scrutiny is that of God in the image of a female as well as a male person; reinterpretation can bring to light the many ways in which the marian symbol has usurped functions of the divine, thus clearing the way for renaming God with female imagery such as Mother.[34]

Finally, for all of its debilities, the marian tradition has borne to the present one of the few female-focused symbols which has persisted in the Christian community. Since we are inheritors of the long marian tradition, it is arguably a vitally important task to probe this tradition from the Scriptures onward, seeking a resymbolization of Mary which could serve the liberating intent of the gospel. There is as yet no coherent renewed theology of Mary as a whole, but I would like to identify three new directions which hold some promise, each one roughly counterpoint to the above critiques.

Proposal I

This approach is imaginatively historical in tone, identifying Mary as a real person in human history, a woman who has more in common with the rest of womankind than she has separating prerogatives. Biblical criticism has led to the realization of how very little is known of the historical Mary, most of the Scripture scenes in which she figures being theological interpretations of the gospel message in narrative form rather than historically accurate reportage.[35] This leaves the woman of Nazareth in historical shadows, but paradoxically makes her more accessible as a human person in her own right, the Mary behind the symbolism, so to speak. She did not live a glorified life but can be identified within the context of the Judaism of the first century as a woman of the people, poor, faithful, expectant; a woman with her own life history, her own very real struggles, and her own journey of faith, about which we know very little. The very paucity of the historical record regarding her is a point of identification with all women, whose history has been largely hidden and unremarked.

The new imagery developing from this approach, while not necessarily historically based, is pervaded with a realism which puts Mary within imaginable reach; for example, she is now addressed in feminist litanies as unwed mother, refugee woman with child, widow, and mother of a son executed as a common criminal. Some suggest that, in solidarity with Mary as a woman of our history, believers now invoke her as our "sister" in faith who reveals to women their own real resources.[36] This line of approach is revaluing the marian symbol not because of Mary's glorious difference from all the rest but because as a real woman with much to contend with she gave herself to her life and to her God, in her own time and place and way. We are associated with her by the bond of human history and still more in the communion of saints. She is one of the cloud of witnesses (Heb 11-12) whose story encourages our own faith. As the fourth Eucharistic prayer of the renewed Catholic liturgy so well expresses it, we praise God in her company—in the company of Mary and all the saints.

Proposal II

A second promising approach, more theological in its orientation, sees Mary as a type of the church and, more specifically within that broad concept, as a disciple who hears the Word of God and keeps it. She is thereby a type of the community of believing disciples which is the church. The early Christian understanding that Mary is a type of the church was reincorporated into current discussion mainly as a result of Vatican II's statement on Mary and has been the source of fruitful reflection ever since. It holds Mary forth as the symbol of the community of redeemed humanity, gifted with the healing grace of God, responding wholeheartedly, and called to the mission of spreading the gospel in the world. The advance made here over much of the tradition is that as type, Mary represents not just believing women but the *whole* church saved from the enchainment of sin. In her precisely as woman is symbolized the fact that all those needy and oppressed by sin have received the self-communicating grace of the transcendent mystery which we call God, source of both maleness and femaleness; all are therefore called in the Spirit to the mission of working for the coming of the reign of God; all are therefore capable of presencing Christ in the world and have a responsibility to do so.[37] As type of the church which receives the grace of Jesus Christ and which is the sacrament of Christ in the world, the symbol of Mary calls into question by implication the Mary/Christ-based dichotomization of the nature and roles of women and men in the redeemed community.

One specific interpretation of the exemplarity of Mary for the church designates her as a disciple, in fact as a first and preeminent disciple in the community of disciples which is the church. Biblically based, this approach understands that Mary is not to be imitated in terms of the socio-cultural conditions of her historical life, which are scarcely able to be reproduced today, but

> for the way in which in her own particular life she fully and responsibly accepted God's will; because she heard the Word of God and acted on it; and because charity and a spirit of service were the driving force of her action. She is worthy of imitation because she was the first and most perfect of Christ's disciples.[38]

As both biblical scholars and theologians have been showing, there is a great deal of promise here.[39] But a caution needs to be sounded in the light of our history. Hearing the Word of God and keeping it, which are the primary characteristics of Mary as a disciple, cannot be interpreted as a mandate to passive obedience on the part of women. It must be made explicit that the Word of God which one hears may well be a call to critical prophecy, and that the Word of God which one keeps may well impel the hearer toward conflict with the powers which oppress people not only outside the church but also within it. Furthermore, discipleship may well involve the mandate for action in the public sphere, and here again the symbol of Mary cannot be naively applied.

Historically there is no evidence that the mother of Jesus was ever actively engaged in ministry, that she ever preached or taught or evangelized or healed or administered or led a community. Many feminist theologians have discovered in other women of the New Testament, particularly in Mary of Magdala, much more potent models of female discipleship. It is at least historically ascertainable that this Mary followed Jesus during his public ministry, witnessed his death and burial, and was a commissioned witness of his resurrection, which commission she carried out.[40] The lack of Mary of Nazareth's public involvement has led some to make the distinction between Mary as the model of the believing disciple and Peter as the model of the apostolic disciple, a distinction which again turns the marian symbol into a potential tool of patriarchal power. The symbol of Mary as a disciple needs to be interpreted in such a way that she is seen to embody the personal spirit of discipleship while not strict analogy is made between her own personal history and the lives of women today, called to be disciples in a world she never dreamed of.

Proposal III

A third promising approach is concerning itself with specific aspects of the image of Mary, both discovering a new symbolic aspect of Mary as the proclaimer of liberation and reinterpreting the meaning of the traditional qualities of virginity and motherhood.

In a genuinely new movement of interpretation, the Mary of the Magnificat is coming into focus. Proclaiming words of praise and prophecy, she is a symbol of tremendous power as the singer of the song of justice in the new age of redemption. Liberation theologies of all types have claimed Mary under this aspect, recognizing that her proclamation of the greatness of God who puts down the mighty and exalts the humble, fills the hungry with good things but sends the rich away empty, fits well with the understanding of the importance of engagement for justice and peace. Feminist theologians find particular meaning in this symbol. It is noted that the Lukan community found such a proclamation a fitting expression for Mary, with its focus on the social and political rather than on the maternal and private.

With the Magnificat Mary appears as an active agent in salvation rather than the passive handmaiden, an image also countered by the idea of Mary as disciple. She is highly exalted because through her God is working a radically new reality into history, a transformation of the given order of things in which the victims will be justified. It is a revolution in which she finds great joy. And Mary does not just proclaim this. In her own person she herself embodies the humble and the hungry, the oppressed who are being liberated by God's action. Luke's sensitivity to women as members of the poor and despised classes adds this dimension to the image of Mary singing of justice: she herself represents the subjugated who will be lifted up and filled with good things in the messianic revolution. With this insight it becomes particularly appropriate to see in Mary a type of the church. She is the personification of those who, having nothing, are gifted by the action of God and charged to continue the liberating action of God in the world. It is precisely in her femaleness that she is this sign of the new redeemed humanity, the powerless who are empowered in the reign of God. Pray the Magnificat from a feminist perspective, and whole new meanings are declared.

In the Mediterranean world in which the image of Mary grew up, the cults of the great goddesses frequently portrayed them— Venus, Ishtar, Isis, Astarte—as virgins despite their lovers. Virginity symbolized their autonomy, their ability to refuse men or accept them because as female deities they were powerful, independent, self-directed. They were honored as virgins because they retained freedom of choice, not being identified by their relationships with men. Virginity then did not necessarily connote bodily integrity or sexual abstinence, but rather the notion of female independence. A virgin was "one-in-herself," autonomous. It is noted today that in the Scriptures, Mary is never portrayed as subject to Joseph or under control of any man, but in a unique way as free from parental and connubial control. Whatever the actual historicity of the infancy narratives, the image of Mary as a virgin has significance as the image of a woman from whose personal center power wells up, a woman who symbolizes the independence of the identity of woman.

Mary's motherhood is also being revalued. It is a genuine gift to be so creative, to be so fruitful as to be able to bring a new person into the world. The feminist vision rejects making the role of motherhood the exclusive or even necessarily primal role of a woman's life in a sort of biological determinism. But the actual free bearing of children is a thing to be prized, and Mary's freely chosen motherhood is seen as another aspect of her creative womanly being which creates solidarity with other women.

The combination of both of these attributions, virgin and mother, far from being seen as an impossible ideal for other women to emulate, may be understood to embody at least one aspect of a holistic goal for contemporary women. With the joining of the two, the emphasis is placed neither on bodily generativity alone nor on the value of the purely independent woman, but affirmation is given to the woman who combines both, home and career, if you will, or interrelationship and autonomy: mother and virgin.[41]

V. CONCLUSION

The marian tradition has consistently been integrated into the patriarchal framework of Christianity, and has served to legitimate it. Under the guise of a theologically correct understanding of the "feminine," the tradition about Mary has frequently functioned to undermine the real female self and to obstruct both the liberation of women and genuine mutuality between women and men in the church. Women as well as men have had complicity in this. Symbols can be said to participate in the reality which they signify, and thus they are born—and die—according to their ability to bear the power of a reality to people in different situations.[42] Recognition of the complicity of the traditional marian symbol in the assignment of inferiority to women throughout Christian history has resulted at the present time in its fracture or death among those who have entered into the feminist perspective. That symbol is unable to bear the power of a liberating vision of redemption in the lives of women and men.

Is then a resymbolization possible, so that the image of Mary can empower rather than impede the journey of women and indeed of the whole church toward greater wholeness? I dare to think and hope that it is possible, but caution strongly against letting that hope too quickly lead to a state of complacency. One can indeed imagine a renewed tradition about Mary which would include a non-stereotypical understanding of the nature of woman, one which recognizes the values of autonomy, integrity of conscience, courage, correct use of power, the goodness of female sexuality, self-assertion, and the relations of motherhood and sisterhood. One can also imagine such a renewed tradition playing a role as an integral part of a wider renewal which would result in a church that prized mutuality and reciprocity between women and men rather than one which rests content with the patriarchal pattern of domination and subordination. But this imagined renewed marian tradition is not yet reality. The experience of women in the churches is still that of systemic subordination.

If it be true that the image of Mary is tied to the image of woman in any given age,[43] then both images have a history. That history has entered a new phase as far as women are concerned. It seems a sure judgment to say that the future of the marian tradition is closely tied with the future history of women in the church, and that it will be re-generated or remain collapsed of its own weight depending in large measure on what happens in that history. A renewed marian tradition will be credible only in a church which recognizes and embodies in theory and practice the full dimensions of the dignity of women. It will be viable only in a church which as institution and community of persons learns to love and accept its women who have persisted in fi-delity throughout the centuries of explicit and implicit subordination. Theological reflection reaches its limit at this point, and waits upon experience and orthopraxis within the church as the matrix from which a renewed, revitalized marian tradition can grow. Ultimately, what is at stake in this question is not only the redirection of the tradi-tion about Mary, but the search for our common humanity: the essence of woman, of man, and of redeemed humanity, the church it-self.

NOTES

1.   *Lumen Gentium*, ch. 8, in *The Documents of Vatican II*, Walter Abbott, ed. (New York: America Press, 1966). See commentaries by Otto Semmelroth, *Commentary on the Documents of Vatican II*, H. Vorgrimier, eds. (New York: Herder and Herder, 1967),1: pp. 285-96; and René Laurentin, *Pastoral Reform in Church Government*, Concilium 8 (New York: Paulist, 1965), pp. 155-72.

2.   See the papers of the World Council of Churches' Conference in Sheffield, England, 1981, entitled *The Community of Women and Men in the Church*, Constance Parvey, ed. (Philadelphia: Fortress, 1983).

3.   Juniper Carol, *Fundamentals of Mariology* (New York: Benziger, 1956), p. 1.

4.   Rosemary Radford Ruether, "Christology and Feminism: Can a Male Savior Help Women?," *Occasional Papers* (United Methodist Board of Higher Education and Ministry) 1/13 (1976), pp. 5-6.

5.   Rosemary Radford Ruether, *Sexism and God-talk: Toward a Feminist Theology* (Boston: Beacon, 1983), p. 19. This work's first chapter treats of methodology, sources, and norms (pp. 12-46). For other descriptions of the tasks and goals of feminist theology, see Elisabeth Schüssler Fiorenza, "Feminist Theology as a Critical Theory of Liberation," *Theological Studies* 36

(1975), pp. 605-26; and Anne Carr, "Is a Christian Feminist Theology Possible?," *Theological Studies* 43 (1982), pp. 279-97. A fine description of what is meant by "women's experience" is given by Judith Plaskow, *Sex, Sin, and Grace: Women's Experience and the Theologies of Reinhold Niebuhr and Paul Tillich* (Washington, DC: University Press of America, 1980), pp. 9-50.

6. For example of distortion in theory, see Kari Elisabeth Børresen, *Subordination and Equivalence: The Nature and Role of Woman in Augustine and Thomas Aquinas* (Washington, DC: University Press of America, 1981); for analysis of practice, see Mary Daly, *The Church and the Second Sex* (New York: Harper & Row, 1975).

7. Jozef Tomko, *L'Osservatore Romano* (English) 43 (October 26, 1981), p. 6.

8. Patricia Noone, *Mary for Today* (Chicago: Thomas More, 1977), p. 12.

9. Kari Børresen, "Mary in Catholic Theology," in *Mary in the Churches*, Concilium 168, H. Küng and J. Moltmann, eds. (New York: Seabury, 1983), pp. 54-55.

10. Daly, p. 61.

11. Fiorenza, pp. 620-24.

12. Mary Gordon, "Coming to Terms with Mary," *Commonweal* 109 (January 15, 1982), p. 11.

13. Marina Warner, *Alone of All Her Sex* (New York: Knopf, 1976), pp. 49, 338.

14. *Marialis Cultus*, E.T. *Devotion to the Blessed Virgin Mary*, *The Pope Speaks* 19 (1974-1975), #34-37, 73-75.

15. *Catholic Mind* 72 (1974), #142, 60.

16. Noone, p. 12.

17. *De cultu feminarum*, libri duo I, 1, (PL 1, 1418b-19a).

18. Warner, p. 58.

19. See Rosemary Radford Ruether, "Misogynism and Virginal Feminism in the Fathers of the Church," in Ruether, ed., *Religion and Sexism: Images of Women in the Jewish and Christian Traditions* (New York: Simon & Schuster, 1974), pp. 150-83.

20. *Summa Theologiae* I, q. 92; passim; q. 96, art. 3, corp.; q. 99, art. 2; *ST* III, q. 27, passim; q. 30, passim; q. 37, art. 4, corp.; *ST* Suppl., q. 52, passim; q. 81, passim. See William Cole, "Thomas on Mary and Women: A Study in Contrasts," *University of Dayton Review* 12 (1975-76), pp. 25-64.

21. Jean Galot, *L'église et la femme* (Gemblour: J. Duculot, 1965), p. 57.

22. Giles Dimock, "Mary, Model for the Church Today," *Aids in Ministry* (1982), p. 8.

23. Simone de Beauvoir,*The Second Sex* (New York: Knopf, 1953), p. 171.

24. Cahal Daly, "Mary and the Vocation of Women: I," *The Furrow* 25 (1974), p. 648.

25. René Laurentin, "Mary and Womanhood in the Renewal of Christian Anthropology," *Marian Library Studies* 1 (1969), p. 78. While positing equality of nature between men and women, Laurentin nevertheless argues for a "functional hierarchy" between them (p. 89).

26. Karl Rahner, "Mary and the Apostolate" in his *The Christian Commitment* (New York: Sheed and Ward, 1963 [1954]), p. 123.

27. Karl Rahner, "Maria und das christliche Bild der Frau," *Stimmen der Zeit* 193 (1975), pp. 795-800.

28. Cahal Daly, "Mary and the Vocation of Women: II," *The Furrow*.

29. See Hilda Graef, *Mary: A History of Doctrine and Devotion* (New York: Sheed and Ward, 1963), 1: esp. chaps 4-6.

30. Bernadetter Gasslein, "Images de Marie, image de la femme," *Supplement* 127 (1978), pp. 583-92.

31. René Laurentin, *The Question of Mary* (New York: Holt, Rinehart and Winston, 1965), pp. 72ff.

32. See Catharina Halkes, "Mary and Women" in Küng and Moltmann, eds., *Mary in the Churches*, pp. 66-67.

33. See e.g., Ross MacKenzie, "Mariology as an Ecumenical Problem," *Marian Studies* 26 (1975), pp. 204-20; and Lukas Visher, "Mary—Symbol of the Church and Symbol of Humankind," *Mid-Stream* 17 (1978), pp. 1-12.

34. See Ruether, *Sexism and God-Talk*, pp. 47-71; Joan Chamberlain Engelsman, *The Feminine Dimension of the Divine* (Philadelphia: Westminster, 1979); Elaine Pagels, "What Became of God the Mother?" in Carol Christ and Judith Plaskow, eds., *Womanspirit Rising* (San Francisco: Harper & Row, 1979), pp. 107-19; Geoffrey Ashe, *The Virgin* (London: Routledge and Kegan Paul, 1976).

35. See Raymond Brown *et al.*, eds., *Mary in the New Testament: A Collaborative Assessment by Protestant and Roman Catholic Scholars* (Philadelphia: Fortress, and New York: Paulist, 1978).

36. Noone, p. 167. Noone's whole book does an effective job of resymbolization along the lines of this first proposal. See also Glenys Huws and Clare Guzzo Robert, "A New Image of Mary: Protestant, Catholic and Feminist Perspectives," *America* 141 (1979), pp. 403-06.

37. Rosemary Radford Ruether, *Mary—The Feminine Face of the Church* (Philadelphia: Westminster, 1977), pp. 76-88.

38. Paul VI, *Marialis Cultus* #35, p. 74.

39. See Raymond Brown, "The Meaning of Modern New Testament Studies for Ecumenical Understanding of Mary" in his *Biblical Reflections on Crises Facing the Church* (New York: Paulist, 1975), pp. 84-108; Patrick Bearsley, "Mary the Perfect Disciple: A Paradigm for Mariology," *Theological Studies* 41 (1980), pp. 461-504.

40. See Elisabeth Moltmann-Wendel, "Motherhood or Friendship" in Küng and Moltmann, eds., *Mary in the Churches*, pp. 17-22; Ruether, *Sexism and God-Talk*, pp. 8-11; Schüssler Fiorenza, pp. 624-26. See also Elisabeth Schüssler Fiorenza's study of the discipleship of other women (not including Mary of Nazareth), *In Memory of Her: A Feminist Theological Reconstruction of Christian Origins* (New York: Crossroad, 1983).

41. This is still a partial ideal for it omits reference to adult relationships which are constitutive for wholeness. For discussion, see Beatrice Bruteau, "The Image of the Virgin Mother" in J. Plaskow and J. Romero, eds., *Women and Religion* (Missoula, MT: Scholars Press, 1974), pp. 93-104.

42. Paul Tillich, *Theology of Culture* (New York: Oxford University Press, 1964), pp. 54-58.

43. Karl Rahner, "Maria und das christiliche Bild der Frau," p. 800.

5

"Then Honor God in Your Body" (1 Cor. 6:20): Feminist and Sacramental Theology on the Body

Susan A. Ross*

ABSTRACT

Feminist theology and the Roman Catholic sacramental tradition share a common concern for the integrity of the body and the goodness of the natural world. Yet traditional sacramental theology has used its understanding of body and nature to define women as ontologically distinct from and inferior to men. This chapter argues that recent feminist theological writing on the body offers a corrective to the ahistorical and dualistic understanding of the body prevalent in Roman Catholic theology. By including women's interpretation of their own bodily experience, situating this experience in a social and historical context, and celebrating the variety of human embodiment, feminist theology offers a truly "sacramental" understanding of the body as it also criticizes the sexist assumptions of the tradition.

Over the last two decades, the feminist critique of biblical, historical, systematic, and moral theology has developed as a critique of the fun-

---

*Susan A. Ross (Ph.D., University of Chicago Divinity School) is Associate Professor of Theology and Director of Women's Studies at Loyola University of Chicago (Chicago, IL 60626). Her articles have appeared in *Worship*, *Religious Studies Review*, and the *Journal of Religion*, and she has contributed the chapter on Church and Sacraments to *The Praxis of Christian Experience: An Introduction to the Thought of Edward Schillebeeckx*, ed. M. C. Hilkert and R. J. Schreiter (San Francisco: Harper & Row, 1988).

damental assumptions of these disciplines. Basic presuppositions
about historical method, human nature, the divine (to name only a
few issues) have been seriously challenged, as feminist critics have
questioned aims both to expose and "deconstruct" the implicit androcentric bias in western thought and practice and to suggest alternatives inclusive of the experience of women.[1]

This paper attempts to describe a feminist critique of Roman
Catholic sacramental theology: specifically, its fundamental principle
of the intrinsic sacrality of the body and of nature. I have chosen this
"sacramental principle" as a focus because of the concern for the body
shared by both sacramental theology and by many feminist theologians,[2] a concern that results in very different conclusions about the
meaning of human bodiliness, and ultimately, very different and
sometimes opposing conclusions about ethical standards derived
from a concern for the body.

Sacramental theology and feminist theology have hardly been
congenial conversation partners. The most "sacramental" traditions—
Roman Catholicism and Orthodoxy—are the most vehemently opposed to the ordination of women. Despite its professed concern with
enhancing participation on the part of the laity, in its "official" form
sacramental theology both perpetuates the ontological distinction between clergy and laity (which is also a distinction between the "male"
and "female" elements within the Church) and fails to address the
sense of exclusion experienced by women not only regarding priesthood but also in the language and symbols used in sacramental cele-
brations.[3] It would appear, then, that there is little possibility for dialogue.

While my aim in this essay is not a reconciliation of the two theological perspectives, nevertheless an examination of both on the body
can be instructive for at least two reasons. First, both argue for an
ethics based in embodiment. By exploring both understandings of the
body, we can better understand what is meant by the embodied
person and what kinds of consequences result from embodiment. In
other words, the anthropological presuppositions peculiar to both will
be clarified. Second, understanding the feminist critique of the sacramental understanding of the body may help clarify the basic principles involved in feminist thought. If the feminist critique is to be a
systematic one (as it claims to be), a clear understanding of its assumptions will enhance any evaluation of its worth. My argument is that
feminist theology poses a "sacramental critique" to the tradition of
sacramental theology in challenging the presuppositions of that tradition.

PRELIMINARY REMARKS

Before moving into the specifics of this essay, a few remarks on the context of the concern for the body are appropriate. The recent scholarship in patristic and medieval theology has demonstrated that the many stereotypical pictures of Christianity's hatred of the body overlook a highly complex set of attitudes about the body and ascetic practices concerning it.[4] Nevertheless, one of the more serious challenges leveled at Christian theology by feminist theologians and ethicists is that this tradition has misunderstood the body—especially the female body—as inferior to the soul and as a source of sin.[5] To counter this emphasis, feminist thought has both revealed the extent to which the Christian tradition has manifested a negative attitude toward the body (and consequently, toward women)[6] and developed new forms of theology, spirituality and liturgy which attempt constructively to celebrate the goodness of the body.[7]

A concern for the body and the integrity of the natural is found as well in Roman Catholic theology, especially in moral theology, as it deals with particular questions relating to the body (e.g., sexual morality, biomedical ethics). In dealing with these issues, Catholic moral theology appeals to a basic understanding of reality which in this tradition is characterized as sacramental: that is, the body (and nature) are intrinsically good and are symbolic and revelatory of the sacred.[8] Both feminist and sacramental theology seek to affirm the body against denials of its intrinsic sacrality. Yet their respective interpretations of the body, of the significance of sexual differences, and of bodily experiences are very different, and even in opposition to each other. The purpose, then, of this essay is to show how the implications of embodiment inform sacramental theology both critically and constructively.

I. SACRAMENTAL THEOLOGY AND THE BODY

I began by saying that both sacramental and feminist theology are concerned to affirm the importance of the body. Both perspectives express, in symbolic and ethical form, the conviction that the human body is good and that it can be the source of knowledge of self and society. Therefore, the "natural" processes of the human body (not to mention nature itself) are important not only for their instrumental roles in human activity, but have an intrinsic significance of their own. In what follows I will describe what I consider to be two distinct but related approaches to sacramental theology and the body, neither of which addresses embodiment adequately.

Roman Catholic theology has classically defined sacraments as signs of sacred things which participate in and make present the reality they represent: "they effect what they signify."[9] What things are and what they symbolize are, in the sacramental way of thinking, in part "given in nature." One looks to the "natural" function of something to begin to understand its religious meaning.

The Importance of the Body

The importance of the human body and the theological significance of male and female bodies have been central to the theology of the sacraments. In the older, more traditional sacramental theology represented by Aquinas and papal documents such as *Casti Connubii*, the distinction between male and female is an ontological and hierarchical one, rooted in an understanding of human nature as dual. Aquinas, for example, uses the concepts of perfection and imperfection for males and females, as the oft-quoted passage from Q. 92 of the *Summa Theologiae* puts it.[10] He bases his definition of women as "misbegotten males" on his (mistaken) analysis of empirical reality, in which the male sex is demonstrably superior, because it is visibly active.[11] Transcendence and immanence are also used to symbolize the male and the female. In this particular schema, the female is tied not to imperfection but to the body itself, and more precisely, to the body without the redeeming qualities of the soul. What is problematic for women is not their sheer bodiliness (which is obviously shared by men) but rather their *unbalanced* bodiliness. Both Augustine and Thomas Aquinas list the ways in which they perceive women to experience the relation of body to soul in a different way than men do.[12] This, for Aquinas and others, indicates women's lesser rationality and lesser spirituality and is again rooted in an "empirical" observation of the body.

More recent, phenomenologically influenced understandings, represented by such theologians as Hans Urs von Balthasar, Louis Bouyer, and Pope John Paul II, outline a sacramental theology of the body which is no longer *explicitly* hierarchical but which retains an ontological distinction between male and female rooted in nature. This theology is a retrieval of the metaphysics of activity and receptivity and therefore a contemporary development of the traditional approach. Based on a "phenomenological" analysis of the male and female bodies, this view states that the male represents the "source" in generation and the female the "potential." This symbolism is developed further by linking God to the active force and humanity to the receptive, and by the use of bridal imagery to explain the relationship of Christ to church.[13] John Paul II's recent encyclical, "Mulieris Dignitatem," uses the bride/bridegroom analogy extensively to explain the "nature" of women as receptive, as this quotation illustrates: "The bridegroom is the one who loves. The bride *is loved*: it is she who *receives* love, in order to love in return."[14]

These symbolic and sacramental differences are rooted in a concern for the body and its integrity. To ignore or gloss over these basic bodily differences, it is argued, would be to violate the order of creation and of natural law. The result would be chaos. These differences are also *fixed*, understood to be rooted in nature. What is crucial, for example, in the most recent theology of the sacrament of Orders, as it concerns the possible ordination of women, is the *difference* between male and female bodies, and the theological interpretation of this difference. This "complementary" understanding, it is argued, is rooted in an empirical observation of nature and the body.[15] To ignore or to erase these differences, it is further argued, would be to deny the fundamental distinctions implicit in human bodily existence. These differences, or distinctions, are not purportedly indicative of superiority or inferiority; rather, they concern what is "appropriate" for each sex. Therefore, the exclusion of women from the sacramental priesthood is not a moral question of injustice toward women, the argument goes, but rather a question of theological anthropology.[16]

The most recent generation of sacramental theologians, strongly influenced by Edward Schillebeeckx's and Karl Rahner's pioneering work on symbol and sacrament, expresses no such ontological distinction between male and female. Both Rahner and Schillebeeckx, in fact, publicly dissented from the position of the Vatican Declaration and found its argument flawed.[17] The importance of embodiment for sacramental theology is assumed and affirmed in both their pre- and post-Vatican II writing on the sacraments,[18] yet the implications of this principle for theological anthropology remain undeveloped. Neither addresses the implicit contradiction between reverence for the body and the unsuitability of women for Orders on the grounds of embodiment; the issue is discussed in terms of theological methodology and justice. Indeed the problematic relationship of spirit and matter remains ambiguously defined in recent sacramental thought, as I shall show below.

Ambivalence Toward the Body

This positive concern for the body must be set alongside the tradition's ambivalence toward the body. Augustine, one of the major architects of the sacramental understanding of reality, gave expression to his own experience of the body: source of pleasure, but more realistically, source of sin. By focusing on concupiscence as the prime expression of sinful human nature, and by locating concupiscence's chief manifestation in bodily desire, Augustine shared the concerns of his time with both an awe and a suspicion of the body:

> It is not the body as such, but the corruptible body, that is a burden to the soul. Hence the Scriptural statement, . . . "The corruptible body weighs down the soul." The addition of "corruptible" shows that the writer meant that the soul was weighed down, not by any kind of body, but by the body as it became as a result of sin and the punishment that followed.[19]

Augustine's distinction between the "body as such" and the "corruptible body" is an important one; it is because of sin that the body is not completely good (as it was created to be). And because for us there is no "body as such" but only the "corruptible body," the body itself must be treated with caution, if not suspicion.

Augustine's view is characteristic of much of the western tradition's attitude toward the body. Often characterized (or caricatured) as a tradition marked chiefly by its hatred for the body in arguing for the superiority of celibacy over marriage, in its ascetical practices Christianity has, as Margaret Miles has stated, sought to "connect the body, with its inflexible life cycle and intimate affiliation with mortality, to *life*—animation, momentum, and orientation—which by definition is a property of the soul."[20] Thus the ambivalence toward the body, as Miles would argue, is not necessarily a polarization or a dualism of body and soul, but rather an attempt to balance the concerns of both the physical and the spiritual.

Nevertheless, it would be impossible to characterize Christianity's (and, in particular, sacramental Christianity's) attitude toward the body as totally positive. James Nelson, whose understanding of Christianity's attitude toward the body is not as optimistic as Miles's, has detailed much of the tradition's inability to deal with bodily ambiguity in his book *Embodiment: An Approach to Sexuality and Christian Theology.*[21] Nelson argues that Christianity suffers from a "bodily alienation" which has resulted in psychiatric problems, social problems, male sexism, and, most profoundly, alienation from God. Although "there are positive sources of insight in regard to our sexual salvation," Nelson says that Christianity needs to "face honestly those elements of our common tradition which have contributed to the sexual [i.e., bodily] alienation we presently experience."[22]

In a recent, and very influential, work on sacramental theology, David Power expresses ambivalence toward the body's role in the sacraments. In discussing the "immense difference between the historical religion and rites of Judaism and Christianity" and "cosmic religion," Power writes:

> The place of bodily ritual—with its evocation of deep human experience, its relations to cosmos and body and the unconscious— ... can be understood only in the turn to the word ... what is expressed is God's "nonidentity" with what is symbolized in the cosmic and in the bodily manifestations of the sacred.[23]

Later on in the same chapter, Power emphasizes that "[t]he bodily element is essential to Christian worship," but that "bodily actions and cosmic images . . . refer to fellowship in Jesus Christ rather than to a participation in a mythical reality or in cosmic rhythms."[24] While I do not want to deny that bodily actions are symbolic of the Incarnation, the polarization of "cosmic rhythms" with God's actions in history reveals an unfortunate (and, feminists would argue, incorrect) understanding of the relationship of Christianity toward "nature religions." Inherent in this distinction is a separation of nature and history, which places Christianity "above" nature, and consequently, above the body as well. In affirming the importance of the body—essential for sacramental theology—but in qualifying and distinguishing its role in ritual, Power suggests a dualism of body and spirit, nature and history, that is the foundation for the sacramental tradition's dualistic theological anthropology.

The Body as Sacramental Symbol

All sacramental theologies are concerned to affirm the goodness of the body and its symbolic importance. In the more conservative theologies, the body is understood as *sacramental symbol*. One literally sees God's design for human nature in the body itself. In arguing that differences are significant and are reflective of the divine will in the natural order, these sacramental theologies have designated distinct symbolic valuations for male and female bodies. While difference is apparently celebrated—this is the claim of thinkers like Bouyer, von Balthasar and John Paul II—what results instead is a hierarchy of value in which the female "completes" the male and represents the "purely" human (as in the case of the human bride and the divine spouse) without the transcendent qualities characteristic of the male. The ambivalence and ambiguity of bodily experience ultimately result in an ontological dualism, which separates reality into differing (and opposing) spheres which are mutually exclusive.

Yet even the more recent sacramental theologies which explicitly support the equality of women do not develop a theology of the body which is tied to theological anthropology. While the concrete and embodied nature of human religious experience is consistently underscored, the arguments for human equality do not challenge the "natural law" approach characteristic of the more conservative elements of the tradition. While both conservative and more progressive sacramental theologians see embodiment as fundamental to sacramental theology, it is the more conservative theologians who explicitly use a theology of the body to ground their sacramental theology. The more progressive theologians have failed to develop an alternative understanding of the body which is neither "complementary" nor "above" the rhythms of nature. My point here is that unless one addresses the problematic nature of the body for sacramental theology— its dualistic interpretations and ambiguous meaning—the challenges to sexism in Roman Catholic theology will miss the mark.

In the "complementary" understanding of the body, male and female bodily difference is based in a theology of the sacraments as symbols: physical reality represents transcendent reality. But there are at least two flaws in the way that the theory of symbol is used here. First, this theology posits an identity between symbol and symbolized which is at odds with the delicate tension involved in symbolic representation. Second, this theology adopts symbolic meanings uncritically without awareness of their historical roots.

Symbolic representation is both simple and complex. One reality stands for something else: a cross symbolizes the suffering Christ, a swastika symbolizes hatred of Jews. Both of these symbols are powerful because of the complexity, or "multivalency," as Paul Ricoeur terms it, of the associations they evoke in people.[25] If symbols evoked only one meaning, they would be signs—simple substitutions of one reality for another. As symbols, sacraments evoke both the presence and the absence of the divine through analogy. Bread and wine, for example, are appropriate symbols for food, the stuff of life, and by extension, for Christ. Other edible things could serve as symbols, but perhaps none more than bread and wine (at least in the western world) would be more appropriate. Symbols work because of both likeness and unlikeness. When the unlikeness is too great, when the symbol no longer evokes important associations, it is no longer effective and fails to make present the sacred reality it represents.[26] But when there is no tension at all, when the symbol and the reality it represents become identified, there is, to quote Paul Tillich, "idolatry":[27] the infinite is collapsed into the finite.

In part of its rootedness in an empirical understanding of reality and the natural law tradition, conservative sacramental theology has located itself historically on the side of identification. The tension of the divine presence in the human is, in the theology of Orders, reduced to an identification of maleness with divinity and humanity. A recent study of the sexuality of Jesus, intriguing not only for its subject matter but also for its implications, argues that the focus of Renaissance painters on the genitals of Jesus was a corrective to a tendency to spiritualize Christ. By focusing on the sexuality of the newborn Christ and the suffering Christ on the cross, Renaissance artists were both reminding their viewers that, in the infant Jesus, "the humanization of God entails, along with mortality, his assumption of sexuality," and also, that the Christ on the cross returns to sexuality "the aboriginal innocence which in Adam was lost."[28] By employing the sexual images seemingly so far removed from the divine, the *tension* and *ambiguity* of the incarnation were expressed. Yet this tension between human sexuality and divine power has been reduced to an *identification* between maleness and humanity in traditional Roman Catholic sacramental theology, especially in the theology of Orders. Maleness, rather than human vulnerability and sinfulness (symbolically expressed in the focus on the sexuality in Christ), becomes determinative.

This tradition has also tended to ignore the historical and cultural roots of symbols.[29] All symbols develop in historical, agricultural, familial, or linguistic contexts. To use the example mentioned above, bread and wine are sacred symbols in Christianity for many reasons, one of them being that most people ate bread and drank wine regularly. For a culture, however, which regularly partakes of corn and milk, bread and wine may not be appropriate symbols for the stuff of life. And while it has been argued that women have universally symbolized "nature,"[30] the point of this argument is that this meaning is one that is "constructed," not "fixed,"[31] and hence has historical origins. Obviously, a meaning which is constructed is also subject to change. Whether or not there are "natural" symbols remains a lively debate in anthropological circles;[32] my point here is that the historical—and therefore culturally limited—context of human symbols cannot be ignored, and certainly cannot be absolutized.

More recent sacramental theologies have, in large part, overcome this second flaw. The historical and anthropological contexts of human ritual activity have been incorporated into the theology of the sacraments, as recent developments bear rich witness.[33] But the many possibilities for symbolic representation of the body remain insufficiently developed. This is due both to the dominance of the conservative tradition in practice and the undeveloped role of the body in theological anthropology. While both Rahner and Schillebeeckx, for

example, speak frequently of the "concrete" arid "embodied" nature
of the person, and indeed develop this point in significant ways,[34] neither offers an alternative to the traditional application of embodiment
to sex difference. And while one might excuse Rahner and Schillebeeckx for not attending to this issue, since the impact of feminist theology came so late in both their careers, the next generation of sacramental theologians does not develop the implications of embodiment
in ways that challenge the traditional dualism. Recent writings by
such scholars as Michael Lawler and Kenan Osborne provide valuable
historical and cultural analyses of sacramental theology.[35] Yet neither
author considers embodiment in depth. For recent sacramental theology, embodiment is valued in principle, but is undeveloped in its theological and practical dimensions. It is in feminist theology that we
find a real alternative.

II. FEMINIST THEOLOGY AND THE BODY

Feminists have argued that the incarnational, sacramental tradition in
Christian theology has meant an emphasis on the importance of male
bodies, and that one can read Christian history as one of "sacramental
sex discrimination."[36] The denigration of the female body has been evident in ritual proscriptions against female contact with the holy, in
the classification of women as ontologically different from (and consequently, inferior to) men, and in a negatively obsessive concern with
sexual matters in a tradition where women symbolize the sexual to
celibate men. Until the mainstream of Christianity is willing to celebrate the sacrality of female as well as male bodies, feminist theologians argue, the Christian tradition's incarnational foundation will be
essentially hollow.

The Importance of the Body

In contrast to this sexual dualism, feminist theologians argue for a
new (and for some, recalling pre-Jewish and Christian traditions, a renewed) emphasis on the holiness of the body. This is developed in a
number of ways. In theological anthropology, this emphasis is shown
in an equal valuation of men and women, and of male and female
bodies. Here, the female is no longer a symbol for the sinful and the
sexual, nor is she only a symbol of the receptive and the maternal, but
manifests the fullness of humanity, not only as body but as embodied
spirit.[37] Bodily differences are not ignored but do not determine social
or spiritual roles. The exhibition of a sculpture of a crucified woman in

New York's Cathedral of St. John the Divine in the spring of 1984 was a compelling example of feminist theology's affirmation of the body and of sexual difference. In commenting on this sculpture, feminist biblical theologian Phyllis Trible said that ". . . a female crucifixion figure should be seen as an allusion to 'Christ's mystical body that transcends sex' while 'not denying the male Jesus of history.'"[38]

Liturgically, the celebration of the body in dance, gesture, and in the presence of women in ritual roles furthers this concern for the body. Rosemary Ruether, in her recent book *Women-Church: Theology and Practice of Feminist Liturgical Communities*[39] includes a number of rituals incorporating female bodily experience, such as menstruation, childbirth, miscarriage, and menopause.[40] In much of her work, Ruether stresses the enormous evil of the "original sin" of sexist dualism, which manifests itself chiefly in an understanding of females as body and males as spirit.[41] In ethics, an emphasis on ecological issues, linking feminism with a concern for the earth and a criticism of consequentialism show how a renewed concern for the body, and specifically female bodies, can change the tenor and direction of ethical reasoning.[42]

Ambivalence Toward the Body

With all this concern for the bodily, however, there remains here as well an undercurrent of ambivalence. While feminist theologians are critical of any theology which *identifies* women with the body (and consequently, not with the soul or spirit), the reaction to this identification has sometimes been to minimize the body's importance, and in so doing, to assume the dominant western dualistic attitude toward the body. From the earliest "protofeminists" of the convents and monasteries of early Christianity to the nineteenth-century abolitionist/feminist movement, a desire to be "freed from" the constraints of the female body (specifically with regard to its childbearing role) has been a frequent theme in feminist focuses on the nonbodily dimensions of feminine personality. The desire for knowledge and learning, the pursuit of independent and intellectual lives, have been characteristic of women who have rejected their identification with the body but have not always sorted out a positive meaning for the body apart from its traditionally male-defined roles.[43]

Feminist theorists have distinguished three distinct types of feminism—liberal, radical, and Marxist/socialist[44]—and it is liberal feminism which has both been the most influential of the feminist movements in the United States and which has most frequently manifested an ambivalence toward the body. Liberal feminism tends to assume the dualistic tradition of western rationality, where "the characteristic human activity is the exercise of one's reason."[45] While not hostile toward the body, this position sees sexuality as incidental to human nature, and therefore dismisses any attempt to develop a normative theory of sexuality.[46] The concern of the liberal feminist is to achieve equality, as defined according to a western, Enlightenment model, and any differentiation in the valuation of the body threatens equality. Conceptions of "difference" are viewed with suspicion by the liberal feminist, because differences are rarely, if ever, accorded equal treatment.[47]

Similarly, many feminist theologians explicitly reject theories of "complementarity" because of the ways in which so-called complementary differences are valued. Mary Jo Weaver, for example, writes:

> Underlying my interpretation [of American Catholic women] is a reaction against complementarity. I interpret "complementarity" as "completing" or "mirroring," which suggests a nature not complete in its own right. It would follow, therefore, that complementarity and inferiority are at least subliminally linked. If women are not inferior to men, then why does complementarity function to treat them as if they are?[48]

In relation to male and female bodily differences, Rosemary Ruether writes in *Sexism and God-Talk* that "maleness and femaleness exist as reproductive role specialization. There is no necessary (biological) connection between reproductive complementarity in either psychological or social role differentiation. These are the works of culture and socialization, not of 'nature.'"[49]

A second reason for ambivalence toward the body by feminists is in reaction to the ways in which women have historically been denied reproductive control over their bodies. Women have been identified with the body, which is seen as the object to be mastered or controlled by the higher part of the person—the soul, which is identified with men. Therefore, most feminist theologians argue that unless and until women have full reproductive control over their bodies, women will continue to be identified with the lower, carnal (and sinful) dimensions of humanity. Control of women's bodies is control of both women and the body itself. This control becomes not so much a matter of indifference to the body, as liberal feminism might suggest, but rather one of rejecting the predominantly negative bodily symbolism in the western Christian tradition. While some feminists have moved from this point to argue for a moral right to abortion, for example,[50] their point is that the female body has been objectified and alienated from those who inhabit it. Therefore, control of the body is paramount, as Rosemary Ruether writes:

Any theory of women's liberation that stops short of liberating women from male control of their bodies has not reached the root of patriarchy.[51]

The Body as Self

Feminist theology cannot but affirm the importance of the body. In recognizing the consequence of body/soul and female/male dualism, feminist theologians are concerned to return to the body—especially the female body—the essential goodness it naturally possesses. The ambiguity of the body is no less recognized by feminists, but many American feminists, at least, are reluctant to attribute a fixed meaning to bodily difference. Instead, bodily differences and ambivalent attitudes toward the body are held loosely together in an understanding of the body as *self.*

This understanding of the body communicates an intrinsic, indivisible union between body and self, over and against a distanciated or alienated understanding. Beverly Wildung Harrison clearly expresses this understanding:

> We do not merely have bodies. The body-self is the integrated locus of our being in the world. We are related to everything through our body-selves: our bodies ground our connection to the world. Our bodies are the vehicles of relation that put us in touch with reality at every level.[52]

Another feminist scholar of religion, Naomi Goldenberg, argues for a bodily basis for understanding the human person. The essential flaw of Jungian psychology, she argues, lies in its separation of mind and body: indeed Jung's archetypal theory is based on this separation.[53] It is in the work of Freud and post-Freudian analytical theory that a sounder basis for understanding the self is found:

> Psychoanalysis has produced an extensive body of theory based on the idea that human beings are essentially physical creatures whose mental and emotional experience is derived wholly from bodily life.[54]

Not only does this understanding of human nature overcome the alienation of body from soul, it is also grounded in "what is known, what is observable, and what is bodily."[55] Goldenberg uses this point to argue that western thought, in relying on theories of mind-body separation, has perpetuated "the disparagement of sexuality in Western philosophical and religious thought."[56] And, she concludes, "In order to stop disparaging the body, we might well have to give up all forms of theism and take our inspiration from ideas which see human beings as nothing more (or less) than human."[57] Goldenberg's implication here is that theistic understandings of the person necessarily involve a dualistic conception of the self. Feminist theory, in condemning dualism because of its disastrous consequences for women, is suspicious of theism, especially in its western forms. Therefore a turn to the goddess movement (as Goldenberg herself has done) and earth-centered religious traditions is for some the only real alternative.

While not going so far as to suggest that we "give up all forms of theism," Rosemary Ruether shows a similar concern for the bodily basis of human selfhood. The alienated dualism of body and soul has been a recurring theme in Ruether's writings. In *New Woman/New Earth* (1975), Ruether writes:

> The psychic organization of consciousness, the dualistic view of self and the world, the hierarchical concept of society, the relation of humanity and nature, and of God and creation—all these relations have been modeled on sexual dualism.[58]

This concern is reiterated forcefully, and with new insights, in her chapter "Eschatology and Feminism" in *Sexism and God-Talk*. Ruether's point in this chapter is to criticize the ways in which the self has been identified with the spiritual and the effects that this has had on religion and society. The root of this understanding of the self, she argues, is the desire for personal immortality, which she identifies as a predominantly male concern. The "spiritualization" of the self is further manifested in male attitudes toward females: "Femaleness is both symbol and expression of the corruptible bodiliness that one must flee in order to purify the soul for eternal life."[59] The solution to this alienated understanding of the body is to recognize and accept the body as self. Thus Ruether argues for an "agnosticism" about personal immortality,[60] rather than a "flight into the unrealizable future.[61] If, indeed, the body is the self,

> What then has happened to "me"? In effect, our existence ceases as individuated ego-organism and dissolves back into the cosmic matrix of matter/energy, from which new centers of individuation arise.[62]

In this understanding, the search for personal immortality is the attempt to perpetuate the individualism so devastating to both human society and the natural world. Personhood, Ruether writes, lies not in individual ego-centers, but rather in the fundamentally personal basis of reality itself:

> That great matrix that supports the energy-matter of our individuated beings is itself the ground of all personhood as well.[63]

In modeling the body as self, feminist theology primarily seeks to overcome the alienating dualisms of spirit over matter, mind over body, male over female. While distinctions between these two dimensions may be a part of human experience, their dualistic interpretations raise the ancient spectres of Gnosticism, Manichaeanism, witch-hunts, and confirm the persistent sexism that has plagued Christianity. Recent emphasis on ecology employs a similar argument against the alienation of the "natural" from the "human."[64]

What is unspoken in this understanding of the body is its very ambiguity: that is, its toleration of different, and even possibly conflicting meanings. For feminist theologians like Ruether, Goldenberg, and Harrison, "self" means not the mind as distinct from the body but a holding together of the diverse and ambiguous elements of selfhood: the spiritual *as well as* the physical, the positive *as well as* the negative. Feminist theology thus tolerates bodily differences and bodily ambiguity without sacrificing distinctions. Difference is not to be overcome or placed in a hierarchy but valued as distinctive and contributing to the richness and variety of human experience. Ambiguity is not to be dismissed or resolved dualistically, but explored as a way of amplifying and correcting the ways in which human experience is interpreted.

III. DICHOTOMY AND NATURE/ DIFFERENTIATION AND HISTORY

A review of both sacramental and feminist literature on the body reveals a few common areas, but many more differences. First, the common areas. Both perspectives see the body as essentially, or naturally, good. More than being neutral, the body's physicality is an important source of knowledge. For the sacramental traditions, this is knowledge of God's will for human life; for the feminist, this is knowledge of self, and also, in an extended way, knowledge of the natural world.[65] Both also center their ethical principles in the body. The sacramental tradition draws its normative principles from natural bodily processes, leaving it vulnerable to charges of "physicalism." Feminists, while not drawing so directly on the body, nevertheless rely on accounts of women's interpreted bodily experience to ground ethical considerations, leaving them vulnerable to charges of "relativism."

The differences emerge as crucial, however. I will focus on what I consider to be the two most obvious areas of difference: how sexual difference is accounted for, and the roles of history and nature. As shown above, traditional sacramental theology looks upon sexual difference (as contrasted with racial or ethnic difference) as the decisive category in theological anthropology. Sexual difference is absolutely crucial and, given the sacramentality of all reality, is not just biological but metaphysical as well. In *Mulieris Dignitatem*, for example, John Paul II refers to the "naturally spousal predisposition of the feminine personality" and cautions against the " 'masculinization' of women" which involved appropriating "characteristics contrary to their own feminine 'originality.'"[66] While oriented to a single goal, the partners in marriage have essentially different roles, and these roles have metaphysical significance. Dichotomy, rather than complementarity, seems to be the more adequate descriptive term for this theology of sexual difference, since this understanding is centered on a strict separation of roles. Another example, more explicit in its justification of difference, is found in one theologian's speech to the 1987 Synod on the Laity:

> Difficult as it is to describe this complementarity in adequate language, it may be seen from the vantage point of the marital act, or the reproductive act, as characterized by equal dignity and equally active participation but diversity of role.[67]

Note that the entire focus here is on the (relatively brief) moment of intercourse, and not on the larger (personal rather than physiological) context of reproduction: nurturing, educating, socializing, which are not sex-specific roles. The term dichotomy is also descriptive of the way in which the social and religious roles of women and men are understood: whatever social changes may occur, they have no effect on religious roles.

While some radical feminists such as Mary Daly have developed a dichotomous understanding of male and female human nature,[68] most feminist theorists reject dichotomy as an adequate descriptive term for sexual differences. Not surprisingly, many also rejected heterosexuality as the only moral sexual choice. And, as noted above, while sexual difference is not ignored by most feminists, rigid sex-role distinctions are, for the most part, rejected by feminists as ultimately oppressive to women, since, historically, women have had little or no voice in determining social roles. Feminist characterizations of sexual difference can best be classified under the term "differentiation": that is, a recognition of difference without dichotomization. "Differentiation" allows for sexual difference without prior stereotyping, for example, in discussions and parenting, representations of the divine, and attempts to account for the many differences (not only sexual) among men and women, women and women, and men and men. Here, the more progressive sacramental theologies could be characterized as positing a "differentiated" understanding of the person, but, as I have argued above, the importance of the body remains undeveloped.

The other area of difference—closely related to the meaning of sexual difference—is that of the roles of nature and history. The sacramental tradition, as I have described it here, is largely unconcerned with or has not sufficiently attended to the role of history in understanding the body. The body's meaning is rooted in nature, not in history: that is, the religious and metaphysical meaning of the body—male and female—is essentially the same in all periods of history, although social meanings may shift. The female body is equated with "receptivity" (in relation to activity, that of God or of males) and "creation" (in relation to the divine creator).

Feminist theorists reject this understanding of nature as itself a historical construction, and reverse the valuation by giving history a privileged position. In pointing out the constructed nature of human knowledge, feminists argue that not only is this "natural" understanding of the female body inadequate to the experience of women, but that it also serves a historical and political purpose in keeping women subordinate.

IV. CONCLUSION

As I have sketched it here, the possibility of a sacramental theology informed by feminism has remained one largely untried. Despite essential agreement on the goodness of the body and a concern to ground ethics in embodiment, the dichotomous and differentiated understandings of the body seem to be fundamentally at odds with each other. Separation grounded in nature and differentiation grounded in history suggest very different theological, liturgical, and ethical conclusions.

Yet the possibility of a feminist theology informed by a sense of sacramentality has received some recent attention. If one understands sacramentality as an awareness and appreciation of the "spiritual" dimension of the "physical," a "feminist sacramental theology" reveals some fundamental and recurring themes found in writings by feminists on a number of diverse issues. Consider the comments of June O'Connor on "sacramentality":

> Sacramentality implies that the invisible spiritual dimension of life is expressed and discovered in the sensuous dimension of life. Conversely, to go toward spirit is to move through matter, through the sensible, visible aspect of life. The sensual would not be sensual unless it were spirited with beauty, power, life, and meaning. To be attracted to the sensible is to discover its spirited, spiritual dimension.[69]

This feminist appropriation of sacramentality draws on some basic themes in sacramental theology—the potentially revelatory character of all reality, the concern for the integrity of the "natural world"—while emphasizing connection over separation:

> This pervasive presence of the oneness and interconnection of all things that characterizes contemporary feminist and process thought may provide the possibility for a new theology of sacramentality.[70]

A concern for "connection" and the use of such terms as "relation," "interconnection," "interdependence," and "context" is, as O'Connor notes above, characteristic of feminist thought.[71] And it is this understanding of the self—as interrelated, historically situated, and embodied—that constitutes feminist theological anthropology. This is the understanding of the self that is so desperately needed in contemporary theology, and a feminist sacramental theology can provide the resources for its development.

What I have described here as a feminist critique of the sacramental tradition's understanding of the body is not, as the common areas show, a wholesale rejection of any principle of sacramentality. It is, rather, an argument for what I have called a differentiated and historical understanding of the person which includes (or should one say "incorporates") a concern for the body, as well as a concern for the natural world.

While most of the feminist theologians I have considered here (with the notable exception of June O'Connor) would not describe themselves as holding a "sacramental" understanding of the person, nor would most of them consider the Catholic sacramental tradition a helpful resource in reconceiving the Christian tradition, nevertheless, my argument here has been to show that the feminist conception of the body has what I call an "implicit sacramentality" that also serves to critique the tradition itself. In this regard, the feminist concern for the body is the route for reconceiving, minimally, theological anthropology, liturgical and symbolic expression, and ethics. Like the biblical, historical, systematic, and ethical feminist critiques, what I have termed here the "sacramental critique" is an argument for rethinking the fundamental assumptions of the discipline, not merely including the feminine within already-described parameters.

It would take more time and space than is available here to develop fully the implications for theological anthropology and symbolic expression, to say nothing of ethics. But at the least, it should be clear that the feminist understanding of the body constitutes a serious critique of the sacramental tradition, offering a more adequately grounded understanding of the embodied person and suggesting a way of living with the variety and ambiguity of human physical existence.

NOTES

1. Chris Weedon, *Feminist Practice and Poststructuralist Theory* (Oxford: Basil Blackwell, 1987), pp. 1-11. This article has greatly benefited from the careful and critical readings of my colleagues in the Loyola University Theology Department; from the moral and financial support of Loyola University which granted me a paid leave of absence in 1987, during which time I completed this article; from my colleagues in the Institute for the Advanced Study of Religion at the Divinity School of the University of Chicago; and from the editorial readers of this article at *Horizons*. I am deeply grateful for the help of all.

2. In "Feminist Theology and Bioethics" in Barbara Hilkert Andolsen, Christine E. Gudorf, and Mary D. Pellauer, eds., *Women's Consciousness, Women's Conscience: A Reader in Feminist Ethics* (San Francisco: Harper and Row, 1985), Margaret A. Farley describes "embodiment" as a central theme in feminist theology. See also Paula M. Cooey, Sharon A. Farmer, and Mary Ellen Ross, *Embodied Love: Sensuality and Relationship as Feminist Values* (San Francisco: Harper and Row, 1987). The centrality of "embodiment" for feminist thought in general is argued in this essay.

3. A recent example of this attitude is expressed in a speech given to the 1987 Synod on the Laity by Rev. Joseph Fessio, "Reasons Given Against Women Acolytes and Lectors," Origins 17/32 (January 21, 1988), p. 398. For the theological grounding for this position, see "Declaration on the Admission of Women to the Ministerial Priesthood" in Arlene Swidler and Leonard Swidler, eds., *Women Priest: A Catholic Commentary on the Vatican Declaration* (New York: Paulist, 1977); see also John Paul II, "*Mulieris Dignitatem*: On the Dignity and Vocation of Women," Origins 18/17 (October 6, 1988).

4. See Margaret R. Miles, *Fullness of Life: Historical Foundations for a New Asceticism* (Philadelphia: Westminster, 1981); *idem., Image as Insight: Visual Understanding in Western Christianity and Secular Culture* (Boston: Beacon, 1985); Carolyn Walker Bynum, *Holy Feast and Holy Fast: The Religious Significance of Food to Medieval Women* (Berkeley: University of California Press, 1987); Peter Brown, *The Body and Society: Men, Women, and Sexual Renunciation in Early Christianity* (New York: Columbia University Press, 1988).

5. See Rosemary Radford Ruether, *New Woman/New Earth: Sexist Ideologies and Human Liberation* (New York: Seabury, 1975), especially pp. 186-211; *idem., Sexism and God-Talk: Toward a Feminist Theology* (Boston: Beacon, 1983), especially pp. 179-92; Daniel C. Maguire, "The Feminization of God and Ethics," *Christianity and Crisis* 42 (March 15, 1982), pp. 59-67.

6. See, for example, the widely used text (in courses on Women and Religion), Elizabeth Clark and Herbert Richardson, eds., *Women and Religion: A Feminist Sourcebook of Christian Thought* (New York: Harper and Row, 1977), especially the selections from Jerome, Augustine, Aquinas, and the *Malleus Maleficarum*.

7. See Penelope Washbourn, *Becoming Woman: The Quest for Wholeness in Female Experience* (New York: Harper and Row, 1977).

8. For a concise summary of the sacramental in Roman Catholicism, see Richard P. McBrien, *Catholicism* (Minneapolis, MN: Winston, 1980), pp. 731ff. For more recent and extensive discussions on sacramental theology, see the very helpful articles by Kevin W. Irwin, "Recent Sacramental Theology: A Review Discussion," *The Thomist* 47 (October 1983), pp. 592-608, and "Recent Sacramental Theology," *The Thomist* 52 (January 1988), pp. 124-47. Edward Schillebeeckx's *Christ the Sacrament of the Encounter with God*, trans. N.D. Smith (New York: Sheed and Ward, 1967) remains an essential source for contemporary sacramental theology.

9. Thomas Aquinas, *Summa Theologiae*, III, Q. 62, a. 1.

10. Thomas Aquinas, *Summa Theologiae*, I, Q. 92, a. 1.

11. It should be noted here that the Aristotelian metaphysics employed by Aquinas sees activity as prior to and superior to passivity and receptivity; it is God who acts, and human beings who are acted upon. Those who act are ontologically superior to those who receive, as Thomas understands the sexual act. See *ST*, I, Q. 2, a. 3, for the classic "five ways" in which Aquinas demonstrates God's existence. The first way discusses God as "Pure Act." For a compelling refutation of the nature of women as "passive receptacles" in the process of conception, see Margaret Farley, "New Patterns of Relationship: Beginnings of a Moral Revolution," *Theological Studies* 36/4 (December 1975), pp. 627-46, esp. p. 637.

12. See Kari Borreson, *Subordination and Equivalence: The Nature and Role of Woman in Augustine and Thomas Aquinas* (Washington, DC: University Press of America, 1981); for Augustine, see pp. 23-30; for Aquinas, see pp. 174-78.

13. See von Balthasar, esp. pp. 309-22; see also Louis Bouyer, *Woman in the Church* (San Francisco: Ignatius Press, 1985), p. 33: "God, inasmuch as he reveals himself supremely as the unique Father, appears in certain regards as a masculine being, and not feminine."

14. John Paul II, *Mulieris Dignitatem*, par. 29. Emphasis added.

15. "Nevertheless, the Incarnation of the Word took place according to the male sex: this is indeed a question of fact, while not implying an alleged natural superiority of man over women, it cannot be disassociated from the economy of salvation: it is, indeed, in harmony with the entirety of God's plan as God himself has revealed it, and of which the mystery of the Covenant is the nucleus . . . the Covenant . . . took on, from the Old Testament prophets onwards, the privileged form of a nuptial mystery. . ." "Vatican Declaration," par. 28. For critical perspectives on the "complementary" view of human nature, see Mary Buckley, "The Rising of the Woman is the Rising of the Race," *Catholic Theological Society of America Proceedings* 34 (1979), pp. 48-63; Sara Butler, ed., *Research Report: Women in Church and Society* (Mahwah, NJ: Theological Society of America, 1978), esp. the section written by Anne Carr, "Arguments Based on the Nature of Women," pp. 32-40.

16. See "Vatican Declaration," par. 6: "For this reason one cannot see how it is possible to propose the admission of women to the priesthood in virtue of the equality of rights of the human person, an equality which holds good also for Christians."

17. For Rahner, see "Women and the Priesthood" in *Concern for the Church, Theological Investigations* 20, trans. Edward Quinn (New York: Crossroad, 1981), pp. 35-47; for Schillebeeckx, see *Ministry: Leadership in the Community of Jesus Christ*, trans. John Bowden (New York: Crossroad, 1981), pp. 96-98.

18. Schillebeeckx's theology has had a consistent focus on the concrete and sacramental character of God's revelation. See Susan A. Ross, "Church and Sacrament" in Mary Catherine Hilkert and Robert Schreiter, eds., *The Praxis of Christian Experience: An Introduction to the Thought of Edward Schillebeeckx* (San Francisco: Harper and Row, 1989). Rahner addresses this issue in a somewhat different way, but with no less an emphasis on the concrete and embodied form of human religious experience. While his *Foundations of Christian Faith: An Introduction to the Idea of Christianity* (New York: Seabury, 1978) remains the basic introduction to his thought, many of his earlier essays on such issues as "Personal and Sacramental Piety" and "The Resurrection of the Body" (in *Theological Investigations* 2 [Baltimore; Helicon Press, 1963]) remain important sources for his understanding of the body.

19. Augustine, *City of God*, 13, 6, quoted in Miles, *Fullness*, p. 73. See also Miles's full-length study, *Augustine on the Body* (Missoula, MT: Scholars Press, 1979).

20. *Ibid.*, p. 14.

21. James Nelson, *Embodiment: An Approach to Sexuality and Christian Theology* (Minneapolis, MN: Augsburg, 1978).

22. *Ibid.*, p. 57.

23. David Power, *Unsearchable Riches: The Symbolic Nature of Liturgy* (New York: Pueblo, 1984), p. 94.

24. *Ibid.*, pp. 96-97.

25. Paul Ricoeur, *The Rule of Metaphor: Multidisciplinary Studies in the Creation of Meaning in Language,* trans. Robert Czerny (Toronto: University of Toronto Press, 1979), esp. pp. 230ff.

26. Paul Tillich, *The Dynamics of Faith* (New York: Harper and Row, 1957), p. 50. Tillich describes a modern, critical perspective on Christian symbols as one which recognizes their "brokenness," yet still is open to the reality they attempt to represent. See also Paul Ricoeur, *The Symbolism of Evil,* trans. Emerson Buchanan (Boston: Beacon, 1969) for a discussion of "second naiveté," closely related to Tillich's idea.

27. Tillich, p. 52.

28. Leo Steinberg, *The Sexuality of Christ in Renaissance Art and in Modern Oblivion* (New York: Pantheon/October, 1983), p. 23. Carolyn Walker Bynum points out that it is genitality rather than sexuality that is key. See Bynum, p. 307, n. 3.

29. This failure has been addressed in many recent works on sacramental theology. The influence of cultural anthropology has been acknowledged; see George S. Worgul, Jr., *From Magic to Metaphor: A Validation of the Christian Sacraments* (New York: Paulist, 1980). The influence of Mircea Eliade in particular has been immeasurable.

30. Sherry B. Ortner, "Is Female to Male as Nature is to Culture?" in Michelle Rosaldo and Louis Lamphere, eds., *Woman, Culture, and Society* (Stanford: Stanford University Press, 1974).

31. Ortner, p. 87: "Ultimately, it must be stressed again that the whole scheme is a construct of culture rather than a fact of nature."

32. See, for example, Mary Douglas, *Natural Symbols* (New York: Vintage, 1970) and Dan Sperber, *Rethinking Symbolism,* trans. Alice L. Morton (Cambridge: Cambridge University Press, 1975).

33. The Rite of Christian Initiation of Adults is one outstanding example of how sacramental theology had adapted to a changed understanding of the person.

34. See Ross, n. 18 above.

35. Michael G. Lawler, *Symbol and Sacrament: A Contemporary Sacramental Theology* (New York: Paulist, 1987); Kenan B. Osborne, *Sacramental Theology: A General Introduction* (Mahwah: Paulist, 1988).

36. Anne E. Patrick, "Coming of Age: Women's Contribution to Contemporary Theology," *New Catholic World* 228/1364 (March-April 1985), pp. 61-69; the quotation is from p. 64.

37. See Ruether, Sexism, esp. chap. 3: "Woman, Body, and Nature: Sexism and the Theology of Creation," pp. 72-92, and chap. 4: "Anthropology: Humanity as Male and Female," pp. 93-115. See also Anne E. Carr, *Transforming Grace: Christian Tradition and Women's Experience* (San Francisco: Harper and Row, 1988), esp. chap. 6, "Theological Anthropology and the Experience of Women," for a helpful survey of feminist anthropologies and a discussion of interpreting women's experience.

38. *The New York Times,* April 28, 1984.

39. Rosemary Ruether, *Women-Church: Theology and Practice of Feminist Liturgical Communities* (San Francisco: Harper and Row, 1985).

40. See Ruether, *Women-Church*, Part II.

41. See Ruether, *New Woman*, chaps. 4 and 5, where she attributes racism and antisemitism to psychic dualism.

42. See Ruether, *New Woman*; Maguire, "Feminization"; see also Carol Gilligan, *In a Different Voice: Psychological Theory and Women's Development* (Cambridge: Harvard University Press, 1982); Andolsen et al. (See n. 2 above).

43. See Elizabeth Castelli, "Virginity and Its Meaning for Women's Sexuality in Early Christianity," *Journal of Feminist Studies in Religion* 2/1 (Spring 1986), pp. 62-88; Bynum, *Holy Feast*, n. 4 above. Bynum's work is especially interesting for the ways in which she shows how women and men differed in their expressions of spirituality and how food was more central for women than for men.

44. See Alison Jaggar, *Feminist Politics and Human Nature* (Totowa, NJ: Rowman and Allenheid, 1983), for an explanation of the use of these categories.

45. Jaggar, p. 179. See also Elizabeth Spelman, "Woman as Body: Ancient and Contemporary Views," *Feminist Studies* 8/1 (Spring 1982), who develops this point at length.

46. Jaggar, p. 180.

47. Here I would note a major difference between the predominant stream of feminist thought in the United States, which tends to be "liberal" in its sympathies (and therefore uncomfortable with ideas of difference) and feminist thought in France, which places a much greater emphasis on "difference" between women and men. See Elaine Marks and Isabelle de Courtivon, eds., *New French Feminisms: An Anthology* (New York: Schocken Books, 1981) and Toril Moi, ed., *French Feminist Thought: A Reader* (Oxford: Basil Blackwell, 1987).

48. Mary Jo Weaver, *New Catholic Women: A Contemporary Challenge to Traditional Religious Authority* (San Francisco: Harper and Row, 1985), p. xiv.

49. Ruether, *Sexism*, p. 228.

50. Beverly Wildung Harrison, *Our Right to Choose: Toward a New Ethic of Abortion* (Boston: Beacon, 1983).

51. Ruether, *Sexism*, p. 228.

52. Harrison, p. 106. She notes the title of the book on women's health, *Our Bodies/Our Selves*, Boston Women's Health Collective (New York: Simon & Schuster, 1976), as further evidence for this understanding.

53. Naomi Goldenberg, "Archetypal Theory and the Separation of Mind and Body: Reason Enough to Turn to Freud?" *Journal of Feminist Studies in Religion* 1/1 (Winter 1985), pp. 55-72. But see also Judith Van Herik, *Freud on Femininity and Faith* (Berkeley: University of California Press, 1983) for some reasons *not* to turn to Freud.

54. Goldenberg, p. 65.

55. *Ibid.*, p. 68.

56. *Ibid.*, p. 72.

57. *Ibid.*

58. Ruether, *New Woman*, p. 3.

59. Ruether, *Sexism*, p. 245.

60. *Ibid.*, p. 257.

61. *Ibid.*, p. 256.

62. *Ibid.*, p. 257.

63. *Ibid.*, p. 258.

64. See, for example, William C. French, "Christianity and the Domination of Nature," unpublished Ph.D. dissertation, University of Chicago, 1985.

65. This is especially true of goddess-oriented feminists who see the woman's connection to natural cycles as significant. My major focus in this essay is not goddess feminists (although their influence on feminist thought as a whole cannot be dismissed), but the more "mainstream" feminists who are reluctant to posit a female and not a male connection to natural cycles.

66. *Mulieris Dignitatem*, par. 10.

67. Fessio, "Reasons," p. 398.

68. See Mary Daly, *Gyn/Ecology: The Metaethics of Radical Feminism* (Boston: Beacon, 1979). The more "mainstream" feminists I consider here, while not agreeing with many of Daly's conclusions, nevertheless consider her an important and valuable thinker. See, *e.g.*, Ruether, *Sexism*, p. 187.

69. June O'Connor, "Sensuality, Spirituality, Sacramentality," *Union Seminary Quarterly Review* 40/1-2 (May 1985), p. 64.

70. O'Connor, p. 68.

71. Feminist writing in ethics, psychology, and educational theory bears out this characterization. See Gilligan, n. 37 above; Nancy Chodorow, *The Reproduction of Mother: Psychoanalysis and the Sociology of Gender* (Berkeley: University of California Press, 1978); Mary Field Belenky, Blythe McVicker Clinchy, Nancy Rule Goldberger, Jill Mattock Tarule, *Women's Ways of Knowing: The Development of Self, Voice, and Mind* (New York: Basic Books, 1986). Gilligan describes the "web of responsibility" involved in women's ethical decision making, in contrast to a process of adjudicating competing "rights"; Chodorow argues against both the exaggerated and highly individualistic sense of self characteristic of male development and the lack of individuation characteristic of female; and the four authors of *Women's Ways* argue for an educational process based on connection with what is known rather than separation.

II

Spiritual Realizations

6

On Feminist Spirituality

Anne E. Carr*

ABSTRACT

This chapter defines spirituality and notes characteristics of women's and men's spirituality. It then relates these issues to Christian feminism.

Discussion about women and spirituality can range from romanticized claims of special privilege to insistence that equality means sameness. Some typical questions focus the issues. "What is a women's spirituality?" "How is it different from male spirituality?" "What is spirituality, anyway?" And, "what is a feminist spirituality?" "Is it androgynous?" "Is it a stage on the way to something else?"[1]

I. SPIRITUALITY

Spirituality can be described as the whole of our deepest religious beliefs, convictions, and patterns of thought, emotion, and behavior in respect to what is ultimate, to God. Spirituality is holistic, encompassing our relationships to all of creation—to others, to society and nature, to work and recreation—in a fundamentally religious orientation. Spirituality is larger than a theology or set of values precisely because it is all-encompassing and pervasive. Unlike theology as an explicit intellectual position, spirituality reaches into our unconscious

*Anne E. Carr is Professor of Theology at the Divinity School of the University of Chicago (Chicago, IL 60637), where she received the Ph.D. An original associate editor of *Horizons* and a co-editor of the *Journal of Religion*, her many articles and books include *A Search for Wisdom and Spirit: Thomas Merton's Theology of the Self* (Notre Dame, IN: University of Notre Dame Press, 1988) and *Transforming Grace: Christian Tradition and Women's Experience* (San Francisco: Harper & Row, 1988).

or half-conscious depths. And while it shapes behavior and attitudes, spirituality is more than a conscious moral code. In relation to God, it is who we *really* are, the deepest self, not entirely accessible to our comprehensive self-reflection. In a Christian context, God's love goes before us in a way we can never fully name.

Spirituality can be a predominantly unconscious pattern of relating seldom reflected on, activated only in certain situations, as at Sunday Mass or during a personal crisis. As such it is a dimension of life for the most part unexamined, resting on convention, upbringing, or social expectations. But spirituality can also be made conscious, explicitly reflected on, developed, changed, and understood in a context of growth and cultivation of the fundamental self in a situation of response and relationship. Christian spirituality entails the conviction that God is indeed personal and that we are in immediate personal relationship to another, an Other who "speaks" and can be spoken to, who really affects our lives.

Although it is deeply personal, spirituality is not necessarily individualistic, because within the relationship to the ultimate, to God, it touches on everything: our relations to others, to community, to politics, society, the world. Spirituality can be consciously oriented toward the inclusive social context in which we live.

Spirituality is expressed in everything we do. It is a style, unique to the self, that catches up all our attitudes: in communal and personal prayer, in behavior, bodily expressions, life choices, in what we support and affirm and what we protest and deny. As our deepest self in relation to God, to the whole, and so literally to everything, spirituality changes, grows, or diminishes in the whole context of life. Consciously cultivated, nourished, cared about, it often takes the character of struggle as we strive to integrate new perceptions or convictions. And it bears the character of grace as we are lifted beyond previous levels of integration by a power greater than our own.

Spirituality is deeply informed by family, teachers, friends, community, class, race, culture, sex, and by our time in history, just as it is influenced by beliefs, intellectual positions, and moral options. These influences may be unconscious or made explicit through reading, reflection, conversation, even conversion. And so spirituality includes and expresses our self-conscious or critical appraisal of our situation in time, in history, and in culture.

As a style of response, spirituality is individually patterned yet culturally shaped. Implicit metaphors, images, or stories drawn from our culture are embodied in a particular spiritual style; these can be made explicit through reflection, journal keeping, conversations with friends, or therapy. We each live a personal story that is part of a wider familial, cultural, racial, and sexual myth. When our myths are made conscious, we can affirm or deny them, accept parts and reject others, as we grow in relationship to God, to others, to our world. Personal, familial, religious, cultural, racial, sexual stories answer the great questions: Where do I come from? How should I live? What is the meaning of the end, of death? Making myths explicit means that we have already moved beyond them and that they become available for criticism.

II. WOMEN'S AND MEN'S SPIRITUALITIES

Even with affirmations of equality between women and men, of a single-nature anthropology in contrast to a dual-nature view,[2] it seems clear that there are differences between the sexes in basic style of understanding and relationship. Thus, there are probably differences in women's and men's spiritualities. Recognition of difference, while admitting real equality, need not entail subversive notions of complementarity that really means subordination or inferiority of one in relation to the other. What are these differences, prescinding from the question (unanswerable, I think) of whether these are the result of nature or nurture?

In a helpful book, *Women's Reality*,[3] Anne Wilson Schaef describes the differences between what she calls the White Male System and an emergent Female System on the basis of her consultant work with both women and men. The White Male System is the dominant one in our culture. While there are other systems (Black, Native American, Hispanic) the White Male System, she argues, views itself as (1) the only one, (2) innately superior, (3) knowing and understanding everything, and (4) believing that it is possible to be totally logical, objective, and rational. Schaef lists a set of contrasts that might help us get at differences in women's and men's spiritualities. These contrasts, of course, describe abstract types; no one is completely one type or another. And some men are in fact in the Female System, while some women are in the White Male System. The following indicate some of these different gender based perspectives.

Issues	White Male System	Female System
Time	Clock	Process
Relationships	Hierarchy	Peer
Center of focus	Self and work	Relationship (self-others)
Sexuality	Central	Part in whole
Intimacy	Physical	Verbal
Friendship	Team effort	Knowing and being known

Power	Zero sum (scarcity)	Limitless
Money	Absolute, real	Relative, symbolic
Leadership	To lead	To enable
Negotiation	Fun = winning	Fun = creativity

In sum, the White Male System is analytic, concerned with definition, explanation, either/or, and is goal-centered. The Female System is synthetic, concerned with understanding, both/and, and is process-centered.

Feminist consciousness, as critical of religious and cultural ideologies which reach into our very perception, thought, and language, must be a little suspicious here. Rather than delimiting a female spirituality to one side of the list, would not a critical feminist consciousness try to hold elements of both sides together, in critical correlation with one another? Do we not need to preserve the values of traditional female characteristics while recognizing certain values in the traditional male traits?

Schaef performs an exercise with her groups (male, female, mixed) in which she asks participants to list characteristics of God (whether they believe in God or not) and of humankind; then characteristics of male and female. Invariably, she writes, the lists look like this:

God	*Humankind*	*Male*	*Female*
Male	Childlike	Intelligent	Emotional
Omnipotent	Sinful	Powerful	Weak
Omniscient	Weak	Brave	Fearful
Omnipresent	Stupid/dumb	Good	Sinful
Eternal	Mortal	Strong	Like children

She concludes that male is to female as God is to humankind. And this, she argues, is the mythology of the White Male System, whose basic hierarchical structure is God—men—women—children—animals—earth, in a system of dominance. Schaef says our traditional theology supports this myth. Clearly feminist theology, and other forms of contemporary theology, do not.

III. FEMINIST SPIRITUALITY

A feminist spirituality would be distinguished from any other as a spiritual orientation which has integrated into itself the central elements of feminist consciousness. It is the spirituality of those who have experienced feminist consciousness raising.

Feminist spirituality is thus different from women's spirituality, that is, the distinctive female relationship to the divine in contrast to the male. Women's spirituality might be studied across particular historical periods, or within particular religions, or racial or cultural groups (e.g., puritan, Muslim, Black or, as above, White, middle class, Western) and certain "female" characteristics delineated. For example, in contrast to male spirituality, women's spirituality might be described as more related to nature and natural processes than to culture; more personal and relational than objective and structural; more diffuse, concrete, and general than focused, universal, abstract; more emotional than intellectual, etc.

A specifically feminist spirituality, on the other hand, would be that mode of relating to God, and everyone and everything in relation to God, exhibited by those who are deeply aware of the historical and cultural restriction of women to a narrowly defined "place" within the wider human (male) "world." Such awareness would mean that we are self-consciously critical of the cultural and religious ideologies which deny women full opportunities for self-actualization and self-transcendence. This critical stance is both negative and positive. Negatively, it bears a healthy suspicion and vigilance toward taken-for-granted cultural and religious views that, in a variety of subtle ways, continue to limit the expectations of women to passive, subordinate, auxiliary roles and rewards. Positively, this critical stance includes a vision of the world in which genuine mutuality, reciprocity, and equality might prevail. A fully developed feminist spirituality would bear the traces of the central elements of feminist consciousness, integrated within a wider religious framework.

Such a spirituality would affirm and be deeply at home in the reality of sisterhood. It would recognize the importance of the supportive network among women of all ages, races, and classes and would espouse non-competitive, non-hierarchical, non-dominating modes of relationship among human beings. As critical, it would recognize the competitive and non-supportive ways in which women have sometimes related to one another in the past and would consciously struggle to achieve authentic, interdependent modes of relationship. As religious, and as Christian, such a spirituality would strive to integrate the model of feminist sisterhood into a wider vision of human community with men as brothers. Thus, it would be open to all people and would not cease calling the brothers to task for their failings and to wider vision of human mutuality, reciprocity, and interdependence before a God who wills our unity and community.

As feminist, such a spirituality would encourage the autonomy, self-actualization, and self-transcendence of all women (and men). It would recognize the uniqueness of each individual as she tells her own story (there is no universal women's experience) and affirm each one as she strives to make her own choices. As critical, it would recognize the cultural and religious limitations placed on women in the past and present; and as self-critical, it would recognize the the temptation of the feminist group to impose another ideology as oppressive as the old obedience to the fathers. Feminist spirituality would consciously struggle to free itself from ideologies in favor of the authentic freedom of the individual and the group as it attempts to be faithful to its own experience. As religious, and as Christian, a feminist spirituality would strive for an ever freer, but always human, self-transcendence before a God who does not call us servants but friends.

In its encouragement of sisterhood and autonomy, feminist spirituality understands the wider dimensions of human oppression, especially the relationships of racism, classism, sexism, and elitism in our society, and affirms the liberation of all oppressed groups. As critical, it would resist limiting the women's movement to a luxury only the affluent can afford, but would embrace the plight of women of all colors and all classes, that is, be genuinely self-critical. As religious, and as Christian, such a spirituality would strive to become global in its concerns, in its prayer as in action, to become truly inclusive of the whole of God's world, to pray and to act with the inclusive mind of God, that is, to be self-transcendent.

A Christian feminist spirituality is universal in its vision and relates the struggle of the individual woman—black, brown, yellow or white, rich or poor, educated or illiterate—to the massive global problems of our day. For in recognizing the problem (the sin) of human exploitation, violence, and domination of male over female, rich over poor, white over color, in-group over out-group, strong over weak, force over freedom, man over nature, it sees the whole through the part. Such a spirituality strives to be not elitist but inclusive. It invites men, and all the other oppressor groups, to conversion. Yet it remains critical, on guard against the easy cooptation that can dim its radical vision of human mutuality and cooperation. Wise as a serpent, cunning as a dove, Christian feminist spirituality resorts to prayer as the only hope for its vision even as it struggles to act, here and now, to bring it into reality.

Given the possible scope of feminist spirituality as it views the whole through the lens of women's situation, what can be said about female and male spirituality? That each has its values and limitations. That the emergent female spirituality has strong humanistic and corrective elements for contemporary society. The *feminist* spirituality is, I think, new. With the exception, perhaps, of the nineteenth-century Protestant feminists, the feminist spirituality I have described differs not only from male spirituality, past and present, but from a good deal of female spirituality as well. Clearly, it would be available for everyone, male and female. And clearly, it would be androgynous, if by the term is meant focus on the person as integrating the full range of human possibilities, with choices dependent on talents and attractions rather than the stereotypes of race, class, and sex. (The oppressors are oppressed, too, by limited horizons.) Strictly feminist spirituality, with its particular stress on female bonding in sisterhood, affirmation of the self-actualization and self-transcendence of women, and interrelationships among sexism, racism, and classism, is, one hopes, a temporary stage on the way to a fuller human spirituality.

In the present, however, it remains a stage that has only begun to be explored. Analogies with the experience of other oppressed or minority groups might be helpful. One who has worked in and with any of these groups, shared in their struggle and their prayer, even if she is not a member of the group, can to some extent know what that experience is, can be "converted." So, too, any man who has identified with the struggle of women can participate in the feminist experience, share in a feminist spirituality. Given the massive distortions of both the religious and the cultural traditions, I would say that in truth any man should. All the spiritualities of liberation, notwithstanding the distinctive and never to be totally assimilated experience of the "minority," do have a convergent unity. But it is precisely through the particularities of the individual group that some purchase on the broader vision can be had.

The feminist experience is unique in that it potentially covers the world, every human group. It is this that has led some feminists to maintain that male-female domination is not only the oldest, but the source of all oppressor-oppressed relationships. And because of the close familial, personal, ethnic, and class ties involved, it is also often seen as the most difficult to deal with. And yet that very closeness of male-female, in whatever group, may offer stronger possibilities for overcoming the split, for healing the wound, particularly in the religious context that spirituality encompasses. For here, in the Christian framework at least, human beings understand themselves in relation to a God who is ultimate, yet incarnate, whose name is love, who calls us to unity, whose revelation is in the death and resurrection of Jesus, who is among us in the Spirit (our experience of spirituality) that our joy may be complete. The Spirit is advocate, comforter, clarifier of sin and of truth.

A feminist spirituality, with its sources in women's experience of friendship and sisterhood, might express the experience of joy in the divine-human relationship, as suggested by Judith Plaskow in her study of Protestant theologies of sin and grace in relation to the experience of women. This is the experience of grace or the Spirit which is neither "shattering" (Niebuhr) as by an authoritarian father-judge nor a quietistic "acceptance" as by an understanding mother (Tillich), neither "subordination nor participation which threatens the boundaries of the individual self." It is an experience of grace or the Spirit "best expressed in words using the prefix 'co'—co-creating, co-shaping, co-stewardship; and in non-objectifying process words, aliveness, changing, loving, pushing, etc."[4] The suggestion is similar to one made by Elisabeth Schüssler Fiorenza about the metaphor of friend/friendship in relation to God.[5]

What if one were to envision God as friend, even as a feminist friend, rather than father or mother? What if God is friend to humanity as a whole, and even more intimately, friend to the individual, to me? A friend whose presence is joy, ever-deepening relationship and love, ever available in direct address, in communion and presence? A friend whose person is fundamentally a mystery, inexhaustible, never fully known, always surprising? Yet a friend, familiar, comforting, at home with us: a friend who urges our freedom and autonomy in decision, yet who is present in the community of interdependence and in fact creates it? A friend who widens our perspectives daily and who deepens our passion for freedom—our own and that of others? What if? Jesus' relationship to his disciples was that of friendship, chosen friends; he was rather critical of familial ties. His friendship transformed their lives—both women and men—expanded their horizons; his Spirit pressed them forward. Can we pray to the God of Jesus, through the Spirit, as friends?

NOTES

1. An earlier version of these reflections was presented at a seminar on feminist spirituality organized by Mary Jo Weaver of Indiana University, Bloomington, in October, 1981, and supported by a grant from Lilly Endowment.

2. See *Research Report: Women in Church and Society*, Sara Butler, M.S.B.T., ed. (Mahwah, NJ: Catholic Theological Society of America, 1978), pp. 32-40.

3. (Minneapolis: Winston, 1981).

4. *Sex, Sin and Grace: Women's Experience and the Theologies of Reinhold Niebuhr and Paul Tillich* (Washington, DC: University Press of America, 1980), p. 172.

5. "Why Not the Category Friend/Friendship?" *Horizons* 2/1 (Spring 1975), pp. 117-18.

7

Dorothy Day and Gender Identity: The Rhetoric and the Reality

June O'Connor*

ABSTRACT

*Dorothy Day's sense of herself as a woman and as a mother fea-
ture prominently in her writings. In light of recent inquiries into
gender identity and gender ideology, and given Dorothy Day's
prominence as editor, social activist, anarchist, pacifist, and religious author, questions about her views regarding woman's role
and related feminist concerns invite investigation. This chapter
argues that although Dorothy Day did not become a vocal advocate nor public ally of the women's movements in twentieth-century American life because of some fundamental differences in
viewpoint and loyalty, she did share a number of affinities with
feminist perspectives. To investigate her thought on this topic enables us to understand Dorothy Day more fully and to bring a
critical eye to selected features of feminism, discerning (from
Day's standpoint) both strengths and weaknesses.*

The writings of Dorothy Day (1897-1980) reflect a woman acutely
conscious of her identity as a woman and as a mother. This sense of
self as woman and as mother feature prominently in Day's observations and reflections and in her ethic of caring for the poor. Given recent research interests in gender identity and ideology, and given

---

*June O'Connor, Professor and Chair of the Program in Religious Stud-
ies at the University of California, Riverside (Riverside, CA 92521), holds a
Ph.D. in Religion from Temple University and is the author of articles and review essays on theology and religious ethics in *Horizons, Religious Studies Review, Cross Currents, Listening: Journal of Religion and Culture, The Hastings Center Report*, and *Union Seminary Quarterly Review*. Her recent book is *The Moral
Vision of Dorothy Day: A Feminist Perspective* (New York: Crossroad, 1991).

Dorothy Day's prominence as editor of *The Catholic Worker*, as social critic, dissenter, anarchist, pacifist, and religious author, questions about her views on the role of woman and her position vis-à-vis contemporary feminist concerns invite investigation. Some questions: Did Day's views about women conform to and reflect the conventional patriarchal outlook of her mentor Peter Maurin whose theology identified man with spirit and woman with matter?[1] Or is it accurate to describe Dorothy Day as a "feminist" as at least one scholar has done?[2] If accurate, in what sense was Day a feminist? If inaccurate, what were her views about women and women's roles? What did she think of the women's movements she lived through, particularly women's suffrage before 1920 and feminism of the 1960s and 1970s? How did she describe women, reflect on them, present them to her readers?

A study of Dorothy Day's writings, specifically her books,[3] yields numerous observations about women that conform to a conventional patriarchal outlook wherein women are accepted as naturally and instinctively different from men and inferior to them. The inferiority is at times named. At other times it is implied. Yet these observations are punctuated with comments that suggest that Day subscribed to a much more egalitarian theological and ethical perspective regarding gender identity than some of her words suggest. The "women's movement" was not a cause Day committed herself to. She became a voice on behalf of laborers, pacifists, and nonviolent protestors for social change, the majority of whom were men. But along the way Day did voice some critical complaints about inequities between the sexes, illustrating some affinities with the feminist critique, and she placed theological value on the fact that a greater balance or integration of gender roles was possible in the Catholic Worker setting.

To develop this thesis, this paper is cast in two sections. Part one examines representative examples of Day's language (the "rhetoric") regarding women's roles and identity. Part two discusses her views in light of her life work and life choices (the "reality") and in light of selected questions and values being expressed in contemporary feminist thought.

I. THE RHETORIC

Day grew up during the early twentieth-century suffrage movement, joined her first march in Washington, DC, on its behalf in 1917, and received a sentence of thirty days in jail for her actions. (She was released after sixteen days when President Wilson signed a pardon for the whole group.) A mere citation of these facts might suggest that

Day supported the cause of suffrage and identified with the movement of equality for women.

But her account of this event tells us something altogether different. "The cause for which we were in jail seemed utterly unimportant," she wrote.

> I had not much interest in the vote, and it seemed to me our protest should have been not for ourselves but for all those thousands of prisoners throughout the country, victims of a materialistic system (*US*, 86).

Day's dissatisfaction with the suffrage movement can be understood in three ways: as a feature of her anarchist sympathies, as one aspect of her critique of American socioeconomic values, and as what she perceived to be an isolated effort to effect change in only one area, when many areas of life were in need of radical change. As a person attracted to anarchism, Day never used the vote women won (*OPS*, 304). She distrusted government, valuing personal responsibility in the context of caring community far more highly than state structures. The vote, she thought, simply provided for women an opportunity to participate in a way of life that had a skewed sense of values: materialism, violence, and social patterns that promoted injustice and indifference toward the unemployed, the poor, and the homeless. Day could not envision what good women's suffrage would do when it came, for she found those women who would most likely use the vote to be blindly patriotic and supportive of the American system. Her fundamental experience while in jail with the suffrage marchers was that of solitude, not solidarity (*US*, 86).

The radical philosophy that attracted Day for its social and economic analysis distanced her in its often liberal approach to sexuality. Day was offended by Emma Goldman's advocacy of free love and of the tendency of women revolutionaries to complicate social analysis and social change by emphasizing personal needs. Her critique of this viewpoint led her to universalize that "men are the single-minded, the pure of heart, in these movements. Women by their very nature are more materialistic, thinking of the home, the children, and of all things needful to them, especially love" (*LL*, 68-69). In constantly searching to meet these needs, she felt, women "go against their own best interests" (*LL*, 69).

Day was drawn to the possibility of a profound revolution in values, sensing, even as she emerged from jail after that march, that the success of such a revolution would be dependent on a deeply personal conversion to those values.

In the voice of June, the protagonist of her autobiographical novel, *The Eleventh Virgin*, Day highlights the limitations of the suffragette vision, the conflicting concerns of the participants, and their failure to work together. (Some fought for the vote, others for birth control, still others for street women or for pacifism, and often one group criticized the other.)[4] June voices Day's discontent: "if I worked among these people with their single-track minds, I'd go crazy. . . . I feel that all these people with their causes are one-sided" (*EV*, 217). What was needed, she felt, "was a radical party whose platform would include such planks as birth control, pacifism, suffrage" all in one (*EV*, 209). Day's interest in the dignity and respect due the worker and her later support for the labor movement, however, led her to appreciate the leadership of those women who led labor strikes in order to limit the working day to ten hours, to increase wages, and to support worker organization and participation in policy decisions.

> My heart thrilled at those unknown women in New England who led the first strikes to liberate the women and children from the cotton mills (*US*, 49; see also *LL*, 51).

Day's well-known conversion to religious faith, reported in *From Union Square to Rome*, was deeply connected to her experiences as lover, wife, and mother. Her story of conversion to religious faith in the context of the Catholic Church is a statement of the excitement and beauty and illuminating power that the experience of marital love and pregnancy can generate. Day waxes eloquently about the fact that it was precisely in these direct and creative actions that she was drawn to acknowledge the creative source of all:

> I had known Forster a long time before we contracted our common-law relationship, and I have always felt that it was life with him that brought me natural happiness, that brought me to God.
> His ardent love of creation brought me to the Creator of all things. . . .
> I could not see that love between a man and woman was incompatible with love of God. God is the Creator, and the very fact that we were begetting a child made me have a sense that we were made in the image and likeness of God, co-creators with him (*LL*, 153).

In her occasional references to marriage, we see an acceptance of conventional views. When describing a marital decision to become involved in social action, for example, she writes that "as head of the household" the husband need not consider the wife when making social action commitments, though the wife "of course" (*OP*, 159) must consider her husband when making such decisions. Day generally does not question the traditional roles assigned to men and women, but rather finds them operative and confirmed in her experience.

> Women do love to be active, it is natural to them, they are most happy in doing that for which they are made, when they are cooking and serving others. They are the nourishers, starting with the babies at the breast and from there on their work is to nourish and strengthen and console (*OP*, 40; see also 174, 34),

Day's journals provide vivid detail of women's work. When reading about the life of a mother on a farm, for example, the reader feels the never-ending bending and lifting which mark the woman's day: "cooking, dishwashing, clothes washing, drawing water, keeping two fires going, feeding babies, consoling babies, picking up after babies" (*OP*, 7).

This back-breaking work leads her to muse about hardened gender roles:

> One cannot help thinking that the men have an easier time of it. It is wonderful to work out on such a day as this with the snow falling lightly all around, chopping wood, dragging in fodder, working with the animals. Women are held pretty constantly to the house (*OP*, 27; see also *M*, 36, 43-44).

Day registers a more pronounced measure of discontent regarding gender roles when giving an account of the first issue of *The Catholic Worker*. Explaining her decision as editor not to give the lead editorial to Peter Maurin's three-point program, she speculates about her reasons for this decision: "Perhaps it sounded too utopian for my tastes; perhaps I was irked because women were left out in his description of a house of hospitality, where he spoke of a group of men living under a priest" (*LF*, 22).[5]

Day rarely registers an analysis of ideas. She functions, rather, as *reporter* of events. A skilled and skillful journalist, she records ideas as well as events and often offers response and commentary but generally avoids extensive analysis. This may be due to a feeling of ambivalence about her intellectual skills. On the one hand she sounds self-confident when she registers annoyance at the way "men, even priests" insult women's intelligence with "pious pap" (*BL*, 189). And yet she seems to have internalized the insult, for she often attributes to her identity as a woman her "stupidity" (*HH*, xxxvi), her "wandering mind" (*HH*, 2), and her inability to understand theological subtleties (*US*, 169; Coles, 117).

This sampling of materials from Dorothy Day's books illustrate that Day was not an advocate of women's suffrage, was not a feminist in any intentional way, that is to say, did not see herself as a feminist, did not identify with, nor join, the feminist movement.

She did observe inequities in socially assigned gender roles and expectations and voiced these as journalistic observations and personal musings. At times she represents and reflects the patriarchal attitude toward women whose difference from men is interpreted as a kind of inferiority. The accepted inferiority then functions on her behalf as a way of explaining to her readers her limitations as author. Because she is a woman, she does not display theological sophistication (*US*, 169); because she is a woman, ordinary "daily things" (*HH*, 2) pervade her writings.

As an activist, Day believed stoutly in the importance of putting ideas into direct action and of using actions to arouse the conscience and to stimulate thought. Her words, by her own standards, then, need to be interpreted in light of her choices, in light of the actions and patterns and commitments that comprise her life. Proceeding this way enables us to see more fully and to probe more deeply Dorothy Day's views on the theological and ethical dimensions of gender identity.

II. THE REALITY

Although Day remembers her father as a stern and distant man who believed that the place for women and children was in the home, Dorothy the young adult apparently felt otherwise, for she began living and working independently after spending two years at the University of Illinois as a student. Her father's discomfort and impatience with her radical ideas moved him, she felt, to treat her in her adult years as a casual friend, thus sustaining the sense of distance she had always felt from him as a child. Nonetheless, she pursued her interests, which were observing and writing about people in American society who were squeezed into poverty, hunger, and discrimination.

Living and working among radical writers of the early twentieth century (Floyd Dell and Max Eastman, editors of the leftist monthly *Masses*, Mike Gold, assistant editor of the Socialist *Call*, and John Reed), Dorothy pursued direct experience with dissenters, anarchists, and labor organizers (such as the I.W.W.s) who often poised themselves in conflict with the law. Strikes, acts of civil disobedience, and other forms of protest brought with them risk of arrest, abuse, and imprisonment. She recounts an experience of imprisonment in Chicago in 1922 in which she felt victimized. Contrasting this event with her imprisonment in Washington, DC, five years earlier, where the collective presence of the feminist marchers made that experience more bearable, Day introduces the Chicago episode by accenting the injustices of the men who mistreated her. "Now I was to have a solitary taste of the injustice, or the ugliness of men's justice, which set me more squarely on the side of the revolution" (*LL*, 114). Specifically this meant the humiliating experiences of the arrest: being "forced to dress . . . in the presence of two detectives, leering"; being wrongly booked as an inmate of a disorderly house; being forced to stand on the street under the gaze of passers-by while awaiting the police wagon; being put in a room that smelled foul and had an unscreened toilet; being examined for venereal diseases; being unfree to contact lawyer or friend; being judged guilty before trial; being stripped naked and searched for drugs (*LL*, 115-21). (Eventually Dorothy was released and the case dismissed.)

Reflecting on the Chicago arrest years later, recording it from some distance and in light of her faith and religious sensibilities, Day broadens her view, faulting also her own naïveté, her stubbornness in flouting convention, and resisting the red hysteria of the time (*LL*, 116). But it is interesting to note the way she initially labels the Chicago experience: "the ugliness of men's justice which set me more squarely on the side of the revolution."[6]

The revolution Day wanted in those early years, well before her religious conversion in the late 1920s, is notably of a piece with the revolution she sought to create through *The Catholic Worker* from 1933 on. She and her mentor Peter Maurin placed a high degree of value on personal responsibility, voluntary poverty, and meeting the needs of others by enacting the works of mercy (feeding the hungry, instructing the ignorant, clothing the naked, visiting the sick, counseling the doubtful, etc.). As newspaper writers and frequent lecturers, Maurin and Day both saw themselves at work at a task that sought to create the news, not merely to report the news. The news they wished to create was a more just society wherein the social teachings of the Catholic encyclicals were brought alive and made practical to the lives of workers and of the unemployed in the United States.

Feeding the hungry became the primary vehicle for reaching people in need. "A man has to eat," Day said, in characteristic simplicity and definitiveness (*OPS*, 81). There may be murderers among them in their soup kitchen, she admitted, but no matter, no questions, a man has to eat.

Feeding the hungry, however, was not sufficient. There had to be learning, discussion of the ideas that would foster a new society where it would be easier for people to be good. Thus, through round-table discussions over meals, promulgation of their views in newspaper format, explanatory lectures, and letters of appeal, Day and Maurin sought to carry on a revolution. It was a revolution stimulated by the values of empathy for others, personal responsibility in meeting the needs of others, political actions which resist the materialism, consumerism, and violence of American society. It is a revolution which alerts people to a sense of interdependence and solidarity in an effort to rectify a system which favors the bright, the wealthy, and the powerful.

A prominent theme in contemporary feminist ethics is recognition of the connections among a wide range of social injustices: discrimination on the basis of gender, color, culture, age, sexuality, and, some would add, species.[7] Day shared this point of view; she remarks, for example, that sex and its place in life is as pertinent to questions of social justice as the discussion of war, overpopulation, capital punishment, birth control, abortion, euthanasia, and the role of the state in human life: "The entire question of man's control over the life of others, over the life forces within man, is one of the most profound importance today" (*OPS*, 90). In the early years of *The Catholic Worker* movement, Day focused attention on the labor movement, on the evils of war, and on the poverty of destitution. Yet in the course of time, she continued to identify and to identify with newly emerging causes of justice: the Cuban revolution, the civil rights quests of the Black community in the U.S., the work on behalf of better conditions for migrant workers in California and elsewhere, the resistance to U.S. involvement in Vietnam. She spoke and wrote admiringly and with empathy for Fidel Castro,[8] Martin Luther King, Jr., César Chavez; and she encouraged young men to refuse being drafted into the war in Indochina. Notably absent in this list of issues that won Day's attention and public support is the women's movement of the 1960s and 1970s.

Given feminist critiques of American society because of its history of exclusion and discrimination regarding women, the women's movement might be construed to be a likely recipient of Dorothy Day's empathy. Yet this is not the case. Why this was not the case, I suggest, can be accounted for in several ways.

First, to the extent that "the women's movement" was initially and primarily voiced by an educated, middle-class (and most often white) woman, arguing for legal, economic, and political reforms, its call for change was insufficiently radical to converge with Day's criticisms of American life and empathy for the underclass. Middle-class women may indeed be excluded from power and position in American life, but "middle class" means "privilege" from the standpoint of the poor, the homeless, the unemployed and unemployable. The critique of the educated urban and suburban feminists did not penetrate the experience of women in the slum, ghetto, and Bowery, where Day lived and thought, felt and worked.[9]

Second, to the extent that the publicized and televised voices of feminism placed a decided emphasis on *freedom* (as a means of securing a broad range of rights for women and arguing for full participation by women in social, political, economic, educational, commercial, and religious structures), they and Day differed in emphases.

Dorothy Day's approach to "increasing" the "amount" of justice in the world is not one of accenting freedom but of accenting responsibility. She believed in freedom and was jailed on behalf of freedom. But she does not *speak* in terms of freedom as much as she *acts* in freedom, for freedom, highlighting always that the important point is *how one uses one's freedom*, namely, on behalf of justice. Her appeal to social justice brought with it an insistence on a sense of personal responsibility that involved self-discipline, personal conversion, and a willingness to take action.[10]

Responsibility focuses attention on the communitarian features of human existence and of the obligations to one another that arise from the social nature of human persons. Community consistently received the accent in her reading of the interdependent relationship between individual and community. Her interest was less on rights, more on responsibilities, less on "me," more on "we." Ideally, the worker would strike in order to secure attention to the workers' condition of the indignity of wage-slave status; the unemployed would demonstrate in order to draw attention to the dehumanizing impact of nonparticipation in the economic order. Insofar as the women's movement emphasized rights over responsibilities and focused on freedom rather than justice, it would have failed to engage Dorothy Day's ear. She was never drawn to petition nor demand equality for women; rather she was driven to expose and to criticize the system that prevented it, whether in the labor movement, the prison system, or in her work for peace. "Equality," indeed, was not one of her words. "Participation" better captures her ideal. As a humanistic socialist by inclination and a Catholic by choice, she affirmed the dignity and respect due to human persons regardless of gender, class, employment status, religion, or race. Her concern was with their participation, particularly economic participation in the face of social marginalization and exclusion.[11] She held "distributism" and the "cooperative ideal" to offer hopeful models of social arrangements that would foster the common good (*HH*, 142-49; *OPS*, 105-07).[12]

Third, to the extent that the "sexual liberation" of women was a component of women's liberation more generally conceived, Day would have been distanced from the cause, as she had been in the second decade of the century.

Day knew from experience something of what a sexuality liberated from marital commitment could be like. In *The Eleventh Virgin* she explores the experience of sexual awakening, seduction, and surrender, and with it humiliation, insult, and abandonment. In *The Long Loneliness* she alludes to a similar life experience which she later chooses to repudiate. Her dislike of Emma Goldman's ethic of free love sustained itself throughout Day's life. Indeed, her views became solidified and deepened by her religious commitments and the theology of her chosen church. Day regarded sex as a profound life force having to do with the God-like capacity of creation, as fundamentally related to the integrity and life of the family, as the context for children's growth and understanding of stability and commitment (*OPS*, 159 and *AIG*, 164-71). To the extent that the "women's liberation movement" connoted a sexual liberation which separated sexual activity from marital commitment and from the possibility of (procreative) "co-creation," it would fail to win Day's interest and support.

Fourth, during the 1970s, the final decade of her life, Day wrote and published less often, due to failing health. As the feminist critique deepened and broadened and expanded beyond its white middle-class origins with the passage of time, Day's physical health weakened. As the movement was gaining energy and strength, Dorothy Day was losing energy and strength. And so for these historical and philosophical reasons, feminism and Dorothy failed to meet as public allies.

Nonetheless, given the conflicts between them, there are several areas in which one finds compatibility between stated feminist concerns and Dorothy Day's views and choices, areas where one notes a convergence of views. One has been noted above, namely the deep sense of connection among diverse social problems (sex, race, war, capital punishment, abortion, and the like) and a desire to address these problems from a fundamental and integral vision of justice. A second pertains to the feminist affirmation of the legitimacy, need, and wisdom of women's participation in the work force. Dorothy Day is herself a model of full and active participation. Though she did not work for a salary at *The Catholic Worker*, but lived frugally from contributions in order to distribute such funds to the poor and to voice their needs in lectures and articles, she did work. Conscious always of the need to pay the bills (rent, grocer, post office, and printer), she wrote in order to secure income for that end as well as to make known her views on life. She edited a newspaper, lectured widely, fed the hungry, clothed the poor, found housing for the homeless, purchased farms for the cultivation of the land and employment of the unemployed. She publicly protested the advocacy and acceptance of war through marches, pickets, sit-ins, and vigils of support. She herself thus lived the life of working woman and working mother, meeting the demands of multiple commitments, though in an admittedly unconventional way.

In 1965, reflecting on her daughter Tamar's opportunity to train as a nurse, Day further reveals her approving thoughts about women working outside the home. She encouraged her daughter's decision to attend nursing school by pledging to care for Tamar's children during the four months training time Tamar would be away. Day explains her thinking:

> With children all day in school women have come to feel the isolation of the home, the lack of community facilities such as day nurseries. They know they have a contribution to make to the common good. Their talents are unused and undeveloped. And above all, there is the crucial need to earn money to help support and to educate and provide training in turn for the young ones (*OPS*, 202).

Here we note Day's recognition of the multiple motivations that move women to work in the public sphere: economic necessity, the need to overcome the isolation of the nuclear family context, and the desire to make a contribution to the larger community in addition to one's immediate family.

Day would not, I propose, be sympathetic to the feminist slogan of "having it all." To the extent that this is an expression of feminism, it would lose Dorothy Day who spent her life praising simplicity and detachment, fidelity and constancy, life lived by little and by little. Yet Day would, I think, be quite sympathetic to women who want to "do it all" (as distinct from "have it all"). By this I refer to the desire for multiple and diverse commitments: to contribute to the larger, public sphere, to marry, and to mother, simultaneously. The accent here is on attending to the world, contributing to the world, working in the world and on behalf of the world, utilizing one's talents and inclinations for those who might be aided by them. To have it all taps a metaphor of consumption; to do it all suggests action in and with others. The second of these slogans fits with Day's outlook in a way the first cannot.

Third, *The Catholic Worker* mission to feed the hungry, clothe the naked, and instruct the ignorant was a mission that engaged men and women alike. In this setting, men, as women, were called upon to purchase food, prepare and serve meals, and perform the cleaning and dishwashing tasks required by meal service. Traditionally "woman's work," such tasks shared across gender lines and gender roles were for Day a source of eschatological hope, rooted in a biblically based theology. At *The Catholic Worker*,

> . . . men joined in the healing and the nourishing, the building and the spinning and the weaving, the cultivation and the preservation of the good earth. Now there is neither bond nor free, Greek or Hebrew, male or female—we are a little nearer to the heavenly kingdom when men are feeding the hungry. It is real action as well as symbolic action (*OPS*, 378).

This very concrete ethic of women and men caring and working in family and community without regard to socially assigned gender roles is a theme regularly voiced in feminist discourse. For Day, this insistence on mutually-engaged-in work was not only advisable from a human point of view, but symbolized the heavenly kingdom promised in the gospels.

Fourth, Day's views about women touch a prominent feminist hope: recovery of the integral, intimate connections between the personal and the political, the spiritual and the material, the religious and the social-historical features of human experience.[13] For example, Day registers esteem for women's inclination to see the "whole" (*BL*, 270), women's ability to keep a "balance" (*OPS*, 378), and women's tendency to "think with their whole bodies" (*BL*, 270). Thus, upon hearing from Peter Maurin an "obscure Thomistic utterance" that "man is spirit, woman is matter" (*OPS*, 362-63), Dorothy Day interpreted this in a very interesting way: "Woman is close to the material things of life and accepts them, this integration of soul and body and its interaction" (*OPS*, 363). Rather than perceive it as a view which bespeaks discrimination by relegating woman to inferior status, as was often the case in the history of Christian thought, Day accepted this claim as true, and proceeded to understand it in terms of woman's capacity to integrate conflicting features of human life.

Finally, one notes that Dorothy Day's interest in ideas, understanding of ideas and her testing of ideas are all activated by attending to her experience. In this respect, too, her writings exemplify an important feature of feminist thought and ethics: woman's experience as starting point. Her writings are a record of that experience and the insights drawn from experience. It is a basic experience of learning from others as well as from self, from recognized authorities in positions of knowledge and power and from unrecognized authorities met on the streets of New York City, from people who share her religious faith and from people who repudiate or ignore her faith, from people who agree with her anarchist perspective and from those who are uneasy with it or even shocked by it. But in all of her encounters, reflections, and records, Dorothy Day's experiences of herself as woman and mother inform, punctuate, and direct her observations and judgments.

III. CONCLUSION

Day's books, articles, and columns regularly reflect the view that women's nature and instincts are different from those of men. At times her acceptance of this difference leads her to fault women for being preoccupied with concerns that constrict their social vision. At other times she accepts this difference as a complimentary statement about women's greater strength and ability to respond to the vicissitudes of life (*OPS*, 378). As a thinker and a writer about life as experienced, Day does not indulge in speculation about the origin of the differences she observes between women and men. She does not become engaged by nature/nurture theories nor biological/cultural explanations. She simply notes her experience and records it, making it available for whatever insight and usefulness it may have for readers.

What contemporary readers note is that, with respect to feminist questions of gender identity and gender ideology which have received widespread attention in our time, Day's views can serve to stimulate our thinking and to refine and give nuance to our own thought and decision on these matters. Feminist ethicist Mary Pellauer reminds us that although feminism insists upon a commitment to listening to women's experience with open ears, the substance of women's well-being is not necessarily known in advance.[14] It is precisely this effort to define women's well-being that gives rise to the diverse views and conflicting values we find among feminist voices. In itself, "feminism is not . . . a set of *a priori* answers, nor a commitment to a particular ideology. It is rather a willingness to follow questions wherever they lead us."[15] In this instance, questions of gender identity and gender ideology have led us to listen to one whose viewpoint on feminism was that of both critic and ally.

NOTES

1. Dorothy Day, *On Pilgrimage: The Sixties* (New York: Curtis Books, 1972), p. 362.

2. Patricia F. McNeal, *The American Catholic Peace Movement 1928-1972* (New York: Arno Press, 1978), p. 37.

3. Dorothy Day's books, in order of original publication, are listed below with the abbreviations used for textual citations: *The Eleventh Virgin* *[EV]* (New York: A. and C. Boni, 1924); *From Union Square to Rome [US]* (New York: Arno Press, 1978 reprint of the original 1938 edition); *House of Hospitality [HH]* (New York: Sheed and Ward, 1939); *On Pilgrimage [OP]* (New York: Catholic Worker Books, 1948); *The Long Loneliness: The Autobiography of Dorothy Day [LL]* (New York: Harper and Row, 1952); *Therese* (Notre Dame, IN: Fides, 1960); *Loaves and Fishes [LF]* (New York: Harper and Row, 1963); *Meditations [M]*, edited by Stanley Vishnewski (New York: Newman Press, 1970); *On Pilgrimage: The Sixties [OPS]* (see n. 1). An anthology of her writings is available in *By Little and By Little: The Selected Writings of Dorothy Day [BL]* edited by Robert Ellsberg (New York: Knopf, 1983).

William D. Miller, Day's biographer (*Dorothy Day: A Biography* [San Francisco: Harper and Row, 1982]), has made available much of Day's unpublished manuscript "All Is Grace" in *All Is Grace: The Spirituality of Dorothy Day [AIG]* (Garden City, NY: Doubleday, 1987). Robert Coles's conversations and tape-recorded interviews with Dorothy Day form the basis of *Dorothy Day: A Radical Devotion* (Reading, MA: Addison-Wesley, 1987). A complete listing of Dorothy Day's writings is available in Anne Klejment and Alice Klejment, *Dorothy Day and the Catholic Worker: A Bibliography and Index* (New York: Garland, 1986).

4. In *Anarchist Women 1870-1920* (Philadelphia: Temple University Press, 1981), p. 47, scholar Margaret Marsh offers a supporting judgment: "Feminism was not a set of specific beliefs and demands, despite the tendency of a later generation of scholars to subsume the whole movement into the drive for suffrage; it was a vast, complicated, and often contradictory movement."

5. Maurin's three-point program (round-table discussions, houses of hospitality, and agronomic universities) appeared in the second issue of *The Catholic Worker* 1/2 (June-July 1933). A more extensive presentation, where he speaks of the role of priests and bishops, appears in 1/5 (October 1933). A collection of Peter Maurin's *Easy Essays* (Chicago: Franciscan Herald Press, 1984) has been published with an introduction by Dorothy Day and a foreword by Eileen Egan.

6. The reader wonders in what way Day intends the phrase, "men's justice." Is this a generic use of the term, as in human justice? Or is it a gender use of the term as in male-expressed justice? The context of her comment, in which Day contrasts the two jail experiences as the collective vs. the solitary, and the supportive presence of the women vs. the humiliating treatment by men, renders the gender interpretation more likely.

7.   See Beverly Harrison, *Making the Connections: Essays in Feminist Social Ethics*, Carol S. Robb, ed. (Boston: Beacon, 1985); Rosemary Radford Ruether, *Sexism and God-Talk: Toward a Feminist Theology* (Boston: Beacon, 1983); and Sallie McFague, *Models of God: Theology for an Ecological, Nuclear Age* (Nashville, TN: Abingdon, 1987).

8.   "We are certainly not Marxist socialists, nor do we believe in violent revolution. Yet we do believe it is better to revolt, to fight, as Castro did with his handful of men, than to do nothing" (*OPS*, 301-02).

9.   Recognition of these differences in women's experiences is becoming a point of examination and self-critical reflection among feminists today. See, e.g., Cherrie Moraga and Gloria Anzaldua, eds., *This Bridge Called My Back: Writings by Radical Women of Color* (Watertown, MA: Persephone Press, 1981), Barbara Hilkert Andolsen, "*Daughters of Jefferson, Daughters of Bootblacks*": *Racism and American Feminism* (Macon, GA: Mercer University Press, 1986), and a forthcoming collection of selected papers from a February 1987 conference on gender, class, and race sponsored by the UCLA Center for the Study of Women, in *Women's Studies: An Interdisciplinary Journal*.

10.   Sally Cunneen and Debra Campbell highlight this direct-action feature of Dorothy Day's approach to change, namely that the primary creative responsibility for change lay in our own hands. Day felt that one should not look for permission or approval but should marshal one's energies personally to resist the giant injustices of the day. See Sally Cunneen, "Dorothy Day: The Storyteller as Human Model" (p. 292) and Debra Campbell, "The Catholic Earth Mother: Dorothy Day and Women's Power in the Church" (p. 276), *Cross Currents* 34/3 (Fall 1984).

David O'Brien's more generalized portrait of Personalism in America corroborates this interpretation of Day: "Perfectionist and unsystematic, focusing on the giver rather than the recipient, on the action itself rather than the social change that such action might bring about, personalism sought to realize love of neighbor through personal commitment and voluntary action. While others directed attention to legislation, organization, and institutional reconstruction, personalists concentrated on reforming themselves and changing society by the example of Christian love. . . . American personalism received its strongest support from sociologist Paul Henley Furfey, liturgist Virgil Michel, and the founders of the Catholic Worker movement." See *American Catholics and Social Reform: The New Deal Years* (New York: Oxford University Press, 1968), p. 185.

11.   In *Holding Their Own: American Women in the 1930s* [Boston: Twayne, 1982], p. 136, Susan Ware wonders why women on the left in the 1930s were not "fueled by feminist consciousness" in the way their counterparts were in the 1960s. The fruits of her thoughts are threefold: (1) that their participation in the radical movements of the 1930s might have allowed them more scope than the New Left allowed in the 1960s; (2) "that they were unwilling or unable to generalize from their own experiences to a full-scale critique of women's roles in society"; and (3) that their commitment to revolutionary socialism with an emphasis on economic solutions to address social

problems subsumed their hopes for a feminist vision (which they read, rightly or wrongly, as selfish, personal, and divorced from economic issues).

12. A summary of her work, in her own words, captures this focus on the common good: "There has been what Cardinal Newman would term a development of doctrine in the pages of *The Catholic Worker*, and we are still learning. But there has been a consistent theme throughout the thirty-six years, and it is that we must work for the common good, that men are responsible for each other, that God has a special love for the poor and the destitute, the insulted and the injured, and that where they are, we must be, too. We have been consistent in our pacifism and our endeavor to portray nonviolent means of bringing about a new social order. We have opposed the Japanese-Chinese War, the Ethiopian War, the Spanish Civil War, World War II, the Korean War, the Vietnam War, and can point with pride to the many editors of *The Catholic Worker* who have spent time in prison for their refusal to serve in the Vietnam War. We advocate the nonpayment of income tax and a life of voluntary poverty in order to have more to share with others." See "Dorothy Day Writes of the Catholic Worker" in Joseph R. Conlin, ed., *The American Radical Press 1880-1960* (London: Greenwood, 1974), 2: p. 468.

13. See, e.g., Charlene Spretnak, ed., *The Politics of Women's Spirituality: Essays on the Rise of Spiritual Power within the Feminist Movement* (Garden City, NY: Doubleday, 1982) and Daniel Maguire, "The Feminization of God and Ethics" (pp. 105-21) and "The Feminist Turn in Ethics" (pp. 122-29) in his *The Moral Revolution: A Christian Humanist Vision* (San Francisco: Harper and Row, 1986).

14. Mary Pellauer, "Moral Callousness and Moral Sensitivity" in Barbara H. Andolsen *et al.*, eds., *Women's Consciousness, Women's Conscience: A Reader in Feminist Ethics* (Minneapolis: Seabury/Winston, 1985), p. 34.

15. Ibid.

8

Spiritual Discernment in
The Dialogue of
Saint Catherine of Siena

Sandra M. Schneiders, I.H.M.*

ABSTRACT

This chapter is divided into two parts. The first deals with the subject of spiritual discernment in Christian tradition: its nature, importance in the spiritual life, and the aspects of the spiritual life on which it bears. The second part deals with Catherine of Siena's particular approach to the subject of discernment: an explanation of the three images she uses to illuminate the meaning and operation of discernment and an exploration of the theological sources of her teaching on this subject.

Although the term "spiritual discernment" or "spiritual discretion" (which Catherine of Siena prefers) is probably associated most readily with the Christian spiritual tradition, the reality which the term denotes has been a major concern of all religious traditions in which personal spiritual transformation is central.[1] The term "discern-

*Sandra M. Schneiders, I.H.M., is Professor of New Testament and Spirituality at the Jesuit School of Theology at Berkeley and the Graduate Theological Union (Berkeley, CA 94709). She received the S.T.L. from Institut Catholique, Paris, and the S.T.D. from the Gregorian University, Rome. She serves on the editorial boards of the *Catholic Biblical Quarterly* and of the Paulist "Classics of Western Spirituality." She has published many articles in reviews such as *Thought, Theological Studies, Biblical Theology Bulletin, Chicago Studies, Spirituality Today,* and *Horizons.* Her books include *The Revelatory Text: Interpreting the New Testament as Sacred Scripture* (San Francisco: Harper, 1991) and *Beyond Patching: Faith and Feminism in the Catholic Church* (New York: Paulist, 1991).

ment" refers both to a personal characteristic of the spiritually mature individual and to the process of using that virtue in concrete situations concerning oneself or others. Thus, we speak of a person of discernment and of the process of discerning.

In this chapter I will deal first with the topic of discernment in general within the Christian tradition,[2] what it is, why it is so important, to what it applies, and then discuss the particular approach to discernment manifest in Catherine of Siena's major work, *The Dialogue*.[3] For the purpose of clarity I am limiting myself to the more theoretical treatment of discernment in *The Dialogue*. However, anyone interested in the practice of discernment will find the letters of Catherine, which provide good examples of her use of discernment with her disciples,[4] extremely helpful.

I. SPIRITUAL DISCERNMENT
IN THE CHRISTIAN TRADITION

Discernment is a characteristic or virtue which grounds three distinguishable but intimately related activities. First, and basically, discernment is the ability to tell when something is not what it seems and secondly what the disputed phenomenon really means. The discerning person can tell, for example, when prayer is not genuine contact with God but a conversation with oneself, when apparent humility is actually a twisted form of pride; when a vision is really an hallucination and an ecstasy a psychosomatic disturbance; when inspirations are projections of suspect desires and when a vocation to celibacy is more a flight from intimacy than a call from God. Although it is relatively easy for a person with a certain amount of human and spiritual experience to recognize the falsity of certain interpretations of supposedly religious phenomena, it is much more difficult to arrive at a more true and adequate interpretation. Even greater spiritual wisdom is required for the third operation of discernment, discovering the appropriate response to the phenomenon once it has been correctly interpreted. Discernment, then, involves the evaluative judgment as to whether or not the phenomenon in question is really what it seems to be, the hermeneutical judgment by which the true meaning of the phenomenon is grasped, and the practical judgment about how to respond to it.

Discernment is crucial in the spiritual life because the realities of that life are, by definition, not open to empirical investigation and verification. More exactly, the phenomenal aspects of spiritual realities, the aspects which are amenable to empirical investigation, are not the aspects which are most important for growth and development in the person's life with God. One can, for example, observe that a person habitually gives way before the importunity of others. But there is no way to establish empirically if this behavior springs from genuine humility, cowardice in the face of opposition, passive aggression, or the natural good humor of someone who has an underdeveloped sense of the significance of most issues. If cowardice, or aggression, or immaturity is masquerading as humility the person's progress in the Christian life will be retarded until the lack of genuine humility is recognized and addressed.

Discernment, which is important in any spiritual tradition, takes on a special importance in the Christian tradition because for Christianity the primary locus of divine revelation, both public and personal, is history. This means that God communicates with human beings not exclusively, or even primarily, in direct mystical experience but in and through the ordinary persons and events of everyday life. According to Christian tradition, in other words, revelation is usually ambiguous because historical events can virtually always be interpreted in more than one way. Discernment is the ability to see the revelatory meaning in the ongoing process of one's own or another's life, to see, as the saints say, "with the eyes of faith" the salvific significance of what seem to be ordinary events.

Classically, discernment has a double object: God's action in a person's experience and the person's own response to that action. The question is twofold: to what is God inviting the person and how is the person to respond to that invitation? Consequently, the areas of the spiritual life within which discernment is critical are numerous. The most easily delineated area is that of vocation. Whether the call is to conversion in the more global sense or to the choice of a particular state of life such as marriage or religious life, the question is, on the one hand, whence the impulse and to what is one called, and on the other, how is one to respond?

In the second area, that of personal and social morality, discernment bears upon temptation, sin, and virtue.[5] To recognize temptation one must distinguish it on the one hand from harmless attraction and on the other from sin itself. One must learn to recognize sin for what it is and to distinguish *ersatz* virtue from the real thing. In the classical literature, discernment in this area is often discussed in terms of the influence of the devil and of the good angel in one's decision-making processes.[6] But it is not necessary to personify the sources of our attractions and repulsions in order to recognize that we experience both and that we are not always spontaneously attracted by the genuine good and repelled by real evil.

In a third area, the life of prayer, discernment is especially important and particularly difficult because the prayer process is almost totally intrapsychic. In the classical literature, the process of discernment in prayer is usually discussed in relationship to positive and negative feeling states which are variously called consolation and desolation, delight and dryness, comfort and disgust, and so on.[7] The problem is to discern whence the positive or negative feeling comes, what it signifies, and how one should respond. People experienced in the life of prayer realize that painful feelings can have a wide variety of meanings, e.g., they may be a healthy warning that one's moral or spiritual life is not what it should be, or a sign of progress in prayer, or a temptation, or a result of physical or psychic debility, or a form of interior purification. On the other hand, joyful feelings in prayer may be a gift from God, a product of self-delusion or immaturity, a sign of progress or regress, natural buoyancy, psychological denial of reality, or remote preparation for the increased suffering of interior purification. Discernment is particularly important in this area of prayer if one is not to be deluded into seeking oneself rather than God and so short circuiting the entire process. And, as the person advances from ordinary prayer, which processes are relatively easily articulated, into mystical prayer, in which the experience is truly ineffable, the problems become ever more difficult and delicate, especially if the person's experience involves not only growing interior union with God but such ambiguous experiences as visions, ecstasies, and raptures.[8] Finally, at all stages of the life of prayer one must discern the quality of the relationship between what is experienced actively and passively in formal prayer and what is happening in the person's ordinary life in its social, psychological, sexual, intellectual, moral, and ministerial dimensions.

This leads to another important area of the spiritual life in which discernment is needed, namely the active life of virtue and ministry. If the total life of the Christian is to be an active response to and service of God, one must learn to recognize God's invitation in the needs of one's neighbors, in the address of authority, and in those phenomena which are peculiar to one's own historical setting and which have been called "the signs of the times."[9] In all of these situations the Christian response is open to much ambiguity. In responding to the needs of one's neighbors, one must learn to avoid not only selfishness but also imprudent zeal, naivete, over-extension, and that short-sightedness and pusillanimity which would relieve symptoms while ignoring structures. In one's dealings with authority, one is confronted not only with the challenge to docility and obedience but also with problems of personal responsibility and the common good which might call one to resist authority or to confront superiors. And the complexities of discerning what really are "signs of the times" and what they mean in our personal and collective lives are too evident to need elaboration. It is particularly in this area of the active life that the conflict is most often not between good and evil but between good and better. Here, too, the classic delusion, evil appearing in the guise of good, is most common.[10] Beginners go to excess and become obstinate in their practice of austerities[11] and the more mature wear themselves out in excessive apostolic service.[12]

A final sphere of discernment, one particularly important to Catherine of Siena as we shall see, is that of "providence" or God's work in the world. Here the problem is not so much to understand what God is doing in one's own life and thus to what one is personally being called, but to understand how the turbulence, disorder, suffering, and chance evil which abound in our world can be reconciled with faith in a loving God. Only the person who can make some sense of the evil in the world, who can discern the hand of God in the overall scheme of things, can resist the temptation to despair and cynicism and continue to respond in faith, hope, and love to God's ongoing self-revelation. To find God in an imperfect world is a work of discernment, particularly as it grounds the act of interpretation in faith.

In summary, discernment is a transformation by faith of one's intelligence, imagination, and intuition enabling one to interpret correctly and respond rightly to God's revelatory initiative in all the areas of one's life and to find oneself within the overall salvific scheme operating in world history.

II. SPIRITUAL DISCERNMENT ACCORDING TO CATHERINE OF SIENA'S *DIALOGUE*

In the second part of this chapter I would like to explain, first, the three images Catherine uses to illuminate the meaning and operation of spiritual discernment. Secondly, I will attempt to show how this teaching about discernment is actually a function of certain major tenets of Catherine's theology, a theology heavily influenced by Thomism and decisively colored by the turbulent historical setting of Catherine's own life.

The presiding metaphor for discernment in *The Dialogue* is the complex and carefully elaborated image of the tree which is developed in chapters nine and ten.[13] God, the revealer in *The Dialogue*,[14] explains to Catherine that discernment is a small shoot which grows on the tree of charity whose marrow is patience. This tree is planted in the soil of humility and the branch of discernment bears the fruit of virtues which are plucked by the hand of free will and consumed by the soul. The soil of humility in which the tree of charity is rooted Catherine pictures as a circular plot which seems to be generated by its circumference. This circumference is the circular spiritual movement of knowledge of self and knowledge of God.

Let us begin our analysis with the circle which describes the ground of humility. Catherine insists repeatedly on the absolute necessity for the soul which would advance in the spiritual life to dwell in the "house" or the "cell" of self-knowledge.[15] Self-knowledge according to Catherine is not so much an intellectual act by which we grasp our sins and shortcomings as an abiding state of awareness of the ontological fact that, as creatures, we simply do not exist since we exist only by a continuing and non-necessary act of divine creation.[16] This is why self-knowledge must never be detached from an equally abiding knowledge of God as the one whose infinite love continuously calls us out of our nothingness into being. Catherine says that self-knowledge which is not in a constant dialectic with knowledge of God will produce a disastrous confusion in the soul,[17] the confusion of despair and self-hatred. Catherine's prayer to know herself and to know God is answered by the divine revelation that God is the one who is and Catherine is she who is not.[18] It is the experiential grasp of this creative dialectic which generates true humility, the sure foundation of the spiritual life.

As we will note later, Catherine's spirituality is characterized by a passionate love of truth.[19] For her, the foundational truth is precisely the allness of God and the nothingness of the creature. To dwell in this truth is what it means to be humble, for it is this truth which both prevents the person from appropriating to herself what is not hers and leads her to give what is due to God and to others.[20] The great enemy in the spiritual life, according to Catherine, is selfish self-centeredness, self-complacency, self-opinionatedness, selfish sensuality.[21] All these terms denote the same thing, namely the soul's departure from the foundation truth that God, not the human being, is the center and goal of the universe.

This humility is the only soil in which the tree of charity or divine love can grow. Charity is the ordered love of God, oneself, and one's neighbors. To love in reality, according to truth, one must value the other rightly and act accordingly. Therefore, the soul grounded in truth, the humble soul, will love God without measure, will love itself to the ultimate degree of never sinning, and will love all others even unto death.[22] This rightly ordered love is what produces the shoot of discretion or spiritual discernment which fills all the actions of the person with truth. Thus, the branch of discernment bears the fruit of virtue by which the soul expresses its ordered love. Although this has three objects, God, self, and neighbor, Catherine learns from God that love's expression is always directed toward the neighbor.[23] When Catherine wants to know how she can show her burning love for God, God replies, "Such is the means I have given you to practice and prove your virtue. The service you cannot render me you must do for your neighbor."[24] This is, of course, a purely evangelical insight corresponding to Christ's last judgment criterion in Mt 25, to the glorified Christ's question to the stricken Saul on the road to Damascus, to the injunctions in I John and the Epistle of James.[25] What is striking in Catherine's appropriation of this traditional Christian doctrine is her insistence on its exclusivity. Service to our neighbor is not one way of expressing our love of God; it is the only way.[26] Catherine insists that love which does not find expression in virtue is not love and that virtue which does not find expression in works of service toward our neighbor is not virtue.[27] She goes even further by insisting that all virtue, as well as all vice, is practiced only by means of our neighbors.[28] This is true even of the most interior and private acts of virtue and vice because these either strengthen or weaken the Christian community, drawing God's grace and blessing upon it and all its members or impeding that grace.[29]

Catherine mentions often that the "marrow" of the tree of love, the core of love, is patience.[30] This seems strange unless one remembers that love, for Catherine is not simply an affection or emotion. It is the right relation of the soul to God, self, and others. Impatience, says Catherine, arises when our will is thwarted. But if we dwelt in truth we would have no will other than to do God's will. In Catherine's view of divine providence, which we will examine later, everything that happens is somehow governed by God's will. Impatience is our reaction when we do not accept what is occurring, do not, in other words, discern God's will, design, and providence in the persons and events of our lives. Impatience manifests the fact that we have set ourselves up as autonomous judges of how things should be.[31] We have ceased to dwell in the truth of our own nothingness and God's all-sufficient being and providence. Consequently, there is no true love which is not filled and nourished with that union of the person's will with the will of God that expresses itself as patience. Patience, then, is the marrow or core of the tree of love which generates the branch of discernment which in turn bears the fruit of virtue.

By means of this presiding metaphor Catherine organizes her rich insight into the paradoxical simplicity and complexity of the spiritual life. She shows us how each of the essential elements is, in its own way, primary, and yet how they form together an organic whole in which each is dependent upon and finds meaning only in relation to the others. This unity of the spiritual life is a function of truth, namely grasping and being grasped by reality which is strictly identical with the God whom Catherine calls sweet First Truth.

Catherine's other two metaphors for discernment are less elaborate and relate only to certain aspects of discernment's place in the spiritual life as a whole. In chapter eleven she calls the virtue of discernment a knife "that kills and cuts off all selfish love to its foundation in self-will"[32] because when the soul comes to know herself she takes for herself only what is her due. By implication, she gives to God and neighbor also what is due to them.

We see in this image of the knife essentially the same doctrine of discernment under a different light. Discernment functions differently, Catherine tells us, at different stages in the spiritual life.[33] In the person still caught up in deadly sin, discernment activates the conscience. In the progressing but still imperfect soul, discernment illuminates the difference between temptation and sin and fosters the soul's growing ability to handle interior suffering and joy prudently.[34] In the perfect soul, discernment orders love so that it produces the fruit of virtue as we have already seen.

The image of discernment as a knife is more appropriate to the first two stages. The first task of discernment is to uproot the tree of self-love from the soil of pride so that the tree of love which can live only in the soil of humility can begin to grow.[35] The root of the tree of self-love is what the knife of discernment strikes, for discernment is actually loving truth in action. Discernment first cuts through the lie of self-sufficiency which makes the person choose her falsely autonomous self over God and neighbor. Then, in the succeeding stage, when the soul is initially established in the truth, the knife of discernment is used to prune away the falsity which is mingled with the truth. Discernment attacks the selfishness and self-will still present in the soul's practice of virtue. For example, Catherine repeatedly warns against a stubborn clinging to penitential practices when the claims of obedience, the needs of the neighbor, or common sense in the care of one's health make it clear that the penance should be left aside.[36] Discernment thus keeps the soul from making an end out of what should be means, i.e., from departing from the truth that love alone is ultimate.[37] In this second stage the knife of discernment also prunes away the selfishness which leads the soul to take pleasure in its own spiritual perfection rather than in God or to overestimate the purity of its love for God.[38] The image of the knife, in short, puts the emphasis on the distinguishing quality of discernment, its function in separating the real from the apparent and the good from the better.

Catherine's third image for discernment is that of light.[39] Discernment is a light which is born of charity and which enlightens charity. Love which is grounded in the truth of who we are and who God is gives birth to a light in which the soul sees and judges rightly what is due to God, self, and neighbor. And this light then illuminates the practice of love, setting it in order, so that the soul actually loves God without measure, itself to the extent of banishing all sin from its life, and its neighbor even unto death if this is required for the other's salvation.[40] The image of light places the emphasis on the illuminating quality of discernment. At each stage of the spiritual life this light is in proportion to the love operative in the person's life. At first it barely reveals the difference between truth and lie, sin and virtue. In the next stage it enables the person to make finer distinctions between ends and means, acts and the virtue which grounds them, good and better. In the perfect soul the light of discernment illuminates the whole of the spiritual life making it resplendent with the beauty of unalloyed truth.

Let us now turn from Catherine's own treatment of discernment to an examination of the relationship of this doctrine to her central theological concerns. This examination will also show how Catherine's teaching deals with each of the four major areas of discernment which were discussed in part one: the interior life, morality, exterior action, and divine providence.

The influences on Catherine's theology have long been debated.[41] I do not wish to enter into that debate except to say that two of the most evident influences are the scholastic theology of Thomas Aquinas which she imbibed from her Dominican ambiance, and the spiritual exegesis of Scripture which she seems to have imbibed from liturgical preaching and spiritual reading. These two influences, particularly the first, are most evident in the theological foundations of her teaching on discernment.

As we have already noted, the keystone of Catherine's spirituality is her passionate love of truth. She habitually calls God "gentle First Truth" or "Eternal Truth" and God the Father refers to the Son as "my truth."[42] Thus, the essence of the spiritual life is the full appropriation of God as Truth. God is Truth because God alone is being.[43] The human person enters into the truth to the extent that he or she grasps experientially that God alone is. The greater obstacle to experiencing the ontological allness of God is the illusion the creature has and promotes that he or she has an autonomous existence. In Catherine's terminology this is self-centeredness, self-love, the existential untruth which fills the soul with darkness and poisons the tree of the spiritual life at its root making even the soul's virtues rotten.[44] Discernment, as it bears on the interior life, is experienced ontological truth in operation and that is why Catherine says that the healthy spiritual life begins in the humility generated by reciprocal self-knowledge and knowledge of God and that the tree of love rooted in this humility can alone produce the branch of discernment which will bear the fruit of authentic virtue.

A second major tenet of Catherine's theology, again immediately recognizable as a Thomistic element,[45] is her doctrine of the virtues which affects her teaching on discernment as it applies to the moral life. Catherine insists on the unity of the virtues whose form is charity, and on the necessity of virtue's self-expression in action. On the one hand, acts are never to be confused with virtue. Acts are virtue only to the extent that they are informed by love.[46] Consequently, discernment must not only distinguish the acts which are means from the end which is love but also know when an act is to be done and when dropped in favor of another which is demanded by love. On the other hand, virtue which does not come to birth in action, according to Catherine, is stillborn and inauthentic.[47] This is why Catherine insists on the fact that virtue does not really exist until it is tried by its opposite[48] and thereby called into operation. Discernment not only makes clear what is the proper response in the face of provocation and temptation but also distinguishes *ersatz* virtue, which operates only when unopposed, from genuine virtue, which shines forth precisely when challenged. Meekness appears when we are abused; chastity surfaces in the face of seduction, and so on. But the touchstone of all the virtues is patience which manifests the soul's full identification with God's will precisely when that will runs counter to the soul's selfish designs.

A third major tenet of Catherine's theology which affects her teaching on discernment especially in relation to the life of action is her teaching that all good and evil are done through our neighbor.[49] No doubt Catherine's historical situation[50] as well as her own spiritual history influenced her radicalization of this Gospel teaching. Catherine lived in the fourteenth century (1347-1380) when the Black Death generated such overwhelming human misery that no one could avoid the incessant cry of the suffering poor for immediate aid. She also lived at a time when the Church, divided by the Avignon papacy, was in seeming ruins and the political situation was explosive. Catherine spent the first three years of her adult spiritual life (1365-1368), from age eighteen to twenty-one, in virtual solitude. There she experienced extraordinary mystical graces to which she became attached. Her own formation in discernment was effected by Christ himself who drove her from her solitude and its consolations into a life of incessant activity serving the poor and the sick, lobbying the political powers for peace, and challenging a vacillating pope to reform the Church. It was in the crucible of action that Catherine's own virtues were tested and that she learned the importance of discernment if one's action was not to be vitiated by imprudence and selfishness. Here also she learned the practical process of discerning. Catherine lived well before the sixteenth century with its fascination with method, technique, and rules in the spiritual life. She offers us no "rules for spiritual discernment." But she does share the fruits of her concrete experience by alerting us to certain observable manifestations of genuine spirituality.

In one particularly beautiful passage,[51] she tells us that when a person is in the second stage of the spiritual life, that of the imperfect but progressing soul, the quality of one's love for God can be discerned by examining the quality of one's love for a special spiritual friend. If jealousy and selfishness mark the human relationship one can be certain that one's love of God is also imperfect because real spiritual friendship is based on and is an expression of love of God.

In the perfect soul there are other indications that can be observed. Catherine notes that compassion for those who abuse one is a certain manifestation of divine love. On the other hand, growing impatience over small frustrations can manifest the real lack of virtue in a person whose patience in the face of great trials seems a proof of mature virtue. How a person deals with the "thorn in the flesh," the human imperfections which one cannot overcome in oneself, is another touchstone for discerning the maturity of one's spiritual life.[52]

We note immediately that Catherine proposes always our relationship with others rather than our interior states of soul as the locus of discernment. She explicitly states that all virtue and all vice are practiced through our neighbor. Even the most interior acts affect others in the community of the church and the world and it is precisely because they do that they are virtue or vice. The externality and relationality of Catherine's teaching on virtue lend a realism and practicality to her mysticism which is especially relevant today. The litmus test of mysticism is prophecy, action in the world. But this action must be constantly tested for its mystical root and content by a spiritual discernment, the locus of which is not one's personal prayer life but one's concrete relationship with others.

The fourth and final tenet of Catherine's theology which bears directly on her teaching about discernment is her belief in providence.[53] She was convinced that, in some mysterious way, God was infallibly directing history and individuals according to his love. Given

Catherine's historical context it is not hard to see why this conviction
was so important to her. External evidence suggested that the only reasonable attitude was utter despair. The world, the church, her religious order were in shambles, and everything was getting steadily
worse. For Catherine a major spiritual challenge was to believe in a
good God in the face of overwhelming evidence to the contrary. She
saw this as a problem of spiritual discernment, of seeing in what was
happening to herself, to others, to the church, to the world, something
other than the evil which appeared. The challenge was to see God's
will, God's loving design, in what appeared to be chaos. We get a
glimpse into Catherine's own struggle in those attitudes she claims are
signs that the soul has truly discerned God's will in history, namely
patience, resistance to scandal, and reverence.[54]

Patience, for Catherine, was the expression of obedience, i.e., of
full identity with the will of God. As long as one wants things other
than they are one feels thwarted and is therefore impatient. The person who sees God's will in events and identifies with that will does
not become impatient. This in no way suggests a passive indifference
to evil or an apathetic abandonment to the *status quo*. Catherine struggled with the sickness and death and poverty around her, denounced
corruption in the church, badgered popes and politic leaders, struggled in every way to overcome the evil in her world. But she saw the
supreme importance in doing so in the firm confidence that God was
finally in charge, that evil did not have the last word. For her, patience, even in the midst of fierce struggle, was the sign that one's faith
rested in God, not in oneself, and that one ultimately trusted God's
power for good despite the apparent supremacy of evil.

Closely related to this patience was another sign that one had
truly discerned God's presence and action even in apparently godless
situations. This was the refusal to take scandal at God, oneself, or
one's neighbor. The person who is scandalized has accepted that
things are as they seem, namely completely evil. The experienced soul
knows that even the most evil actions or events can be used by God
for good, that no evil is totally beyond the reach of grace. Therefore,
the ultimate moral shock, what we call scandal, does not touch the
truly discerning soul.

Finally, reverence for all things manifests the presence of discernment in the soul. Only the person who sees God at work every-
where, even in the most unlikely persons, places, and events, is
moved to that continual reverence which is the proper attitude in the
face of the divine presence and activity.

The Dialogue of Catherine of Siena is strewn with beautiful and
insightful remarks about discernment which have found no place in

this treatment. I have attempted to systematize her teaching in order to manifest its unity, coherence, and completeness but in so doing have necessarily passed over much wealth and beauty. My hope is that what I have presented will whet readers' appetite for what I have not presented and lead them to read *The Dialogue* itself and savor the wisdom of this great woman, discerning spiritual guide, and doctor of the church.

NOTES

1. An excellent source book on spiritual direction, including the approach to discernment, in various historical and cultural settings and among a variety of world religions is J. T. McNeill, *A History of the Cure of Souls* (San Francisco: Harper & Row, 1977), first published in 1951.

2. For a history of discernment within the Christian tradition see *Discernment of Spirits*, ed. E. Malatesta, tr. I. Richards (Collegeville, MN: Liturgical Press, 1970) which is an English translation of the article "Discernements des esprits" in the *Dictionnaire de Spiritualité Ascétique et Mystique*, Vol. III (Paris: Beauchesne, 1957), cols. 1222-91. A briefer, but more readable, treatment can be found in K. Leech, *Soul Friend: The Practice of Christian Spirituality* (San Francisco: Harper & Row, 1977), pp. 34-89.

3. Catherine of Siena, *The Dialogue*, tr. and introd. S. Noffke, *The Classics of Western Spirituality* (New York: Paulist, 1980) is an excellent new translation with a fine introduction to Catherine and her work. Hereafter, this volume will be cited as Noffke with page reference.

4. It is interesting to see, for example, how clearly Catherine's teaching on discernment in her letter on discretion to Sister Daniella of Orvieto (let. CCXIII) parallels the teaching Catherine receives from God in *The Dialogue*, 9 and 10 (see Noffke, pp. 39-45). For Catherine's letter, see *Le lettere di s. Caterina da Siena*, P. Misciatelli, ed. (Florence: G. Barbéra, 1860) 4 vol.

5. A good example of a classical treatment of discernment in the area of morality is *The Cloud of Unknowing*, tr. C. Wolters (Baltimore: Penguin, 1961), pp. 65-68, i.e., chapters 9-11.

6. The best known treatment of good and evil spirits is probably the "Rules for the Discernment of Spirits" in *The Spiritual Exercises* of St. Ignatius of Loyola. A good English edition is *The Spiritual Exercises*, tr. T. Corbishley (Wheathampstead, Hertfordshire: Anthony Clarke Books, 1963), pp. 107-14.

7. Two particularly valuable treatments of positive and negative feeling states in prayer and how their significance is to be judged are Julian of Norwich, *Showings*, tr. and introd. E. Colledge and J. Walsh, *Classics of Western Spirituality* (New York: Paulist, 1978), pp. 204-205, i.e., "The Seventh Revelation," chapter 15, in the long text; and Teresa of Avila, *The Interior Castle*, tr. K. Kavanaugh and O. Rodriguez, *The Classics of Western Spirituality* (New York: Paulist, 1979), pp. 67-84, i.e., "The Fourth Dwelling Place."

8.   One of the best records of the problems of discernment in prayer encountered as the soul progresses from ordinary to mystical prayer is *The Life of Teresa of Jesus: The Autobiography of St. Teresa of Avila*, tr. and ed. E. A. Peers (Garden City, NY: Doubleday Image, 1960). A very valuable source for those who face problems of discernment in the area of prayer is John of the Cross' *Dark Night of the Soul*, tr., ed., and introd. E. A. Peers, 3rd rev. ed. (Garden City, NY: Doubleday Image, 1959).

9.   As will be clear in Part II, Catherine of Siena devotes special attention to the problems of discernment in the active life.

10.   Ignatius of Loyola treats of this in his Rules for Discernment for those who are advancing from good to better.

11.   This temptation to excessive attachment to penance was one Catherine of Siena knew from personal experience; therefore she gives copious advice on the subject in both *The Dialogue* and the letters.

12.   Particular attention is being given to this problem of the spiritual life of our own times. In the last few years an increasing number of articles have appeared on the subject of apostolic "burn-out." See, e.g., M. Oliva, "Burnout," *Ministries* 1 (May-June 1980), pp. 23, 26-27.

13.   Noffke, pp. 39-42. See also Let. CCXIII in which Catherine develops the same image, adding the detail of the "hand of free will" that plucks the virtues which the soul consumes.

14.   In *The Dialogue* God the Father is presented as the speaker but since Catherine is author of the book I usually refer to the teaching as Catherine's.

15.   See, e.g., *Dialogue* 1 and 63 and elsewhere (Noffke, pp. 25, 118).

16.   *Dialogue* 4 (Noffke, p. 29); 155 (Noffke, p. 330).

17.   *Dialogue* 10 (Noffke, p. 42).

18.   See *Dialogue* 9 (Noffke, p. 40). See also *The Life of Catherine of Siena* by Raymond of Capua, trans., introd., and annot. by C. Kearns (Wilmington, DE: Glazier, 1980) Part 1, ch. X, no, 92, p. 85.

19.   See Noffke, "Introduction," pp. 8-9.

20.   *Dialogue* 9 (Noffke, p. 41).

21.   See, e.g., *Dialogue*, 137-39 (Noffke, pp. 282-86) and 147 (Noffke, p. 311).

22.   *Dialogue* 11 (Noffke, pp. 43-45).

23.   See, e.g., *Dialogue* 6 (Noffke, p. 33); 6 (Noffke, p. 35); 7 (Noffke, p. 35) and elsewhere.

24.   *Dialogue* 7 (Noffke, p. 36).

25.   See Mt 25:31-46; Acts 9:4-5; I Jn 2:7-11; 3:14-18; James 1:27; 2:14-19.

26.   *Dialogue* 6 (Noffke, p. 33).

27.   E.g., *Dialogue* 7 (Noffke, p. 36); 11 (Noffke, p. 45) and elsewhere.

28.   *Dialogue* 6 (Noffke, p. 33); 145 (Noffke, p. 304).

29.   *Dialogue* 6 (Noffke, pp. 33-34) and elsewhere.

30.   E.g., *Dialogue* 128 (Noffke, p. 252).

31.   E.g., *Dialogue* 141 (Noffke, pp. 289-93).

32.   E.g., *Dialogue* 155 (Noffke, p. 331); 156 (Noffke, p. 333).

33.   *Dialogue* 11 (Noffke, p. 43).

34.   Cf. *Dialogue* 144-45 (Noffke, pp. 299-307).

35. *Dialogue* 93 (Noffke, pp. 171-74).

36. *Dialogue* 9 (Noffke, p. 40); 11 (Noffke, pp. 42-44); Let. CCXIII.

37. *Dialogue* 11 (Noffke, p. 43).

38. *Dialogue* 144 (Noffke, pp. 301-303); 9 (Noffke, p. 41).

39. *Dialogue* 11 (Noffke, pp. 44-45).

40. *Dialogue* 11 (Noffke, p. 44).

41. See the summary by Noffke, "Introduction," pp. 9-11.

42. See, e.g., *Dialogue* 3 (Noffke, p. 28); 12 (Noffke, p. 45); 27 (Noffke, p. 67); 108 (Noffke, p. 202) and elsewhere.

43. This is a clear case of the influence of Thomas Aquinas on Catherine. See, e.g., *Summa Contra Gentiles* I, pp. 60-61.

44. *Dialogue* 161 (Noffke, p. 349).

45. See *Summa Theologiae* I-II, q. 65, arts. 1-5.

46. On the unity of the virtues, see *Dialogue* 7 (Noffke, pp. 37-38). On charity as form of all the virtues *Dialogue* 11 (Noffke, pp. 42-45).

47. *Dialogue* 7 (Noffke, p. 36); 11 (Noffke, p. 45) and elsewhere.

48. *Dialogue* 8 (Noffke, pp. 38-39); 11 (Noffke, p. 45); 145 (Noffke, p. 303) and elsewhere.

49. See note 28 above.

50. See Noffke, "Introduction," pp. 3-7.

51. *Dialogue* 144 (Noffke, pp. 302-303).

52. *Dialogue* 145 (Noffke, pp. 303-307).

53. Chapters 135-153 of *The Dialogue* are devoted to this subject. Again, the influence of Thomas is evident. See, e.g., *Summa Contra Gentiles* III.

54. *Dialogue* 137 (Noffke, p. 283); 141 (Noffke, p. 292).

9

The Mystical Vision of Simone Weil in Relationship to Roman Catholicism

F. Ellen Weaver*

ABSTRACT

Simone Weil was a mystic obsessed with the search for absolutes and with a holistic vision of the world. At the same time she was deeply concerned about the plight of the outcasts of society. This concern rooted her mysticism in reality and, like the biblical prophets, she decried societal abuses. She saw the church as larger than the institution she was invited to enter through baptism. Her refusal to enter symbolically united her with the members of "common humanity" who were excluded from the institutional church. This mystical vision was prophetic of the church of Vatican II.

Heureux ceux pour qui le malheur entré dans la chair est le malheur du monde lui-même à leur époque. Ceux-la ont la possibilité et la fonction de connaitre dans sa vérité , de contempler dans sa réalité le malheur du monde. C'est là la fonction rédemptrice elle même.

—Lettre à Joë Bousquet

*F. Ellen Weaver earned her Ph.D. at Princeton University in the History of Christianity with emphases on Liturgies, History of Spirituality in the West, and Jansenism in Early Modern France. She has published a book, *The Evolution of the Reform of Port-Royal: From the Role of Citeaux to Jansenism* (Paris, 1978) and numerous articles on spirituality, counter-reformation in France, and the neo-gallican liturgies. She is retired from the Department of Theology at the University of Notre Dame (Notre Dame, IN 46556), where she taught liturgical studies and historical theology, and now lives in Paris.

"Fortunate are those for whom the affliction which enters their flesh is the very affliction of the world itself in their time. They have the opportunity and the function of knowing the truth of the world's affliction and contemplating its reality. That is the redemptive function itself."[1] In these words Simone Weil, Jewess and philosopher, has captured the theological principle of incarnational redemption in a remarkable synthesis. Christian theology over the centuries has explored the meaning of the article of faith that declares: Christ died for our sins that we might live for God in Christ. Theologians have also sought to understand and explain how the redemptive suffering and death of Jesus continues through the ages in the person of the Christian. Through her power of vision Weil has grasped this foundational principle of Christianity and has translated it in the real life of a friend.

Simone Weil wrote these words to Joë Bousquet in 1942, about a year before her death. In the midst of the second world war she wrote to this man who was permanently paralyzed as a result of a wound in the first world war, assuring him that his affliction was a privilege: the privilege of vision through identity. Since Joë was a profoundly Christian man, he would have understood her allusion to the cross as a similar—as the paradigm—experience. She continued: "Twenty centuries ago in the Roman Empire, slavery was the affliction of the age, and crucifixion was its extreme expression."[2] She had prepared him to enter into the mystical significance of her words by her comments on his "privilege":

> You are specially privileged in that the present state of the world is a reality for you. Perhaps even more so than for those who at this moment are killing and dying, wounding and being wounded, because they are taken unawares. . . . But you, on the other hand, for twenty years you have been repeating in thought the destiny which seized and then released so many men, but which seized you permanently. . . . You are now really equipped to think it . . . you have at least only a thin shell to break before emerging from the darkness inside the egg into the light of truth. It is a very ancient image. The egg is this world we see. The bird in it is Love, the Love which is God himself and which lives in the depths of every man, though at first as an invisible seed. When the shell is broken and the being is released, it still has this same world before it. But it is no longer inside. Space is opened and torn apart. The spirit, leaving the miserable body in some corner, is transported to a point outside space, which is not a point of view, which has no perspective, but from which this world is seen as it is, unconfused by perspective. Compared to what is inside the egg, space has become an infinity to the second

or even third power. The moment stands still. The whole of space is filled, even though sounds can be heard, with a dense silence which is not an absence of sound, but is a positive object of sensation; it is the secret word, the word of Love who holds us in his arms from the beginning.[3]

This remarkable letter catches the essence of Simone Weil's mysticism: the two poles are affliction and love; the goal is knowledge, the way is attention,[4] and experiencing through identity.

It is as a mystic that I seek to understand Simone Weil: her thought and her curious relationship to Roman Catholicism. The facts of that relationship are well known: her long attraction to Catholicism, her mystical experience of encounter with Christ, her dialogue with the Church through meeting and writing to Catholic friends and teachers, her desire for eucharistic communion, and her adamant refusal to be baptized. The response to Weil from within Roman Catholicism has never been indifferent. For some she is, in Georges Hourdin's words, "prophet and witness of the absolute at the same time."[5] For others like Charles Moeller, "Simone Weil's thought, a new Catharism, is one of the gravest dangers which can attack Christian consciences."[6] Approaching her as a mystic goes a long way towards understanding both her "flirtation" with the Church, and the contradictory responses of its members to her life and thought.

I. THE CATHOLIC MILIEU OF SIMONE WEIL

Before demonstrating how this key may work, it will help to sketch briefly the Catholicism of her time, and the place of mystics and mysticism in the church. It will then be possible to examine her mystical vision with its emphasis on identification with the oppressed, and how this excluded her from the church in her own conscience. Finally, this perception of Weil as a mystic makes it easier to see how she fits into the history and consciousness of the church.

Simone Weil was born and educated as a Parisian of the upper middle class, a bourgeoise. She was born into a Jewish family of free thinkers, and has stated that since she simply did not think one could know anything about God she did not consider belief or unbelief as a personal option. However, she had friends and contacts in Catholicism. Through them, as well as through the schools in which she received her early education, she came to know a great deal about the doctrine and ethos of Catholicism. It is important to know that this Catholicism with which she came in contact was that of the French bourgeoisie and some classical sources like Pascal, which she read in school. What were some of the characteristics of that Catholicism?

In the early twentieth century the Roman Catholic Church was still a "post-tridentine" church with all that implies of defensiveness toward anything outside Roman Catholicism, and heavy stress on dogmatic teaching. Simone Weil's Catholic friends would have learned their catechism by heart and would have been formidably prepared to give an apologia of their faith. It was also a period of renewal in intellectual Catholic circles, and she would have met many Catholics of serious and informed piety. French Catholicism, especially in the bourgeois circles, was still influenced by Jansenism. It was a Catholicism where moral rigor was combined with a profound awe of the exalted holiness of the sacraments. These tendencies were concretized in the legalism of the *anathama sit*, which became such a powerful symbol of exclusion for Weil, especially in the papal condemnations of "modernism" which extended this exclusion to so much of what she admired.

On the more positive side, there was a revival of Thomism in France which offered an intellectual, deep, and absolutist presentation of the faith which attracted Weil and at the same time placed seemingly insurmountable obstacles in her way. It was also the period when the liturgical movement was still dominated by the romantic, neo-gothic, and monastic style of Dom Guéranger, who founded the Benedictine monastery of Solesmes in the previous century. Weil visited Solesmes with her mother to enjoy the aesthetic experience of hearing the Gregorian chant by monks whose lives were dedicated to its perfection in a setting of ceremonial magnificence. Here she was most strongly drawn to Catholicism, and had one of her most profound mystical experiences.[7]

This, then, was the Catholicism Simone Weil, the philosopher and free thinker, encountered. No wonder she was both attracted and alienated. It was pre-ecumenism, prebiblical renewal, prepatristic renewal. In all of these later movements Weil would have found greater acceptance of herself, and of some of her views of Christianity.

II. WEIL'S MYSTICISM: THE GNOSTIC ELEMENT

It is interesting to realize that within the church, during the same period, there was a young Jesuit priest whose life and work parallels Weil's in some regards. Teilhard de Chardin also had a mystical vision of Christianity, and for it his works were suspect and repressed until after his death in 1955. In one of his early writings Teilhard defines mystical vision and the mystic. It is a definition which describes well the mysticism of Simone Weil:

> The real incessantly reawakens us to an impassioned awareness of a wider expansion and an all embracing unity. It is in the arousing of this restless yearning that the hallowed function of sense-perception finds its consummation. . . . But this [sense-perception of external reality] is merely the surface of the mystery of knowledge; the deeper truth is that when the world reveals itself to us it draws us into itself: it causes us to flow outward into something belonging to it, everywhere present in it, and more perfect than it. The man . . . whose sole interest is in the outward appearance of things seldom gains more than a glimpse, at best, of this second phase in our perceptions, that in which the world, having entered into us, then withdraws from us and bears us away with it: he can have only a very dim awareness of that aureole, thrilling and inundating our being, through which is disclosed to us at every point of contact the unique essence of the universe. *The mystic is the man who is born to give first place in his experience to that aureole.* The mystic only gradually becomes aware of the faculty he has been given of perceiving the indefinite fringe of reality surrounding the totality of all created things, with more intensity than the precise, individual core of their being.[8]

Teilhard's mention of the "mystery of knowledge" points to the gnostic element in mysticism. For the intellectual, I suspect, mystical experience will usually be understood as access to deeper perception of reality, to that "secret knowledge" which gives *Gnosticism* its name. Perhaps this is why Christianity, with its emphasis on universal accessibility of the gospel, has always been suspicious of mystics and of Gnosticism. Yet there has been a mystical element, even a gnostic element, in Christianity throughout its history from its very beginnings.

There is an orthodox Gnosticism in Christian theology, although the West lost sight of it. The Eastern fathers theologize about Christ as Logos, the Divine Word who reveals the secret of God. The Gospel of John and much of the Pauline writings speak of salvation through knowledge—even secret knowledge: the mystery hidden from all ages now made known in Jesus Christ. Eternal life, in John's Gospel, is "to *know* God and to *know* him who was sent, Jesus Christ."

Although Christian spirituality in the Latin West, and to some extent theology, came to emphasize will more than intellect—loving more than knowing God—the tradition of Greek theology never died. Its mode of contemplative expression was the "way of unknowing" in order to come to union with the source of all knowledge. Pseudo-Dionysius (fifth century) and Meister Eckhart (fourteenth century) and John of the Cross (sixteenth century), whom Simone Weil read and admired, are in this tradition.

Toward the great mystics the church has been ambiguous. Some of the propositions of Meister Eckhart were condemned. Nicholas of Cusa, whose "reconciliation of opposites" would have made perfect sense to Weil, was never quite accepted. Yet their writings are treasured classics of Christian literature, and the church has often admitted, although sometimes long after the fact, that their vision was prophetic. Thus, responding to mystics within the fold, the church has recognized them as special and gifted and sometimes acknowledged them as prophets. At the same time, they have often been suspected, even persecuted (John of the Cross wrote some of his most inspired mystical poetry while imprisoned by members of his own Carmelite community), and now and then condemned as heretical. How could the attitude toward Simone Weil not be ambiguous?

I would now like to explore the question from the other direction in the form of the thesis that Simone Weil's mystical vision combined with the central concern of her life for identification with the oppressed, the afflicted, to affect her view of all existence, and in the end "excluded" her from the church.

First, I am convinced that Simone Weil was a true mystic of the apophatic type as defined above. The passage quoted earlier about the egg of the world is highly significant. Weil used similar words to describe her experiences in her spiritual biography. At Solesmes she says she was able

> . . . to rise above this wretched flesh, to leave it to suffer by itself, heaped up in a corner, and to find a pure and perfect joy in the unimaginable beauty of the chanting and the words. This experience enabled me by analogy to get a better understanding of the possibility of loving divine love in the midst of affliction.[9]

In describing what she experienced, whenever she recited the *Pater* in Greek, during the period of her work in the vineyards of Southern France, she says:

> The very first words tear my thoughts from my body and transport it to a place outside space where there is neither perspective nor point of view. . . . There is silence which is not an absence of sound but which is the object of a positive sensation, more positive than that of sound. Noises if there are any only reach me after crossing the silence.[10]

This was the full blossom of the seed of mystical vision which she always bore within. Some would consider her mystical life began with the experience of Christ's visit after Solesmes in 1938-39.[11] Extending the definition of "mystic" to include, in the sense of the definition of Teilhard de Chardin, all those with the ability to see beneath the surface of things an abiding reality, and accepting Weil's own witness to her intense love of and quest for truth from a very early age, I believe that she was always a mystic, and that her gift of vision illumined all her experiences. As a young student she was a mystic in the platonic sense: the philosopher for whom the ultimate knowledge is gained through contemplation. Some signs are her intense desire for intellectual honesty and, especially, her practice from the age of fourteen of concentrated *attention* in the quest of knowledge.[12] In reference to her envy of her brother's brilliant intellectual achievement, she spoke of her grief at being excluded from "that transcendent kingdom to which only the truly great have access and wherein truth abides."[13] She continues:

> I suddenly had the everlasting conviction that any human being even though practically devoid of natural facilities, can penetrate to the kingdom of truth reserved for genius, if only he longs for truth and perpetually concentrates all his attention upon its attainment.[14]

This concentrated attention, and the techniques she developed to maintain it, are very similar to the practice of contemplation in Christianity. Even incidents that strike the unprepared reader as bizarre— e.g., the self-inflicted cigarette burns—may have been tests of concentration, of "mind over matter," to which she subjected herself. As such they are not very different from the ascetic feats described in the lives of some of the desert monks. The heavy work and the meager diet she imposed on her frail constitution also served as an ascetic training for mystical vision.

Weil states that she never sought God, and was thus surprised to encounter the loving presence she recognized as Christ. Yet she did seek with all her being platonic Truth, Good, Beauty. Neo-Thomistic theology comes close to identifying the Good of Greek philosophy and the God of Christianity, and it is possible that she had read some of the writings of the French theologians of her era.

This, however, is conjecture. What is certain is that when Simone Weil writes of her admiration of Catholicism, all of the early experiences of it which she recounts share a mystical quality. Following her factory experience in Paris, during the period in Portugal (1935-36), she tells of how, listening to the songs of the peasants in the fishing village, she had the sudden perception of Catholicism as the "religion of slaves."[15] At Assisi, after one of the rare joyful moments recounted in her autobiography, when she had indulged her deep appreciation of beauty in her Italian tour, she speaks of being overcome and "forced" to her knees.[16] At Solesmes, through liturgy and art—Beauty—she describes an "out of the body" experience.[17] The coming(s) of Christ, and the raptures associated with the recitation of the *Pater*, developed out of her practice of *attention*. The lines from platonic contemplating to these mystical experiences are clear.

III. WEIL'S MYSTICISM:
IDENTIFICATION WITH THE OPPRESSED

But it is the other element of Simone Weil's mysticism that roots it in reality, makes it truly prophetic and significant, and, incidentally, makes it a moral impossibility for her to join the Catholic Church. That is her identification with the oppressed. The collection entitled *La Condition Ouvrière* is exceptionally revealing of the mystical significance of this lifelong obsession. In her letter to Joë Bousquet, Weil said "Blessed are they for whom the affliction which enters their flesh is the very affliction of the world itself in their time." This suggests the mystical significance that such identification had for her. The *Condition Ouvrière* delineates it. We know that Weil shifted from a position as a radical Marxist to a critic of Marxism. Her major criticism was that Marxism was itself as much an opiate of the people as religion. "The name 'opium of the people' which Marx applies to religion can apply to it when it betrays itself, but it applies essentially to the revolution. The hope of the revolution is always a tranquilizer."[18] In the end, she concludes, Marxism substitutes the imperialism of the worker for national imperialism. What she deeply objected to was the domination of collectivity over humanity as a whole, over human life in all its aspects. Parenthetically, this is probably the basis for much of her objection to the church. For Weil the ultimate value is individual freedom. By that she means freedom of the *mind* through obedience to God (necessity), and she thinks all other freedom is illusory.

Weil's concern for the plight of the proletariat, combined with her obsession for intellectual honesty, dictated that she could truly know their problem by entering into it. Thus, in 1934-35 she took a leave of absence from her teaching and took a job in a factory in the Paris region. The *Condition Ouvrière* contains her factory journal, the record of her personal experience. It was an experience which, she says, branded her as a slave forever. (Hence, the sense of identification with Catholicism when she recognized it as "a religion of slaves.") She experienced the full degradation of the life of the worker in the era before social reforms. Although she tells us that she felt herself reduced to animal state—a suffering, hungering body—yet she was able to transcend that condition at least to the degree of keeping a journal.

In 1941, in Marseilles, at a period when she had entered into a state of continual mystical union, she wrote a reflection on the experience which is one of her finest essays, "Condition première d'un travail non servile." It is here that we see the intersection of her vision and her concern. Her theme is "the point of unity between intellectual and manual work is contemplation," and she carefully lays down the conditions under which manual labor can become a life of union with God. This can be done, she says, only through the transformation of the very objects of work into symbols of God. Imposing symbols from without—pictures of saints, prayers to say while working—will not accomplish the transcendence of the condition of the worker. The tools, the furnaces, the fixtures of the factory must be seen as symbols of the eternal in time, the divine presence. She is calling for the kind of mystical vision which enabled her to recognize this "aureole" (in the sense of Teilhard de Chardin). On a more practical level she calls for the kind of reforms which will respect the human dignity of the worker.

It is not the task of this essay to comment on the value of Simone Weil's program for transforming the condition of the worker.[19] It is time to return to the topic under consideration and to examine how Weil's mystical vision and her mystical identification with the oppressed excluded her from the church. Let us enter, if we can, Weil's perception of the church.

IV. WEIL'S MYSTICAL VISION AND THE CHURCH

Her mystical vision gives her a view of the whole—the view from "outside the egg," lofted there by Love. The church as she sees it, the church of the saved in Christ, is much larger than the church she was invited to enter through baptism. Through her identification with the alienated she is irretrievably identified with those whom the *anathama sit* has excluded. She has always identified with the outsiders of society. What she mainly objects to is the church *as a society*. It is logical that with such a view of the church—and it is the only view available to her in her time and milieu—she finds herself irrevocably bound to those whom the church as a society has rejected. It is her natural place. Her final statement regarding her refusal to be baptized sums this up admirably. Known as the "Dernier Texte," it is found in the *Pensées sans ordre concernant l'amour de Dieu*.

She begins this final text with a credo: "I believe in God, the Trinity, the Incarnation, Redemption, the Eucharist, and the teachings of the Gospel." She quickly qualifies this:

> When I say "I believe" I do not mean that I take over for myself what the Church says on these matters, affirming them as one might affirm empirical facts or geometrical theorems, but that, through love, I hold on to the perfect, unseizable, truth which these mysteries contain, and that I try to open my soul to it so that its light may penetrate into me.
>
> I do not recognize that the Church has any right to limit the operations of intelligence or the illuminations of love in the domain of thought.
>
> I recognize that, as steward of the sacraments and guardian of the sacred texts, she has the task of formulating judgments on a few essential points, but only as a guideline for the faithful.
>
> I do not recognize her right to set up, as being the truth, the commentaries with which she surrounds the mysteries of faith, and much less still the right to use intimidation when, in imposing these commentaries, she exercises her power to deprive people of the sacraments.[20]

When Simone Weil goes on to enumerate her doubts, many of them have to do with her studies of comparative religions and her recognition of Christ and/or Christian truth and love in other religions.[21] She admits that she is fallible and that she always doubts her own judgments. Yet, she says, this is true of all her thoughts: those in accord as well as those in disaccord with the teachings of the church. This doubt is an effort to maintain intellectual honesty, and to change would be "a crime against my vocation which demands of me absolute intellectual honesty."[22]

Weil recognizes that to baptize her in this attitude of mind would be "a break . . . with a tradition which has lasted at least seventeen centuries." Then follows the critical text:

> If this break is just and desirable, if precisely in our time is found to be of more than vital urgency for the well-being of Christianity—which seems clear to me—for the sake of the Church and the world it should then take place with bursting impact and not with the isolated initiative of one priest performing one obscure and little known baptism."[23]

What she wishes for herself—to be accepted into the church with all her doubts, or, rather, with her vision of a larger church—she wishes for all those like her, of whom she prophetically realizes there will be more and more. Earlier she had written to Père Perrin in the same vein:

> When so large a proportion of humanity is submerged in materialism [she wonders whether] God does not want there to be some men and women who have given themselves to him and to Christ and who yet remain outside the Church.[24]

She cannot accept the security of a "patriotic Catholicism" when so many whom she loves are excluded. Her mystical sense of vocation is summed up in her desire "to remain anonymous—ready to be mixed into the paste of common humanity.[25]

Considering the relevance of Simone Weil for the present, perhaps one of her most prophetic statements was:

> In order that the present attitude of the Church should be effective and that she should really penetrate like a wedge into social existence, she would have to say openly that she had changed or wished to change.[26]

Twenty years after the death of Simone Weil, in the documents of the Second Vatican Council, the church did admit the fact that there had been change in the past, and there was need for change in the future. Perhaps Weil would have recognized more of her vision of the church in the church of John XXIII. She would have found others—for example, the members of the Protestant monastic community of Taizé—who recognized a vocation to call for reform by remaining outside of the Roman Catholic Church.

But, again, this is conjecture. What is important is that Simone Weil fulfilled the role of true prophet in the biblical sense of the term: the prophet stands out against whatever is unfaithful—to God and to humanity—in the present age and accuses it. Weil did just that. To the church she proclaimed that the church of Christ is larger than the Roman Catholic Church. She indicted the social system of inhumanity, and called for the kind of social reforms that, in fact, did come in France. She attested to the presence of a God who is Love, and to the power of that presence to enable one to transcend the deepest human misery. She still reminds all of us that reality is more than appearances. She calls us to absolutes of intellectual honesty and to contemplation—in her term concentrated *attention*. She is perhaps no more heretical than most of the mystics within the Catholic Church. She is surely as prophetic.

NOTES

1.   Simone Weil, *Seventy Letters*, trans. Richard Rees (New York: Oxford University Press, 1965), p. 137.

2.   *Ibid.*

3.   *Ibid.*, pp. 136-37.

4.   The concept of "attention" in Weil's thought is an important one for understanding my analysis of her mysticism. The way that she defines "attention" is close to the classical definition of contemplation in works of Christian spirituality. In one place she says it is "the sole faculty of the soul which gives access to God. . . . Attention consists of suspending our thought, leaving it detached, empty." Furthermore, "Since prayer is but attention in its pure form, and since studies constitute a gymnastic of attention, it follows that every school exercise should be a refraction of spiritual life." These quotations are taken from *The Notebooks of Simone Weil*, trans. Arthur Wills (London: Routledge & Kegan Paul, 1952), 2: p. 597. But see also S. Weil, "Reflections on the Right Use of School Studies" in her *Waiting for God*, trans. Emma Cranford (New York: Putnam's Sons, 1951), pp. 105-16; and S. Weil, "Attention" in her *Lectures on Philosophy*, trans. Hugh Price (New York: Cambridge University Press, 1978), pp. 205-06.

5.   My translation of "à la fois prophète et témoin de l'absolu" from his "Introduction" to S. Weil, *Le pesanteur et la Grace* (Paris: Plon, 1948), p. 9. Available in translation by Emma Cranford as *Gravity and Grace* (London: Routledge & Kegan Paul, 1952).

6.   My translation of "la pensée de Simone Weil, un nouveau catharisme, constitue un des dangers les plus graves que puissent affronter les consciences chrétiennes" in Charles Moeller, *Literature du XXe Siècle et Christianisme*, Vol. 1: *Silence de Dieu* (Paris: Casterman, 1954), p. 280.

7.   Simone Weil, "Spiritual Autobiography" in *Waiting for God*, pp. 68-69.

8.   Pierre Teilhard de Chardin, *The Prayer of the Universe*, selected from *Writings in Time of War*, trans. René Hague (New York: Harper and Row, 1965), pp. 110-11.

9.   Weil, *Waiting for God*, p. 68.

10.   *Ibid.*, p. 72.

11.   See Jacques Cabaud, *Simone Weil: A Fellowship in Love* (New York: Channel Press, 1965), pp. 636-89 for discussion of the possible literary nature of Weil's description of this encounter and for the text.

12.   See note 4 above.

13.   Weil, *Waiting for God*, p. 64.

14.   *Ibid.*

15.   *Ibid.*, p. 67.

16.   *Ibid.*, pp, 67-68.

17.   *Ibid.*

18.   My translation for "Le nom d'opium du peuple que Marx appliquait à la religion a pu lui convenir quand elle se trahissait elle-même, mais il

convient essentiellement à la revolution. L'espoir de la revolution est toujours un stupéfiant" from S. Weil, "Condition première d'un travail non servile," *La Condition Ouvrière* (Paris: Gallimard, 1951). English translation is available in *The Simone Weil Reader*, George Panichas, ed. (New York: David McKay, 1977).

19. Claire Benedicks Fischer has done this well in a Graduate Theology Union-Berkeley dissertation, "The Fiery Bridge: Simone Weil's Theology of Work" (Ann Arbor, MI: University Microfilms International, 1980).

20. Simone Weil, *Gateway to God*, David Raper, ed. (New York: Crossroad, 1982), pp. 62-63.

21. See, e.g., S. Weil, "Forms of the Implicit Love of God" in *Waiting for God*, pp. 137-215.

22. Weil, "Last Text" in *Gateway to God*, p. 63.

23. *Ibid.*, p. 64.

24. Weil, *Waiting for God*, pp. 47-48.

25. *Ibid.*, p. 49.

26. *Ibid.*, p. 82.

III

Methodological Reflections

10

Widening the Sphere of Discourse: Reflections on the Feminist Perspective in Religious Studies

Mary Jo Weaver*

ABSTRACT

After setting the present academic context of religion and feminism through autobiographical reflections, this chapter outlines two basic models: integrating feminist perspectives into departmental instruction, and discrete Women's Studies programs. Reflections on six steps in a feminist religious studies project are presented, followed by a consideration of the impact of nonacademic feminist activities on the attempt to redefine theological and religious studies.

I. INTRODUCTION

This past February I spent a bracing weekend with two feminist pioneers in their own fields. Joan Huber is an old friend and early mentor, Dean of Social and Behavioral Sciences at Ohio State, and a well-published feminist sociologist. Susan Gubar, my best friend at Indiana University for more than a decade, is a distinguished literary critic and co-author of landmark books like *The Madwoman in the Attic*, and *The Norton Anthology of Literature by Women*. Both have changed

---

*Mary Jo Weaver (Ph.D., University of Notre Dame) is Professor of Religious Studies at Indiana University (Bloomington, IN 47405). Author of many articles and books, her recent publications include *New Catholic Women: A Contemporary Challenge to Traditional Religious Authority* (San Francisco: Harper & Row, 1985) and *Springs of Water in a Dry Land: Spiritual Survival for Catholic Women Today* (Boston: Beacon, 1992). She is currently directing a major study of Catholic fundamentalism.

the shape of their respective disciplines with their work on women and so carry impeccable feminist credentials. Susan and I went to Columbus to help Joan prepare for her March debate with Carol Gilligan.

Since I grew up next to Joan as a teenager, weekends with her are always wonderful for me because they combine all the comforts of home with all the things I could never do while growing up. When I go to Joan's house I eat wonderful meals, drink too much, abandon all my resolutions about smoking, stay up too late, and engage in fabulous conversation. Adding Susan to this cluster of stimulants tripled the pleasure, and the fact that it took us hours to get there and forced us to reread Gilligan did not dampen the occasion. I looked forward to the visit and secretly hoped that the conversation would so something to renew my flagging feminist spirit.

Let me explain the context of my own downtrodden feelings about Women's Studies. When the Women's Studies Program at Indiana University celebrated its tenth anniversary a couple of years ago, we began to look for ways to make ourselves more secure. As an adjunct faculty member of that Program, I join with more than fifty colleagues on the campus who have adjunct status and whose research interests include gender issues. Most of us offer courses related to women in our own departments, but some of us, myself included, teach specific Women's Studies courses. We have been thinking recently that "adjunct" faculty status is not enough of a statement and so have considered asking some members of the Women's Studies faculty to transfer part of their "line" to Women's Studies so that the program can begin to build its own faculty base. I was one of the early supporters of this move, but lately have reconsidered it and decided that I want to remain totally within Religious Studies and do my feminist teaching within my own department. As we drove to Joan's, I was feeling slightly guilty about this decision and wondering if I just needed a shot in the arm.

The weekend was all I hoped it would be in terms of indulgence, though we are too old to sink into bad habits the ways we could ten years ago. The conversation about Gilligan was mutually reinforcing: we all were ambivalent about her book, found its data base hopelessly insufficient, and were distressed about the ways in which it seemed to glorify stereotypes about women that we had been at pains to deny in our own work. Curiously, however, we spent Saturday morning wandering around quilt stores looking for projects and being rhapsodic about "women's crafts." The real surprise, however, was our collective fatigue about Women's Studies.

Sitting around drinking coffee on Saturday morning, we began to sound vaguely reactionary, like people whose dreams were tired. Had we grown intellectually disinterested in Women's Studies as such, we wondered? Why did we feel more devoted to our own disciplines than to Women's Studies? We told stories of students who were writing papers about a "feminist pedagogy" that simply seemed like any kind of liberal move to decenter authority in the classroom. We were unsympathetic to those who believed that women had a unique way of doing sociology or of being religious, and we were skeptical about the claim that women write, speak, or read in their own distinctive language.

"Women's Studies is *not* a discipline," we said. And we claimed to feeling ourselves often more stimulated by colleagues in our own fields than we were by current feminist discussion. We were not shy in voicing these opinions, and yet felt, I think, a little peculiar about stating them so strongly, rather like being in a sinister consciousness raising group. Part of my own unease quavered around the suspicion that I was simply unable to recognize the deeper questions. I am stuck in that zone between old questions and new ones not yet emerged. When I look back, I am bored to tears, and when I look forward, I cannot see what lies ahead. Joan, Susan, and I left our collective doubts unresolved, and I have been pondering them ever since.

II. TWO BASIC MODELS

I accept the presupposition that feminism ought to be an integral part of any department of theology or religious studies. At the same time, I realize that I owe a great deal to Women's Studies as a discrete program. I do not know to what extent I am simply reflecting my own confusion, but I believe I need to attempt to sort out the differences between these two models in order to understand my own malaise. I should say at the outset that I recognize a third way of making a feminist impact on the academy, political action or writing from outside; but I will not discuss that particular aspect except in passing.

Mainstreaming, as it is used in the book edited by Walter Conn and Arlene Swidler,[1] refers to two different strategies. On the one hand, one works to integrate feminist questions or women's issues into traditional courses so that, for instance, a course on American religious history highlights significant female as well as male religious figures. On the other hand, many believe that one should add new courses to their own departmental curricula so that an enlightened list of courses would include, for example, Women in Biblical Literature, Women's Changing Roles in Buddhism, or Feminist Challenges to Traditional Christianity. Each of these approaches has a clear advantage. By drawing feminist perspectives into already existing courses or by creating new courses based primarily on gender issues, one can make use of the research methods of one's own discipline. Mainstreaming appears to free a teacher from the burdens of having to create new methods or new questions *ex nihilo*. We can teach as we have always taught with the stimulation of new material. Furthermore, some scholars believe that institutional curricular change can only be effected by adding new courses to the curriculum.[2]

Teaching a Women's Studies course, however, requires an additional support system. The university, itself, has to find and maintain a Women's Studies Program which is dedicated to exploring new ways of teaching and which takes on the burdens of interdisciplinary research. Women's Studies programs, however creative and vibrant they might be in a given institution, are often looked upon as stepchildren of the academy: members of such programs—the same is true for area studies in general—must be scrappy defenders of new methods, dedicated to mountains of extra committee work, and available to new processes of community interaction. Evelyn Torton Beck, Director of Women's Studies at the University of Maryland, says that the extra work is necessary and ultimately rewarding. She argues persuasively that "no college or university can any longer lay claim to excellence if it does not have a strong Women's Studies Department" with its own faculty and autonomy.[3]

I am still ambivalent about my own participation in an actual Women's Studies *Department*, but believe strongly that any good university needs to support a Women's Studies Program. In such a program, one can find core courses on feminist theory that go beyond what can normally be done in a specific department. In addition, as Paula Rothenberg has argued, Women's Studies can take a "hard" approach which provides "an analysis of the comprehensive and structural nature of [the] form of oppression" known as sexism rather than leaving our students with "a superficial understanding."[4] In my own university, the Women's Studies Program offers a Ph.D. minor as well as an undergraduate certificate and so is able to draw women from a wide variety of different departments into creative conversation. Those who teach mainstream courses on women and religion are often indebted to the political support of Women's Studies Programs during tenure and promotion considerations: if a university committee or even one's own department has no ideas how to judge the merit of one's feminist research or teaching, interdisciplinary committees of senior feminist scholars can help to clarify those contributions and to place one's work in a wider framework of evaluation.

How can I be a staunch defender of Women's Studies on these grounds and still admit to a kind of drooping skepticism? Partly, as I noted, because the extra work of any Women's Studies program is profoundly wearying; but more, I think, because in the exciting early years of that program, I believed that revolution was imminent, or, to put it in religious terms, that the promised land was in sight. I failed, as many of us did, I think, to see the realities of the struggle as an ongoing effort. To borrow the words of Elaine Showalter:

> a few years ago feminist critics thought we were on a pilgrimage to the promised land in which gender would lose its power, in which all texts would be sexless and equal, like angels. But the more precisely we understand the specificity of women's writing, not as a transient by-product of sexism but as a fundamental and continually determining reality, the more clearly we realize that we have misperceived our destination. We may never reach the promised land at all; for when feminist critics see our task as the study of women's writing, we realize that the land promised to us is not the serenely undifferentiated universality of texts, but the tumultuous and intriguing wilderness of difference itself.[5]

In other words, the stimulating work of early feminist research has led to a nexus of gender relations that involves us in a much more complex and less immediately gratifying task than we had originally envisioned. As teachers and scholars we are now challenged to ask deeper questions and to refuse to be satisfied with the politically correct but now boring conclusions of our feminist salad days.

My own confusion comes in part form a feeling of being stuck in a process I cannot fully understand. I have a sense that there are new questions on the horizon, but I cannot see them yet; and I am not persuaded that some of the new perspectives being suggested by my students and colleagues are the right ones. Maternalist theories, for example, that valorize women's nurturing experience over men's individualist perspective strike me as too simplistic. Carol Gilligan must be commended for exposing the limits of Kohlberg's work,[6] and for insisting on the importance of an "ethic of care"; but that does not obviate the need for an "ethic of justice" or lead inescapably to the conclusion that compassion is a higher moral quality than rights. The notion of gender superiority has, on the whole, been bad for women and our challenge today is to show how maternalist theories served to uphold conservative political aims by restricting women's participation in society.[7] Similarly, Carol P. Christ's claim that we must reject the ethos of objectivity in favor of an ethos of eros and sympathy begs more questions than it answers. The only reasonable position we can take, I believe, is to insist that we include these alternative perspectives in our search for a more adequate and representative understanding of humanity.

III. SIX-STEP FEMINIST PROJECT

In *New Catholic Women*, I schematized the feminist project in six steps and generalized those steps for all disciplines. I think my taxonomy still works as a basic scheme, but I would like to place my emphases a little differently and rescind some of my optimism. My scheme presupposed that academic disciplines as well as ecclesiastical life have been shaped by a false consciousness that believes that female voices, thoughts, work, views, experiences, sense of value, and ways of approaching problems are unimportant and that one can understand the "humanities" as implicitly androcentric. The women's movement challenges this viewpoint in six logical steps: (1) we notice and demonstrate that women have been ignored in the field; (2) we show that what we do know about women, sparse though it may be, is characterized by a high level of hostility, diminishment, frivolity, or mushy mystification; (3) we search out and write about the lost women in the field so that we can add as many figures as possible to an otherwise all-male pantheon; (4) we sustain a revisionary reading of old texts and traditions so that they lose their power to terrorize and exclude women; (5) we challenge the discipline methodologically in order to force it to redefine its borders, goals, and consequences; and (6) we work toward a truly integrated field which is not reduced by its prejudices against women, lower classes, variant sexual preferences, ethnic groups or anything else, but one which represents humanity in all its messy diversity.

About a year ago I believed that the first four steps had been "done" to death, that the fifth was not working, and the sixth was impossible. I would like to probe my own skepticism a little by reviewing the first four steps in the light of some new questions and with specific reference to Religious Studies. Step five needs to be rehearsed in relation to mainstreaming and so will absorb special attention, and step six probably needs to be reassessed in light of Showalter's image of a "wilderness of difference." In any case, let me look at the initial tasks: women's invisibility, male hostility, lost women, and revised texts.

First, we demonstrate that women have been ignored in the field. From Mary Daly's groundbreaking book, *The Church and the Second Sex,*[8] to the helpful anthologies edited by Rosemary Ruether,[9] we know the extent of our invisibility. Since these two pioneers and many others have been working on this first step for twenty years, one can be pardoned for not getting excited about it nowadays. At the same time, what would it mean to involve ourselves in this problem of invisibility? When we cite Gerda Lerner's observation that the most jolting discovery for feminist historians is the fact that women in history are invisible "by design,"[10] do we ask ourselves about the women who are *still* invisible after two decades of feminist research? We have learned from Black women that the women's movement, overwhelmingly white, does not speak for them. Similar criticisms have come from lesbians, Third World women, and others. In light of the extraordinary diversity of women's lives and ideas, and with a nod to the axiom that women ought to be able to speak for themselves, I tend to want to distance myself from all these other perspectives. Since I cannot speak for Chicana women, I say, I will say nothing about them and "let them speak for themselves." It is ever a double bind: by refusing to think about or write about women unlike myself, I help to extend their invisibility whereas a decision to include them in my work invites criticism that I have robbed them of their voices or that I do not know the territory. For many of my students, this problem of invisibility often leads to inadequate but politically correct responses to feminist research. Graduate students think they can dismiss a book like Hester Eisenstein's *Contemporary Feminist Thought*[11] because "it has no lesbians or Black women in it." Perhaps Eisenstein would have written a better book had she included these perspectives; but it is intellectually lazy to criticize the book she did not write while ignoring the very real insights and problems in the book she actually produced.

Maybe we need to ask who benefits from whose invisibility? If women are invisible in history "by design," how did that design support patriarchal structures or politically conservative legislation? The Catholic Church has taken pride in the fact that women are not invisible as models of sanctity; but we can show that they *were* invisible in the corridors of power. The whole notion of sanctity for women rests upon the visibility of obedient, receptive women, not on women as models of power or intellectual acuity. Furthermore, for all its praise of motherhood, the Catholic church has not yet found a "good Catholic mother" to canonize. And, many of the women who were found worthy of official sainthood were those who spent their lives locked away in convents. Why? Who benefitted form legislation about papal cloister?[12] What would we find if we began to look into the economic benefits of women's invisibility? How has the lack of women as a public presence shaped religion in a particular way? How do "women's sins" differ from "men's sins" when one looks, as Carole Myscofski has, at the records of the Inquisition in a particular place and time?[13] And how do those differences shape our theological categories?

We need to show our students that women have been invisible in Catholic history and theology, but we cannot stop there. In order to explain invisibility, we have to begin to ask difficult questions about power and patriarchy and to be prepared to examine our own complicity in situations of oppression. If we concluded our seminars with the mere fact of invisibility, our students might assume that the only thing they need to do in order to have a feminist consciousness is to be able to name a few obscure women. If we believe, however, that invisibility has fed certain ideas and helped men to maintain power over women, then we have to refuse to accept easy answers for ourselves or from our students.

When I turn to step two, I find that I can get overwhelmed by the *motivations* for male hostility. Why do men treat women as second-class citizens or write about them as if they were intellectually and spiritually benighted? Frankly, I find continued attention to that discussion fruitless: I no longer care *why* men have treated women badly, but I want very much to disrupt theories of complementarity which have supported the devaluation of women. That being the case, I think the deeper questions of this step relate to the ways in which gender is a variable in any discussion of women's lives. I am inclined, therefore, to turn my attention to gender theorists, and believe that one of the best places to start might be the writings of Freud.[14] Although there are passages in Freud's work where he sounds like a biological determinist, contemporary interpreters have shown that Freud lays the groundwork for a description of the cultural construction of gender.[15] Read prescriptively, Freudian theory is bad for women, but read descriptively as an explanation for the ways girls are supposed to grow up in a patriarchal society, his work can help to undermine patriarchal systems, including ecclesiastical ones.[16]

Once we begin to read gender theory, we open ourselves to an almost endless list of sources from colleagues in other fields. The work of Levi-Strauss and Marx is surely pertinent, but even more important, I believe, are the ways in which feminist interpreters have deconstructed their theories. Gayle Rubin's groundbreaking essay, "The Traffic in Women,"[17] is a brilliant reading of Freud, Marx, and Levi-Strauss. Adrienne Rich's famous essay on compulsory heterosexuality[18] is another watermark text because whereas Freud asks *how* it is that female children break their natural affectional bond with the mother and transfer their desire to the father (or to men), Rich asks why women would *want* to shift the locus of their love from women to men.

My own reading in gender theory has been limited to these approaches and has helped me to understand the interdisciplinary nature of feminism with new appreciation. I would be intellectually richer if I were able to pay close attention to sociologists, anthropologists, and other social scientists as well. The interdisciplinary imperative in both areas—Religious Studies and Women's Studies—supports the casting of wide nets. Religious Studies professionals cannot get to the deeper questions of male hostility towards women without reference to the work of feminist psychologists, anthropologists, historians, sociologists, and literary critics. At the same time, we need to be much more critical about some of the assumptions of Catholic spirituality that appear to be based on fear of or abhorrence for women. Here the work of medievalists like Carolyn Walker Bynum[19] can give us a whole new set of questions and can also show what happens to a system which restricts access to is sources, languages, and interpretations to clerical elites.

Let me move on to step three while I am lingering over the medieval period. We have now known the thrill of "finding lost women" and so have resuscitated role models that can change the ways we look at religious life. We are also aware of the dangers of finding exceptional women, i.e., however invigorating it is to know about a few female saints, queens, and (both) doctors of the church, we cannot generalize their extraordinary experience to ordinary women. Today we cannot help but be aware of repositories of data about ordinary women and the proliferation of new scholarship based on the diaries of women on the frontier, the records of Hispanic nuns, the works of hundreds of religious orders in the United States, and all this new information is changing the ways we think about history and religion. The work of young scholars like Debra Campbell has virtually created a whole new area of research about the contributions of lay women in early twentieth-century American Catholicism and will give us important new angles on the meaning of parish life in the United States.[20] I would like to raise a different question about recoverable women, however, and use it to urge a higher level of critical appropriation.

One of the results of the search for lost women has been the uncritical valorization of those women. Julian of Norwich's concept of the motherhood of God, for example, leads some to suggest that she was a medieval feminist or an avatar of women's religion. I think we must be very careful with labels and leery of applying them anachronistically. More to the point, in finding solace in a concept like the "motherhood of God," we can fail to be critical of Julian's religious sensibility. Do we *really* want to recommend her kind of religious aspiration to women today? Are we understanding *her* ideas or super-imposing ours upon her work? In what ways do Julian's desire for suffering *undermine* the feminist project rather than uphold it? I find myself increasingly critical about the claims made for medieval women, and again recommend the work of Carolyn Walker Bynum. "The symbols, behaviors, and doctrines [of medieval women] have no direct lessons for the 1980s," she says, "the actual lives of some late medieval women must give us pause."[21] However tempting it is to latch onto someone like Hildegard of Bingen as an extraordinarily ver-satile and gifted women, we must take care not to romanticize her or to create her in our own image. As Barbara Newman has shown, Hildegard "associated moral and spiritual freedom with a dualistic conception of the self and with a pessimistic and even deterministic view of human life."[22] Far from being a pioneer of creation-centered spirituality, Hildegard was censorious about lives not dedicated to virginity, staunchly supportive of papalism, and totally orthodox in her religious beliefs. At the same time, she was a visionary and was concerned enough with gender in God's scheme of things to have a concept of the feminine dimension of the divine.

Since publication on feminist topics has increased dramatically in the last ten years, it is terribly hard to keep up with everything, and I am not urging that we all become medievalists. At the same time, we can be aware that the lives of notable women are not normally trans-latable into contemporary terms and we can keep ourselves constantly critical of the claims made for exceptional women by asking for full expositions of their context and by interpreting them within the framework of their own times rather than moving them forcibly into ours.

The fourth step, the revision of old texts, has been particularly fruitful for feminist scholars of religion. From Phyllis Trible's close reading of some stories in the Hebrew Bible to Elisabeth Schüssler Fiorenza's claims about the egalitarian nature of the early Christian community, we have learned to find central places for women's voices in traditional texts.[23] The work of feminist scholars has led us to chal-lenge traditional interpretations and to undermine the claim that there is only one way to understand the Bible, canon law, or the symbol of divinity itself. In our attempts to include women in all facets of reli-gious life, we have argued that the perceptions of the patriarchs were limited and partial and therefore not universally true. Interestingly, we have based our challenge on the belief that one's knowledge is so-cially constituted: we can confront old reading because, we say, no one can lay claim to universal validity. This move is a good one only if we remember that the same is true for our own conclusions. Feminist readings and new models are also partial and not "true." Our advantage lies in the awareness of our epistemological limits: we can understand our revisions as necessary without needing to claim that they are universal. We can attempt to produce *a* feminist theology and invite others to create different ones. Rosemary Ruether's *Sexism and God-Talk* is, by her own admission, one attempt to reformulate the classical conceptions of theology.[24] Sallie McFague's *Models of God: Theology for an Ecological Nuclear Age* is, as she says, her way of dealing with the conceptual problems of trinitarian theology in a way that makes sense in this time; it is not intended to be eternally valid.[25] One of the strengths of the feminist theological project, I believe, is its openness to a wide variety of experience and interpretation, and one of the values we might pass along to our students is this sense that truth is a metaphysical reality approximated only insofar as we are willing to open ourselves to a chorus of possibilities.

The celebration of diversity is the most important way we have raised a methodological challenge to the discipline. If a goal of feminism as I have described it is to force Religious Studies to redefine its borders, goals, and consequences, one clear way to accomplish that goal is through the demystification of unity. We have learned to be sensitive to differences and enriched by them and so cannot ascribe to the view that we ought to be searching for a single voice. The implications for ecumenical theology, for conservative religion, and for some versions of Catholicism are enormous here because feminism argues against the very presuppositions of those systems. We cannot work for the recovery of Christian unity if we do not believe such unity ever existed; we cannot insist that our way of reading Scripture or evangelizing people is the "one way of Jesus Christ" if our experience has shown us the folly of any claims to such singlemindedness; and we cannot define Roman Catholicism as the "one true church" if the teachings and texts of Catholicism do not reflect the wider and more diverse criteria for truth claims that feminist critics help to provide.

In suggesting that one of the gifts of feminism is a sense of relativity, I know that I am touching upon a real pedagogical problem. It is easy for our students to wake from the dream of pluralism only to be confronted with the nightmare of total relativism, whence to conclude that anything is all right and that we can never know the truth about anything. It is important, therefore, that we do not forswear the hope that some claims can be made that have universal validity. Feminism brings pluralism inside the academy, it forces us and our students to confront differences in *ourselves*, not only in some remote corner of the world. The salubrious effect of this intrusion is its ability to make us aware of the relative nature of our knowledge by insisting that truth claims must be subjected to more rigorous testing than we had heretofore assumed. Feminism, along with other movements, has helped us to forge higher standards for proof, not to abandon them altogether. If we want to attempt to evaluate something against these new standards of universality, then it must be good for women as well as men, inclusive of the poor as well as the rich, sensitive to ethnic and religious differences rather than culturally imperialistic. Feminism adds a new dimension to intellectual awareness: it does not destroy academic discourse or classical culture by overthrowing the desire for universally valid conclusions.

Besides diversity, feminism has claimed to add a new dimension to the academy by way of its reliance on experience. It is now a cliché to say that the feminist contribution to Religious Studies is the introduction of women's experience. I do not know what that means anymore, if I ever did. Women's Studies has four ways of making a contribution to academic life: two of them are versions of mainstreaming—additions to existing courses or the generation of new courses—and one of them is by way of a discrete Women's Studies program. The fourth is, strictly speaking, not within the academy, although its impact has been felt very strongly within academic circles. I am speaking here of contributions by novelists, activists, self-conscious women's communities, and new experiments like Womenchurch. Many of us have benefitted from the insights of these groups and have interacted with them so as to blur the lines between academic discourse and popular culture that some of our male colleagues find so reassuring. As another way to insist on pluralism, I find this an acceptable move and am convinced that we need as many ways as possible to bring invisible women and unheard voices into our discussions of "the humanities." I think we can argue that these are not two different worlds, but two venues of the same intellectual problem. At the same time, I believe that the claims about women from nonacademic sources can be a problem as we try to redefine the discipline.

Suppose, for example, that I am trying to argue the advantages of a feminist systematic theology to traditional theologians. Can I really adopt the rhetoric of a women's retreat? I have been to numerous meetings where women sit in circles and tell their stories, where, predictably, someone will say, "I'd just like to point out that we're doing theology here. Women telling their stories *is* theology." I feel struck when this happens. I do not think that any group of people revealing their feelings is "theology," yet I have been shaped as a feminist by such encounters. I am willing to argue that theologians must pay attention to women's stories based on the insights of contemporary theologians about the relationship between theology and experience; but I am not willing to accept those stories as theology. Perhaps I am only reflecting a tension I have with regard to mainstreaming.

I believe that we need to think about the ways in which feminist perspectives can get absorbed and ghettoized in our discipline. Since Religious Studies has no single methodology, we survive on the creative interaction of multiple perspectives. In our situation, as in anthropology, there is a danger that the "feminist perspective" can become just another way of seeing things in a discipline that prides itself on a variety of viewpoints. If that happens, then we lose part of our power to disrupt the field and challenge its methods and conclusions. And we *will* relinquish our claim to change Religious Studies if we do not make careful, critical use of nonacademic feminist rhetoric.

I do not want to be misunderstood. Without the work of activists, women's communities, and alternative religious experiments, we could not advance some of the positions we now hold dear. I would be impoverished without the courageous work of nonacademic feminists. At the same time, I believe that there is a real difference between academic work and political activism, and that brings me back to the beginning as well as to my final point. As I try to imagine a truly integrated field, I am confronted by Elaine Showalter's "wilderness of difference." When I try to listen to multiple voices, I worry about the lack of intellectual coherence in feminist discourse. When I plead for diversity, I am heartened by an enormous emerging body of literature by women not heard from before now and angered by the predictable attacks from conservatives who ask if that literature is "any good?" Their supercilious attitudes provide us with our most fundamental question: by whose standards do we judge "goodness" and by what criteria do we include nonwhite, non-male, non-privileged perspectives? Florence Howe says that autobiography is the "rage to explain" oneself,[26] which means that we must listen to all those that, I hope, we can finally welcome into the field: we must insist that Religious Studies is an academically incompetent enterprise unless its conclusions take account of the claims and experience of women as well as men, just as we believe that we cannot base our conclusions about religion on Christianity without being cognizant of Buddhism, Judaism, Islam, modern religious experiments and so-called "primitive religions."

IV. CONCLUSION

Where does all this speculation leave me in terms of my initial conflicts? I admit that I am uneasy about some of the claims of Women's Studies, and yet believe that Women's Studies has forced us to rethink the structure and theory of Religious Studies. I believe that we have modified our field, though evidence is more easily garnered in some areas of study than in others, and one cannot rest when the engines of reactionaries are revving up in many quarters. In light of increasing opposition, I think it is clear that Women's Studies cannot fade into oblivion as we trust our colleagues to see the inherent logic of our claims. At the same time, I think we have a new mandate to press those claims as intelligently as possible.

In Religious Studies, where feminist perspectives are only beginning to make an impact, we must rededicate ourselves to the "tumultuous and intriguing wilderness of difference," realizing that we are in for a long struggle *and* an enormously complicated life. the most intriguing aspect of feminism, is akin, I think, to the most compelling dimension of Religious Studies: both are in danger of death when they rest on the assumption that everything is settled. As feminists working in Religious Studies we know that we are in two areas that invite disruption from new perspectives so that we can learn to understand humanity and religion in new, more embracing, but less clear-cut ways. That professional posture is what distinguishes both fields, and what makes our lives both rich and difficult.

The very first essay I ever read by my friend, Joan Huber, opened this way: "a person who maintains a self-definition with no social support is mad; with minimum support, a pioneer; and with broad support, a lemming. Most of us are lemmings. We accept or change our ideas of our own rights and duties only when we perceive social support for doing so."[27] She wrote that essay in 1972, the first year I gave a paper on feminism and the Catholic Church. We were both hopeful, I think, that women and men could create new institutions for themselves and expand the options for everyone. Perhaps we both perceived a burgeoning swell of social support, and maybe my present uneasiness is related to an ominous sense that such support is under attack *and* that the questions for the nineties reconstitute our status so that we do not have the comfort of being lemmings, but must assume the sturdiness of pioneers, again.

As we shoulder the burdens of integrating feminist perspectives into the Religious Studies curriculum I realize that we are not all sisters, that our work will come under attack from women as well as men, from the left as well as the right, and sometimes from the very institutions we hope to change. We know, too, that feminism has the power to undermine traditional religious authority as it challenges some of the dearly held assumptions of religion in general and Catholicism in particular. Politically, I continue to believe that we must support strong Women's Studies programs, and despite my growing frustrations about some aspects of those programs, I believe that I must continue to teach independent Women's Studies courses as I also work to develop new courses and to include feminist perspectives into my general courses. If our new questions are good ones, nothing will happen easily. Perhaps, however, we can learn to find courage in opposition and comfort in the struggle because we know that if what we are doing is acceptable to our colleagues, we are not doing it right.

NOTES

1. *Mainstreaming: Feminist Research for Teaching Religious Studies*, CTS Resources in Religion, 2 (Lanham, MD: University Press of America, 1985).
2. Marilyn R. Schuster and Susan R. Van Dyne, eds., *Women's Place in the Academy: Transforming the Liberal Arts Curriculum* (Totowa, NJ: Rowan & Allanheld, 1985). For a look at some of the ways that feminist research has made an impact on the academy from *within*, see Christie Farnham, ed., *The Impact of Feminist Research in the Academy* (Bloomington: Indiana University Press, 1987).
3. "Asking for the Future," *The Women's Review of Books* 6 (February 1989), pp. 21-22.
4. "The Hand that Pushes the Rock," *The Women's Review of Books* 6 (February 1989), p. 18.
5. "Feminist Criticism in the Wilderness," *Critical Inquiry* (Winter 1981), reprinted in Elaine Showalter, ed., *The New Feminist Criticism* (New York: Pantheon Books, 1985), pp. 243-70.
6. *In a Different Voice: Psychological Theory and Women's Development* (Cambridge, MA: Harvard University Press, 1982).
7. Most Vatican decrees against women's equal access to power in the church are based on theories of complementarity which are based on a binary gender system in which women are said to be either weaker and less human, or, paradoxically, stronger and more spiritual. See my *New Catholic Women: A Contemporary Challenge to Traditional Religious Authority* (San Francisco: Harper and Row, 1985). For a look at the ways in which "women's superiority" functioned to keep women underpaid and undereducated, see Jill K. Conway, "Politics, Pedagogy, and Gender" in Jill K. Conway, Susan C. Bourque and Joan W. Scott, eds., *Learning About Women* (Ann Arbor: University of Michigan Press, 1989), pp. 137-53.
8. Boston: Beacon, 1968.
9. *Religion and Sexism* (New York: Simon and Schuster, 1974); with Eleanor Como McLaughlin, *Women of Spirit* (New York: Simon and Schuster, 1979); and with Rosemary Skinner Keller, *Women and Religion in America*, 3 vols. (San Francisco: Harper and Row, 1981, 1983, and 1986).
10. "Placing Women in History: A 1975 Perspective," originally published in *Feminist Studies* 3 (1975), 5-15, revised and published in Bernice Car-

roll, ed., *Liberating Women's History: Theoretical and Critical Essays* (Urbana: University of Illinois Press, 1976), pp. 357-67.

11. *Contemporary Feminist Thought* (Boston: G. K. Hall, 1983).

12. Peter F. Anson, "Papal Enclosure for Nuns," *Cistercian Studies* 3 (1968), pp. 109-23, 189-206.

13. "Women's Religious Roles in Brazil: A History of Limitations," *Journal of Feminist Studies in Religion* 1 (1985), pp. 43-57. Myscofski noticed that the difference between women's confessed sins and those of men were highly dependent upon the range of ordinary activity for each gender.

14. No theorist of gender can avoid Freud; even those who do not cite his work explicitly are shaped by it in some way. For an introduction to his work in this area see "Female Sexuality" (1931) in Philip Rieff, ed., *Sexuality and the Psychology of Love* (New York: Collier, 1963), pp. 194-211.

15. See, e.g., Nancy Chodorow, *The Reproduction of Mothering: Psycho-analysis and the Sociology of Gender* (Berkeley: University of California Press, 1978).

16. For an illuminating appropriation of Freud by feminist critics, see Sandra Gilbert and Susan Gubar, *No Man's Land: The War of the Words* (New Haven, CT: Yale University Press, 1988), pp. 165-227.

17. "The Traffic in Women: Notes on the 'Political Economy' of Sex," in Rayna R. Reiter, ed., *Towards an Anthropology of Women* (New York: Monthly Review Press, 1975), pp.157-210.

18. "Compulsory Heterosexuality and Lesbian Existence," *Signs* 5 (1980), pp. 631-60.

19. See, e.g., *Gender and Religion: On the Complexity of Symbols* (Boston: Beacon, 1986), and her brilliant analysis of gender in *Jesus as Mother: Studies in the Spirituality of the High Middle Ages* (Berkeley: University of California Press, 1982).

20. Campbell has published numerous articles on heretofore obscure women like Maisie Ward, female evangelists in the 1930s and 1940s, and other important, but neglected figures. See, e.g., "The Catholic Earth Mother: Dorothy Day and Women's Power in the Church," *Cross Currents* 34 (1984), pp. 270-82; "Part Time Female Evangelists of the Thirties and Forties: The Rosary College Catholic Evidence Guild," *U.S. Catholic Historian* 5 (1986), pp. 371-84; "Gleanings of a Laywoman's Ministry" Maisie Ward as Preacher, Publisher and Social Activist," *The Month* 258 (1987), pp. 313-17; or "Hannah Whitall Smith (1832-1911): Theology of the Mother-hearted God," *Signs* 15/1 (Autumn 1989), pp. 79-101.

21. *Holy Feast and Holy Fast: The Religious Significance of Food to Medieval Women* (Berkeley: University of California Press, 1987), p. 299.

22. *Sister of Wisdom: St. Hildegard's Theology of the Feminine* (Berkeley: University of California Press, 1987).

23. Phyllis Trible, *God and the Rhetoric of Sexuality* (Philadelphia: Fortress, 1981); Elisabeth Schüssler Fiorenza, *In Memory of Her: A Feminist Theological Reconstruction of Christian Origins* (New York: Crossroad, 1984).

24. Boston: Beacon, 1987.

25. Philadelphia: Fortress, 1987.

26. "A Symbiotic Relationship," *The Women's Review of Books* 6 (February 1989), p. 16.

27. "Ambiguities in Identity Transformation: From Sugar and Spice to Professor," *Notre Dame Journal of Education* 2 (1972), pp. 338-47.